The Great Household in Late Medieval England

The Great Household in
Late Medieval England

C. M. Woolgar

Yale University Press
New Haven and London

Set in Simoncini Garamond by Servis Filmsetting Ltd, Manchester
Printed in Hong Kong through World Print Ltd

Library of Congress Cataloging-in-Publication Data

Woolgar, C. M.
    The great household in late medieval England/by C. M. Woolgar.
    Includes bibliographical references and index.
    ISBN 0–300–07687–8 (cl.: alk. paper).
    1. England—Social life and customs—1066–1485. 2. Master and servant—England—History—To 1500. 3. Upper class—England—History—To 1500. 4. Households—England—History—To 1500. 5. Family—England—History—To 1500. I. Title.
DA185.W66 1999
306'.0942—dc21   98–44161
                                                                              CIP

A catalogue record for this book is available from the British Library.

10 9 8 7 6 5 4 3 2 1

Contents

Illustration Acknowledgements

Fine Arts Museums of San Francisco, Achenbach Foundation for Graphic Arts, Gift of Osgood Hooker, 1967.4: **1**; National Gallery, L3, from the Gorhambury Collection and reproduced by permission of the Earl of Verulam. Photo: © National Gallery, London: **2**; By permission of the British Library: **3** (BL MS Cotton Julius E IV, f. 22v), **4** (BL MS Royal 20 D IV, f. 1r), **5** (BL Add. MS 47,680, f. 60v), **6** (BL MS Cotton Julius E IV, f. 10v), **7** (BL Add. MS 47,682, f. 21v), **27** (BL MS Cotton Julius E IV, f. 1r), **28** (BL MS Cotton Julius E IV, f. 10r), **31** (BL MS Royal 2 B VII, f. 23v), **33** (BL MS Cotton Julius E IV, f. 26v), **34** (BL Map Library, C.7.d.4), **36** (BL MS Royal 2 B VII, f. 23r), **38** (BL Add. MS 47,682, f. 18r), **39** (BL Add. MS 42,130, f. 202v), **42** (BL MS Cotton Julius E IV, f. 27r), **43** (BL Add. MS 42,130, f. 63r), **44** (BL MS Royal 2 B VII, f. 82v), **46** (BL Add. MS 47,682, f. 37r), **47** (BL MS Royal 2 B VII, f. 16v), **50** (BL Add. MS 42,130, f. 206v), **51** (BL Add. MS 42,130, f. 207r), **52** (BL Add. MS 42,130, f. 207v), **53** (BL Add. MS 42,130, f. 208r), **58** (BL MS Royal 2 B VII, f. 43r), **60** (BL Add. MS 47,682, f. 20v), **61** (BL Add. MS 42,130, f. 90v), **62** (BL MS Royal 2 B VII, f. 29r), **65** (BL MS Cotton Julius E IV, f. 6v), **66** (BL Add. MS 47,680, f. 63v), **67** (BL MS Harley 642, f. 4r), **68** (BL Add. MS 47,682, f. 24v), **69** (BL Add. MS 42,130, f. 97v), **72** (BL Add. MS 42,130, f. 173v), **73** (BL Add. MS 42,130, ff. 181v–182r); British Museum. © Copyright The British Museum: **8** (MLA 1963.10–2.1), **13 and 14** (deposited by the Warden and Fellows of All Souls College, Oxford), **15** (MLA 1947.10–7.1), **29, 59**; Spencer Collection, MS 26, The New York Public Library, Astor, Lenox and Tilden Foundations: **9** (f. 60r), **10** (f. 36v), **32** (f. 71r); © English Heritage/Skyscan Balloon Photography: **11**; By courtesy of the Board of Trustees of the Victoria and Albert Museum: **12** (4–1865), **30, 49** (also by courtesy of the rector and churchwardens of St Mary Magdalen, Bermondsey); Photograph C. M. Woolgar: **16, 17, 18, 19, 20, 21, 23, 25, 26, 40, 41, 45, 48, 55, 56, 70, 74**; Photograph P. A. Stamper: **22**; Photograph A. F. Kersting: **24, 75, 76**; © The National Trust Photographic Library: **35** (Andreas von Einsiedel), **57** (Alasdair Ogilvie); Courtesy of the Museum of London: **37**; From T. H. Turner and J. Parker, *Some account of domestic architecture in England* (3 vols in 4, Oxford, 1851–9) iii, part 2, following p. 276: **54**; By permission of the Master and Fellows of Corpus Christi College, Cambridge: **63**; Courtesy of the Borough Council of King's Lynn and West Norfolk: **64**; Reproduced by courtesy of the Yorkshire Museum. YORYM: 1991.43: **71**.

Figures, Tables and Maps

Figures

Tables

Maps

Acknowledgements

The subject of this book has been in my mind for most of my working life, stretching back now nearly two decades. I owe a great debt to the President and Fellows of Magdalen College, Oxford, work on whose archives at the start of my career first led me to medieval household accounts and then to an investigation of their diplomatic. More recently, I owe to Dr Robert Baldock of Yale University Press the encouragement that has enabled me to bring to fruition my thoughts on a range of matters related to the great household. In the intervening period I have consulted many archives and libraries and incurred debts that are now too numerous to mention singly; that, however, is not to belittle their importance. For permission to consult their papers I am grateful to the Marquis of Bath; His Grace the Archbishop of Canterbury and the Trustees of Lambeth Palace Library; the Dean and Chapter of Westminster Abbey; and the Warden and Fellows of Winchester College.

For permission to use illustrations, I am grateful to the British Library; the Trustees of the British Museum; the Master and Fellows of Corpus Christi College, Cambridge; English Heritage; the Borough Council of King's Lynn and West Norfolk; the National Gallery and the Earl of Verulam; the National Trust; the New York Public Library, Spencer Collection, Astor, Lenox and Tilden Foundations; the Fine Arts Museums of San Francisco, Achenbach Foundation for Graphic Arts; the Board of Trustees of the Victoria and Albert Museum; and the Yorkshire Museum.

This book depends much on the work of others. Beyond the sources cited, B. F. Harvey's *Living and dying in England 1100–1500: the monastic experience* (Oxford, 1993) and C. Dyer's *Standards of living in the later Middle Ages: social change in England c. 1200–1500* (Cambridge, 1989) stimulated many ideas. Two unpublished theses, by L. H. Butler and F. Lachaud, have been particularly useful. Dale Serjeantson, Paul Stamper and Nick Kingwell kindly read the typescript, in part or in whole; and Professor Paul Harvey helpfully discussed some of the ideas with me. Parts of the text were given as papers to the Medieval Diet Group and, at the University of Southampton, to the Wessex Medieval Centre. Barbara Harvey, John Hare, R. Shoesmith and S. Brown kindly gave advice on particular points. To all of these I am grateful for their kindness, thoughtfulness and attention.

The University of Southampton Library, both in the course of my normal duties there and during leave of absence from them, has done much to help the progress of this book. I am grateful to the University Librarian, Mr B. Naylor, for his encouragement; to my immediate colleagues, who have borne much during my absence and forborne it in my presence; to the Inter-Library Loan section, which has made a good library an exceptional one; and to successive Hartley Institute Fellows, who have provided a congenial environment for the development of some of my ideas: the assistance of these and other colleagues is a benefit I value especially.

No writer on the great household can fail to reflect on his own domestic arrangements – and this book is richer for *tute la frape de garcuns* which has sometimes accompanied its composition, for my wife's wry smile at my knowledge of medieval domestic chores and unexpected interests while shopping. To Sue, Thomas, Matthew and Daniel, this book is dedicated with gratitude.

Christopher M. Woolgar
University of Southampton

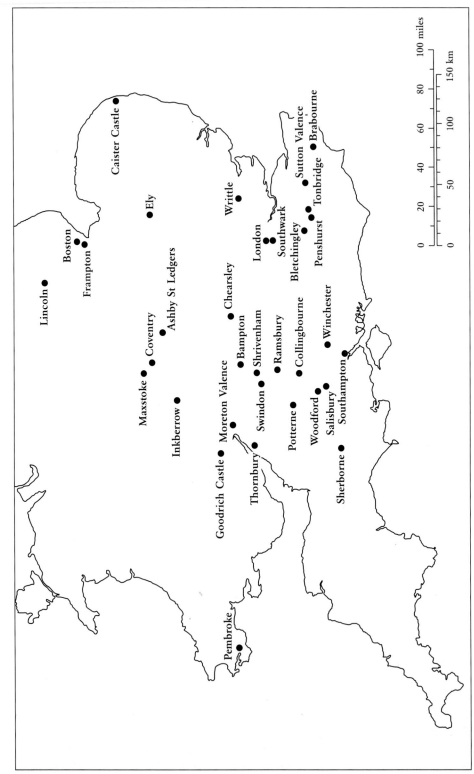

Map 1. Principal places mentioned in the text.

CHAPTER 1

Household Antiquities

It is no exaggeration to see in the historical landscape of the British Isles, in the houses, castles and religious houses, ruined or otherwise, a physical reminder of one of the most potent forces of the Western Middle Ages, the great household. As an institution it is central to the study of medieval history, providing the back-drop for many aspects of life from the development of politics, the conduct of government and international relations, to literature and drama, music, the arts and architecture, and much else besides. Its language is embedded in our own, although it is now rarely perceived as such. Menial servants were those who worked for the *mesnie*, or household; the bar at the pub is a direct descendant of the bar of the pantry and buttery, at which rations were dispensed; the caterer was the individual who purchased (*acater*) the household's requirements; *hotel* was the Anglo-Norman word for the household itself; and whole degrees of service and servants, which now have no function or a very different one, were present – pantlers, butlers, valets, yeomen, grooms and pages, stewards and marshals.

The way in which a household was conducted was a formal expression of lordship and a political statement. Its magnificence and splendour could be quite deliberately stupendous; likewise its size. This was a society in which display, lavish hospitality, prestige and social competition were all important, in which such distinctions came to be carefully weighed, nuances closely regarded and the overwhelming detail of ceremony recorded for posterity.[1] When, c. 1473, Olivier de la Marche, a master of the household of Charles the Bold, Duke of Burgundy, prepared a description of that court and its practices, des-tined for Edward IV, the English monarch must have had in mind how he might more than match the magnificence of his brother-in-law.[2] Even in death, the household was important. The executors of Richard Gravesend, Bishop of London (d. 1303), followed the usual practice of keeping his domestic establish-ment together until after his funeral. In itself, this was not untypical considera-tion for the standing of a bishop, but it was also a practical benefit in terms of organisation of a ceremony equally commensurate with the individual, which included a distribution to 31,968 poor, with arrangements for subsequent commemoration stretching throughout the following decade.[3] On this scale, 'great' may seem an appropriate epithet for the household: *magnum hospicium*. Contemporaries had also in view another distinction, to indicate the principal establishment of a lord, rather than parts domiciled elsewhere or travelling with him.

Outside the present-day royal households and a few aristocratic establishments, there is little now in Britain that can compare with the great household. The break in this tradition of living is no less recent than the early years of the twentieth century. Paradoxically, it is at this point in its demise that the great household is again widely seen: court ceremony, state occasions, accessible through the medium first of newsreel, then of television, are functions at which this form of living is prominent. At the same time, the admission of the public to great houses, the development of the National Trust and government agencies to preserve them, to package them as part of a heritage industry (a process which itself has been in train for some two centuries), make it all the more important to understand the household for what it was. The very longevity of the institution conceals many changes. While the servant in a great household of *c.* 1300 would not have been totally unacquainted with the main features of such an establishment two centuries later, there would have been much that would have struck him as novel.

The study of the medieval great household has never been out of favour. Since the sixteenth century, those engaged in the study of household antiquities, as it was then known, have done much to preserve and explain its remains. All subsequent students must tread in the steps of politicians, like the first Baron Burghley, whose curiosity about contemporary financial management took him to the early fourteenth-century household records of Thomas of Lancaster, and of antiquarians, such as Sir Simonds D'Ewes, to whom we owe the preservation of the Yorkist household ordinances and the best copy of the Black Book of the household of Edward IV.[4] Publication of texts gathered pace through the eighteenth and nineteenth centuries, underpinning studies of manners, meals and daily life, generating a sustained interest: a recondite and substantial document like the Northumberland Household Book of 1512 was published four times between 1770 and 1905. For the sightseers of the Napoleonic period, confined to the British Isles by continental war, the household's remains said something about national identity, about Britishness. They were celebrated in engravings and paintings, they were the backdrop of Walter Scott's novels and a major influence on the architecture of the neo-Gothic (Plate 1).[5]

Household antiquities have held an enduring interest for students of late medieval England. Our knowledge of the great household, however, is largely formed by a focus on single households or families, or individual aspects, or has been driven by historical interpretation. Much work has been coloured by an emphasis on bastard feudalism, the system whereby a lord retained men for service by cash payment rather than land. Other deficiencies lie in those works looking at life in the medieval household which are centred primarily on the architectural setting or its archaeology: there have been few based on a study of the house in use; and the combined study of architecture and etiquette has

1. Painted *c.* 1830–2, at a time of renewed interest in the great household and the medieval past, J. M. W. Turner's watercolour and gouache view of Kenilworth Castle, Warwickshire, shows visitors to the ruins: from left to right, the Strong Tower, John of Gaunt's great hall, the Saintlowe Tower, the remains of the great chamber with the keep behind and the sixteenth-century work of the Earl of Leicester at the right-hand side.

principally concentrated on the post-medieval period, with much work weighted towards the Continent.[6] Our view of English castles is essentially a military one, but a primary function of these sites was as a base for the domestic activities of the great household.[7] Equally, we study aspects of the household which seem of the first importance to us without recognising their significance to contemporaries. Great feasts and entertainments are well known, but what was the common expectation of daily life in the household? There are detailed studies of a single class of servants, such as musicians or players: there are few which tell of the general lot of servants. It is important to see what was usual before we can define what was unusual. This book therefore sets out to examine the basic characteristics of the household – size, membership, dynamics, economics, social context – as these are crucial if we are to place individual studies in perspective. This is not a work in the 'manners and customs' mould, although it touches on these matters, but an attempt at social history that does not shirk the detail of daily living: it is here that there is still much to learn. The main themes are the way the great household developed and functioned, broadly from the start of the thirteenth century to the close of the fifteenth; from the creation of a magnificence underpinned by what might seem to us an exaggerated manner of courtesy, gentility, livery and display, to an investigation of the life and conditions of servants; from the use of castles and residences, the influence of religion, the hot-house of a largely male establishment, to the opaque questions of diet and nutrition. The text touches upon the military retinue within the household at a number of points, but its principal focus is not on that body, falling instead on the grand operations of domestic living that characterised the medieval great household.

Between 1200 and 1500 considerable changes in English society were reflected in the great household. This period saw a definition of the peerage, in the sense of those who were regularly summoned to Parliament, a growth in its membership and an extension in the number of its ranks. In the thirteenth century, a lay magnate who intended to maintain his position in society would have needed an annual net income of about £400, the product of a minimum of 20 to 30 manors. At any one time in that century, there were probably between 80 and 90 individuals who met this criterion, with a further 15 bishops and between 25 and 30 abbots and priors who also had sufficient income to live in similar fashion.[8] There were 11 earldoms in existence at the end of Edward I's reign, at this date the only dignity other than the king's which could be inherited. During the fourteenth century, a further 24 non-royal earldoms were created. With the establishment of other ranks – dukedoms, marquisates – and the persistence of baronies, there were probably 60 to 70 families who were effectively distinguished by what became a hereditary right to receive a summons to Parliament.

The resources available to this group of families varied widely. In the early fourteenth century, two of the earls stood above the others: Thomas of Lancaster, with an annual income at the time of his death in 1322 of about £11,000 gross, and Gilbert de Clare, Earl of Gloucester, with about £6,000 gross. The accepted endowment in land for an earldom under Edward III appears to have been in the region of £1,000 a year and even that could not always be sustained. The assessed value of the wealth of the upper ranks of the peerage – three dukedoms and 11 earldoms – for the 1436 income tax was a little less than £15,000.[9] In one sense this defines the households that might be characterised as 'great', but it is a narrow definition. To examine a pattern of living – and medieval society throve on emulation – there is much to be said for casting the net more widely.

At the apex of society, the royal household was without parallel. The expenditure of the wealthiest earl, Thomas of Lancaster, reached about £7,500 on his household and wardrobe (responsible for special expenditure on cloth, jewels and other luxury goods) in 1313–14 and again in 1318–19, with the domestic household accounting for £3,400 in the first of these years and £4,800 in the second. Edward II's household expenses in 1318–19 totalled less than double this amount, about £8,310.[10] John of Gaunt had revenues on a scale similar to Lancaster, around £11,750 a year in 1394 and 1395, which probably meant an income of £10,000 net.[11] The costs of his household ranged from £5,750 in 1376–7 to a maximum of about £7,000 in 1392–3: the annual charges of the household of Richard II rose from around £19,000 at the start of his reign to about £27,000.[12]

The uniqueness of the Crown's position meant that it was, financially, by the end of the fourteenth century, the only body that could promote a court society of any size. Others might imitate the style of living, but they could no longer match the scale or the political effect.[13] Just as nobles imitated royalty, so the gentry aped the aristocracy. Sir Hamon Le Strange of Hunstanton, who had fought at Crécy and who maintained a modest establishment of 15 persons, would have seen himself as part of this society. His household expenses in the year to 1 August 1348 came to just over £6, with as much again drawn directly from manorial stock.[14] By the end of the fifteenth century there were probably between 1,000 and 2,000 households which aspired to live in the style of the great household. To group these together conceals a disparity in means, at the extremes of the range, of a factor of 100 and, in some instances, 1,000. What united the households was a common set of ideals. There will be found many examples of the use of limited resources husbanded to achieve particular effect on a small number of prestigious occasions, allowing even the lowest gentry to reinforce their standing among their peers and to delineate their difference from the other ranks of society.

To look at developments across this spectrum, a number of households has been selected as a focus for the examples in this book. The leading actors are two aristocratic households, those of Joan de Valence, Countess of Pembroke (d. 1307), and the Stafford Dukes of Buckingham in the fifteenth and early sixteenth centuries; two gentry families in the fourteenth century, the Multons of Frampton, near Boston in Lincolnshire, and the Catesbys of Northamptonshire and Warwickshire; an eminent knight, Sir John Fastolf (1380–1459); and two bishops, Richard Mitford, Bishop of Salisbury (d. 1407), and Thomas Arundel, Bishop of Ely and subsequently Archbishop of York and of Canterbury (1353–1414), with supporting material for the Bishops of Winchester, particularly William of Wykeham (d. 1404) and Cardinal Beaufort (d. 1447).

Joan de Valence was the daughter of Warin de Munchensy and his wife Joan, daughter of William Marshal, Earl of Pembroke. She married William de Valence, half-brother of Henry III, in August 1247, the year in which he acquired Goodrich Castle. He was granted the lordship of Wexford about the same time and, early in the following year, the share of the lordship of Pembroke to which his wife was entitled as coheir of the Earls of Pembroke. To these estates he added properties scattered through more than a dozen counties, largely in southern England, including the castle at Hertford. By the start of Edward I's reign, he had an income of about £2,500 p.a. William had a long career serving both Henry III and Edward I.[15] On William's death in May 1296, his wife held as her dower Goodrich Castle, Pembroke Castle and its lordship, Inkberrow in Worcestershire, Sutton Valence and Brabourne in Kent, half the hundred of Shrivenham, Berkshire, and the lordship of Wexford with other Irish properties, as well as Chearsley, Buckinghamshire; Moreton Valence, Gloucestershire; and Collingbourne and Swindon, Wiltshire.[16] Joan had a house in London, which was set in order for her visit there in May 1297, although she also made use of the Bishop of Winchester's palace in Southwark, possibly as a depot for her household goods.[17] Her annual income was about £1,000 and her household expenses between £400 and £500.[18] Joan had at least seven children, although there were no more than four alive at the time of her husband's death: Aymer, her son and successor to the earldom, and three daughters, Isabella de Hastings, Agnes de Valence and Joan Comyn. Aymer was probably about 26 at the time of his father's death and had recently married Beatrice de Nesle who, from at least 1295 until early 1297, spent much of her time residing with her mother-in-law, before embarking on an independent married life.[19] There are three accounts for the household of Joan de Valence, covering much of October 1295 to September 1297.[20]

The Stafford family, Dukes of Buckingham, had an annual income of about £5,000 at the time of Duke Edward's death in 1521.[21] The legacy of the three Dukes (Humphrey, 1402–60; Henry, d. 1483; and Edward, 1478–1521) and their dowagers (especially Humphrey's widow, Anne, d. 1480) was a group of major residences. These ranged from Stafford Castle, used extensively in the 1440s and 1450s, to the more recent buildings at Maxstoke, Warwickshire, and Writtle, Essex, much favoured by Duke Humphrey and his wife. Tonbridge Castle, in Kent, was also popular with the first Duke; Penshurst, Kent, and Thornbury, Gloucestershire, were used by him and by the third Duke. Thornbury was associated particularly with the third Duke. Bletchingley in Surrey was also conveniently situated for London.[22] In terms of records, the Stafford household is one of the better documented, exceptionally so for the fifteenth and early sixteenth centuries.

The Multons of Frampton, near Boston, were a junior branch of the Multon and Lucy families, Barons Egremont.[23] In 1343–4, the family received about £40 from rents, possibly only for a half-year, from property primarily in three areas of Lincolnshire, at Frampton and Boston; on the coast near Saltfleetby and Somercotes; and between Gainsborough and Lincoln, in Heapham, Sturton by Stow, Stow and Ingleby. Household and necessary expenses at the same time totalled about £60. In addition to several hundred charters and some estate records, there are two household accounts for the family from the 1340s.

By the late fourteenth century, the Catesby family were substantial gentry in Northamptonshire and Warwickshire, with estates based on Ashby St Ledgers, Ladbroke, Radbourn and the Shuckburghs, and Bubbenhall, together with property in Coventry. John Catesby (d. *c.* 1405) was a Member for Warwickshire in the Parliaments of 1372 and 1393, as well as holding royal commissions. The annual value of the estate was about £120 in the mid-1380s and the family was also associated with sheep-farming and cloth manufacture.[24] Besides estate accounts and deeds of title, there survives a group of records of household expenditure which encompass, in 1392–3, building work at Ashby.[25]

Sir John Fastolf was a household servant, in the train of Thomas, Duke of Clarence. He followed a military career in France from 1415, was knighted in 1416, and subsequently served as grand master of the household of the Duke of Bedford. He was a member of the French council of Henry VI from 1422 until 1439.[26] He employed the profits of his service to purchase property in East

Anglia and Southwark, with an outlay of £13,855 over a period of thirty years from 1415, 90% of which was spent in Norfolk, Suffolk and Essex, as well as investing in other profitable areas, notably the cloth-producing estate at Castle Combe, in which he had a life interest.[27] The purchases were marked by a pattern of farming to bring them into profitability and a major programme of building, including £6,000 invested in the construction of Caister Castle, Norfolk, with smaller amounts elsewhere, at his moated house at Horselydown in Southwark.[28] There survives a number of inventories of his possessions, particularly at Caister, of his plate and descriptions of some of his jewels, as well as documentation for his household.[29]

Bishop Mitford of Salisbury had been a clerk in royal service, acting as Richard II's secretary between 1385 and 1388. He held the bishopric of Chichester from 1390 – and his household appears obliquely in the accounts of William of Wykeham, Bishop of Winchester, in 1393, during which time he resided at Wolvesey at Wykeham's expense. In 1395 he was translated to Salisbury where he remained until his death in 1407. The see of Salisbury was worth about £1,000 per annum at this date and there is an extensive account for the Bishop's household during the last eight months of his life, during which about £600 was spent. Mitford resided at this time on his Wiltshire manors of Woodford and Potterne, with parts of his household at Ramsbury and Salisbury.[30] For the household of Thomas Arundel, there survives a group of accounts for parts of the years 1380–4, while he was Bishop of Ely, which have much useful material to contrast with the Mitford household.[31]

A primary motive in selecting these households for closer study has been the existence of documentation for their activities. They also provide examples of a style of living at different ranks of upper-class society and a geographic spread across the country. Since, however, there are so few households for which either extensive domestic records or physical remains survive, reference is made to a broader range of establishments. The focus of the work is England and the much more extensive material illustrative of continental households and practices has largely been excluded.

Chapter 2

Size, Membership and Hospitality

Describing the Burgundian court in *c.* 1473, Olivier de la Marche began with 'the service of God and of the Duke's chapel, which must be the beginning of all things'.[1] Beyond that, the prime purposes of the household were to maintain the honour, status, profit and well-being of the lord. Everything was organised to those ends, providing a way of life as much as a home for the lord, his immediate family and a large group of servants and followers. An economist might characterise the household entirely as a consumer, dependent on the produce of land and rents; an anthropologist would note the vigour of the distinction both between households and between the social groups within them. The majority of the household's inhabitants was male, even in establishments headed by a woman: in 1290, of 148 identifiable members of the household of Eleanor of Castile, Edward I's first wife, fewer than 10% were women.[2] Household members led a public life, with no privacy in any sense that we would recognise. Few individuals would have been alone in the performance of their tasks, in anything that we might regard as leisure or in the conduct of any aspect of life we would consider personal, from washing to sleeping. They were organised in a hierarchical fashion: status, rank and precedence were of supreme rather than nugatory importance. The members of the household did not travel to work, but the household did: to maintain the lord's status and position, it was essentially a peripatetic institution for much of the Middle Ages, although the amount of travel diminished markedly from the fourteenth century onwards.

The household was a legal entity in which rights might be granted. At a pragmatic level this was implicit in the English royal household since at least the 1130s, when the *Constitutio domus regis* (establishment of the king's household) recorded the entitlements and changes of personnel.[3] From around 1300, a more patent definition was applied. Indentures of retinue – that is, those binding an individual to the service of a lord, typically in time of war and peace in return for a money payment – provide details of household membership, specifying the rights granted. These included either a right to food and drink within the household, sometimes known as bouche of court, or a regular payment of wages in lieu. The balance varied from time to time, but, aside from the royal household, where the entitlement to food had been withdrawn from at least a part of the household in 1300,[4] most members of the great household, with the exception of the grooms and pages of the marshalsea (stables), ate within the household. There were standard allowances for those members entitled to food and drink, although the amounts varied between households. The indentures also provided for servants and horses, sometimes for a limited duration.

Indentures of retinue were probably unusual.[5] While they regulated temporary membership, other documents looked at a permanent relationship, much in the way that a religious house might manage a corrody (the privileges, typically food, drink and accommodation, granted to a permanent lodger). In February 1312, the Earl of Hereford exchanged parts of a manor in Essex with William, son of Ralph de Merk, giving him a life interest in a property with 60 acres. At the same time, William was to have reasonable food and drink, fitting for an esquire, together with a horse and a groom, in the Earl's household or that of his wife, as well as a yearly allowance of two sets of clothes, as worn by the Earl's esquires.[6] This sharper definition of household membership established rates of livery and food, even the table in a lord's hall at which an individual was to sit. It was reflected in the construction of checker rolls, much like school attendance registers, or calendars, lists aimed at controlling membership and expenditure, a process refined through the fourteenth century.

The corporate sense of the household was reinforced by marks of identification. Livery – the issue of cloth, or clothing, to members of the household – was a practice at least as old as the middle of the twelfth century.[7] Robert Grosseteste advised the Countess of Lincoln in *c.* 1240–2 that the knights and gentlemen (*gentis hommes*) who received clothing from her, to maintain her honour, should wear it every day, especially at meal times and in her presence and not 'old surcoats, soiled cloaks and cut-off coats'.[8] By the end of the fourteenth century the identity thus conferred applied more widely than the membership of the household, to all a lord's followers; and it became fashionable to extend the group further by the use of livery collars and badges (Plate 2).[9]

How big was the great household? The largest domestic establishments were those of the royal family, especially the king. Throughout the fourteenth century, the royal household had between 400 and 700 servants, four to seven times the adult population of Cuxham, in Oxfordshire, a typical Midlands village, on the eve of the Black Death.[10] The passage of the royal household through the countryside, therefore, had an enormous impact. Its size reflected a recent rise in numbers of servants: there were probably no more than 150 under Henry I. The household ordinance of Edward I of 1279 listed 53 individuals and, though this is not a complete list of members (there were few allocated to the marshalsea), his household was smaller than that of Edward II.[11] In 1279, it had 10 carts, six long and four short; by 1318, Edward II had 20 carts for the household offices, each hauled by five horses, that is, they were all long carts. The 1318 ordinance listed a minimum of 363 servants: 76 in the wardrobe and general officials, such as the steward of the household, the treasurer, other great officers, the chaplains, confessor and almoner; 47 servants for the king's chamber; 39 for the hall; 30 for the pantry and buttery; and 42 for the kitchen and larder. The

2. Edward Grimston, a
diplomat and servant of
Henry VI, with his
Lancastrian livery collar of
SS in his hand. He was
probably conducting
negotiations with the
Duchess of Burgundy at
Brussels when he was
painted by Petrus Christus
in 1446.

largest department was the marshalsea, which totalled at least 129, to which
must be added the grooms and valets for horses located out of court, at a ratio
of one person per horse, and grooms for horses at court, also at a one to one
ratio.[12] The establishments of queens and children, as well as those of royal
wards, domiciled within the king's household, were additional. Numbers calcu-
lated from royal accounts give, for example, 579 servants in 1359–60, and 380
in 1392–3. The royal household continued to increase in size, probably to more
than 800 during the reign of Henry VI, and further still during the sixteenth and
seventeenth centuries.[13]

Whether other households grew is more in debate. Firstly, there was a question of resources and the diminishing landed endowment available in the fourteenth century. As household expenditure was the most important call on a
magnate's income, the size of the great household – if the quality of its membership was to be maintained – was likely to diminish through the fourteenth and
fifteenth centuries. Household size has been addressed largely by historians
interested in service and lordship. Their work has been founded on calendars
of household members, checker rolls and livery rolls, listing those receiving

cloth, extending beyond the immediate establishment of the household.[14] All these records are rare: no more than a handful survives in each case and, of all types, there is only one, a livery roll for Elizabeth de Burgh, Lady of Clare, for 1343–4,[15] which predates the mid-fourteenth century. These documents provide a precise, legalistic definition of size, for a small number of households, and may themselves be the product of a particular formalism. A broader range of information can be obtained by examining domestic records, listing daily expenses. These provide a pragmatic definition of household size, encompassing all who ate or drank there, with some indication as well of how many were guests.

The daily (or diet) accounts of households contain four areas of quantitative information which merit examination: the number of portions served; pantry accounts for bread; buttery accounts for ale; and accounts for servants, particularly of the marshalsea, who were paid wages rather than given food. None of these is straightforward in its interpretation, but where common ground can be established, these figures can indicate the number of individuals present or portions of food served each day. One other area, the number of horses, must be discounted for the purposes of calculating household size. When a household resided in a single place for more than a few days, there were advantages in diminishing the concentration of horses – and horses provisioned elsewhere, but not always their accompanying staff, tended to disappear from the view of household documents, to become charges on the manors where they were billeted. It was the frequency with which a household moved, rather than its size, that determined how many horses it needed.

Numbers of *fercula* (portions) served were recorded in households from the 1270s onwards, but the numbers themselves, beyond a handful for the royal household, are not given before 1320. A single daily figure for *fercula* appears on the accounts of larger households for the remainder of the fourteenth century and into the fifteenth. A *ferculum* sometimes equated with a mess, the unit in which food was served, commonly for four people but fewer for some foods. It was also employed to indicate the number of individuals who were served or the number present that day. Accounts later in the fourteenth century divided the numbers between meals: lunch (*prandium*), supper (*cena*) and, sometimes, breakfast (*jantaculum*).[16]

By correlating the *fercula* with bread and ale accounts, the number of individuals represented can be estimated. In the late fourteenth and early fifteenth centuries each person, on average, received one loaf a day (although in some households the figure was two). With caution, this can be projected backwards by looking at the sums spent on bread in earlier pantry accounts.[17] The accounts for ale are more straightforward. For most purposes, an allowance of ale of about 1 gallon per day was made to household members, although it was sometimes of two different qualities. Those drinking wine rather than ale were no more than a select few.

In combination, these figures give a general indication of the numbers in the household consuming food and drink. What about those who did not? The mar-

Table 1. Household size

Household	Date	Gross income (£)	Total size	Grooms etc.	Poor	Horses
Eleanor de Montfort, Countess of Leicester[1]	1265	–	207	–	14–800[2]	40[3]
Joan de Valence, Countess of Pembroke[4]	1295–6[5]	1,000	122	20	8	32
Joan de Valence, Countess of Pembroke	1296[6]	1,000	194	30	21	53
Joan de Valence, Countess of Pembroke	1296[7]	1,000	154	19	21	40
Joan de Valence, Countess of Pembroke	1296–7[8]	1,000	135	12	21	31[9]
Henry de Lacy, Earl of Lincoln[10]	1299	–	184	52	–	74
Thomas of Lancaster, Earl of Lancaster[11]	1318–19	11,000	708	341	–	402
Hugh Audley the Younger[12]	1320	2,500[13]	96[14]	24	–	42[15]
Ralph of Shrewsbury, Bishop of Bath and Wells	1337–8	–	90+[16]	see note 16	–	see note 16
Thomas Arundel, Bishop of Ely[17]	1380–1	2,500[18]	83	20[19]	–	–
Thomas Arundel, Bishop of Ely[20]	1383–4	2,500[21]	82	16	–	–
Edward Courtenay, Earl of Devon[22]	1384–5	1,000[23]	46[24]	–[25]	–	–
Richard Mitford, Bishop of Salisbury	1406–7[26]	1,000	73	44[27]	–	39[28]
Edward Plantagenet, Duke of York[29]	1409–10	–	91	–	–	–
Thomas Bourgchier, Archbishop of Canterbury[30]	1459	–	68	–	–	60
Edward Stafford, Duke of Buckingham[31]	1501	5,000[32]	67	–	–	–
Edward Stafford, Duke of Buckingham[33]	1503–4	5,000	130	–	–	–
Edward Stafford, Duke of Buckingham (Thornbury)[34]	1507–8	5,000	157	–	–	–
Edward Stafford, Duke of Buckingham (London)	1507–8	5,000	57	–	–	–

Sources and notes

This table has been computed individually for each household based on the information in diet accounts. The total size is the average number of people present in the household, including grooms, poor and guests. A *ferculum* has been treated as representing one person per day. Where there are no figures for *fercula*, an estimate of the loaves baked has been derived, for the thirteenth and fourteenth centuries, from the account of Henry de Lacy. This gives 235 loaves per quarter; this source also provides a standard value of 0.37d. per loaf. The total of loaves has been deflated to 54%, based on the proportion used for *fercula* in the household of Bishop Mitford of Salisbury.

1. *MHE*, pp. 1–86. A small group of servants, away from the main household at wages for part of the account, has not been included.

2. Varying numbers of poor occasionally recorded, but no figures for those constantly present in the household (and some may have been). There was occasional, massive provision for the poor: on 14 April 1265, for 800; but on 5 May 1265, there were 4 bushels of wheat for the poor, spread over 8 days, which suggests a continuing, but smaller, number in the household, probably 14 or 15 per day.

3. There are some hints at the enormous number of horses that could accompany an earl's household: the largest number present was 334, on 19 March 1265, when Eleanor's household was joined by that of her husband: *MHE*, p. 14.

4. PRO E101/505/25–7.

5. 29 September 1295– 5 May 1296, the last day in Joan's accounts before the death of her husband.

6. 18 May 1296–26 June 1296: from the death of her husband to the date she assumed full responsibility for the costs of her household (some costs resulting from her husband's death and affecting her household may have been borne by his executors).

7. 27 June 1296–28 September 1296: all charges borne by Joan de Valence.

8. 29 September 1296–28 September 1297.

9. Includes horses stabled at Moreton Valence while the main household is at Goodrich Castle, 13 December 1296–17 February 1297.

10. *HAME* i, pp. 163–70.

11. PRO DL28/1/14.

12. PRO E101/510/17, E101/372/4, E101/505/17.

13. Rawcliffe, *Staffords*, p. 8.

14. An average of 40.48 *fercula* per day (the first time *fercula* appear in a private household account), but with 1 loaf per person per day (and 24 grooms paid wages), the household had 96 people.

15. Includes a few hackneys, not otherwise mentioned.

16. 'Ralph of Shrewsbury': plus grooms and pages at wages, varying from a maximum of 23 to 0. While they were probably present all the time, they were not recorded for much of it.

17. Based on CUL EDR D5/2–4, accounts for single months, for October 1380, September 1381 and November 1381. The account for September 1381 has the annual totals for the year to 30 September.

18. Gross expenditure on the household, CUL EDR D5/2; Aston, *Arundel*, p. 422.

19. Mainly grooms, but usually includes 1 page per day and the launderer.

20. Based on monthly accounts for November and December 1383 (PRO E101/400/28), August 1384 and September 1384 (CUL EDR D5/5–6).

21. Gross expenditure on the household for the year: CUL EDR D5/6.

22. Based on a household account for Tiverton, for 280 days in 1384–5 (BL Add. Roll 64,803), and the livery roll for the same year (BL Add. Roll 64,320).

23. BL Add. Ch. 13,972, receiver general's account for 1392–3.

24. 85 loaves per day, with deflation to 54%, gives 46 loaves/*fercula* per day. This account gives the price of a loaf as ½d. and 24.3 loaves per bushel. Including the Earl, there are 140 individuals named in the livery roll.

25. 63 servants of rank of valet or below listed in livery roll of 1384–5, but not all based in the household and not all present at one time.

26. *HAME* i, pp. 264–430.

27. Includes both valets and grooms. Pages at Sherborne, paid cash wages in the account on an *ad hoc* basis, are not included.

28. Includes horses resident with the main household and those stabled at Sherborne and Salisbury.

29. Northants RO Westmorland (Apethorpe) 4.xx.4.

30. LPL ED 1973.

31. PRO E101/546/18, probably for the Duke's foreign household, in London.

32. Rawcliffe, *Staffords*, p. 133.

33. Staffs. RO D641/1/3/8.

34. Staffs. RO D1721/1/5: two figures are given, the first for residence at Thornbury, 6 November – 27 January and 28 February–22 March; the second for the intervening period, when the Duke travelled to London and Richmond.

shalsea servants were frequently paid cash wages all the time, as were other servants when away from the household, at rates that changed little throughout the Middle Ages. The wages give a good indication of the size of this part of the household. In the household of Hugh Audley the Younger, in 1320, a cash sum was recorded each day for wages for the marshalsea, with the occasional addition of a schedule sewn to the roll setting out who, precisely, was at wages, what their wage was, and for which horses they were responsible. Here the marshalsea servants were overwhelmingly grooms (*garciones*), entitled to 1½d. a day. There were only one or two pages, who received a lower rate. If the daily wage bill is divided by 1½d., the result is a slight underestimate of the numbers of personnel in this department.[18] The pattern can be replicated in other households. In a few establishments, there were servants in other departments who received wages rather than food, such as the launderer in the household of Thomas Arundel, Bishop of Ely.[19]

These groups – those receiving food and those receiving wages – did not necessarily encompass the totality of the household. Any discussion of size would be incomplete if it ignored the part played by charity and the poor. The accounts suggest an evolving pattern, from large-scale, almost indiscriminate, charity practised in the first two-thirds of the thirteenth century, to more regulated, disciplined distribution later in the century. The household of Eleanor de Montfort, Countess of Leicester, in 1265, with its occasional displays of largess on an impressive scale, for as many as 800, contrasts with that of Joan de Valence, in 1295–7, with its regular group of possibly resident poor. After the death of Joan's husband in May 1296, this amounted to 20 persons each day, with 27 most Saturdays.[20] Where there are separate figures for numbers of poor, these can be taken into account. If the poor shared the bread corn used by the household (already used to calculate its size), they do not increase the overall household numbers, but give an idea of their percentage in its make-up. In the later Middle Ages, charity was formalised further. In Archbishop Bourgchier's household, in 1459, the allowance for the poor probably did not exceed provision for one person (two loaves and 1 gallon of ale per day), but this may have been augmented by distribution of broken meat from the tables, as outlined in later household ordinances.[21]

What conclusions can be drawn from this analysis (Table 1)? The figures are no more than a general guide, as they are based on a small sample and many assumptions have been made in their preparation. They suggest the great household in the period before the Black Death could be very substantial indeed, especially among the upper nobility. Aside from the enormous household of Thomas of Lancaster, the pattern is one of a general decrease in numbers through the fourteenth century, continuing into the fifteenth, but with some possibility of an increase recorded in the figures for the household of the third Duke of Buckingham at the start of the sixteenth century. Military retainers were almost certainly an important element in Lancaster's household in 1318–19. This year saw two Parliaments of long duration and a Scottish war. The military retinue and its followers would have been entitled to bouche of court exactly like the rest of the household. Later, more use was made of a wider range of devices, such as annuities, for maintaining the lord's influence, and the requirement for a member of the lord's connection to attend him in his household was lessened. At the same time, the economic and social stability of the gentry during the fourteenth and fifteenth centuries diminished their need – and desire – for household service. The quality of the household surrounding the lord became a more subtle instrument for ensuring the status of an establishment than presence of numbers. These last, when needed from a military point of view, might increasingly be drawn from a lord's lesser tenants, from the yeomanry rather than the gentry.[22]

A comparison between the households of Thomas of Lancaster and John of Gaunt is instructive, as both had similar financial resources. Unfortunately the fragments of accounts that survive for Gaunt's household are for an untypical period of not much more than a month in 1383, when John of Gaunt was absent.[23] Other sources suggest Gaunt had a household of 115 men. In addition, his indentured retinue was 170 strong: the number of annuitants connected with the household, however, was even larger.[24] There was a marked diminution in the size of other households: that of Archbishop Stratford, in 1347, averaged 191 persons, while Archbishop Bourgchier's establishment, a century later, averaged 68.[25] The biggest households reached their peak in terms of numbers *c.* 1300. After the middle of the fourteenth century the great household, setting aside royal establishments, was never to be as large again, although there may have been some growth towards the end of the fifteenth century. Mirroring this pattern, expenditure per person in the household was at its lowest in the thirteenth century, climbing to a peak of affluence in the late fourteenth and early fifteenth centuries, but declining again by the late fifteenth and early sixteenth centuries (Table 2).

The household was there to serve the lord and his immediate family. This group of individuals could be small. In the household of Joan de Valence, for much of 1296, it probably included three people, Joan herself, her daughter-in-law Beatrice de Nesle and Edward Burnel, a minor whose wardship had been purchased by William de Valence. In 1467, the family of John Howard, later Duke of Norfolk, at Stoke-by-Nayland, included his six children and two wards, John and Thomas Gorge. He had other relations in his household, but they were classed as servants – one of his nephews, Henry Daniel, was listed among his gentlemen at this date.[26]

The formal membership of the household could encompass individuals who were present infrequently, the lord's advisers and council, besides military retainers and others more loosely connected to him. As the household travelled less, it was sometimes divided into separate parts: the great household – the full, permanent establishment; the riding or foreign household, which accompanied the lord when he travelled; and, exceptionally, a secret household, a small group of individuals who remained with the lord when it did not suit him formally to keep household, that is, when the household was 'broken up'. In 1507–8, the great household of the Duke of Buckingham at Thornbury, together with its

Table 2. Daily average costs per person in the household

Household	Gross annual costs of the household (£)	Average cost per person per day (pence)
Joan de Valence 1296–7[1]	414	2
Thomas of Lancaster 1318–19[2]	4,800	4.5
Hugh Audley the Younger 1320	649	4.4
Ralph of Shrewsbury, Bishop of Bath and Wells 1337–8[3]	668	4.9
Thomas Arundel, Bishop of Ely 1380–1	1,729	13.7
Thomas Arundel, Bishop of Ely 1383–4	1,452	11.6
Edward Courtenay, Earl of Devon 1384–5[4]	513	7.3
Richard Mitford, Bishop of Salisbury 1406–7	1,000	9
Edward Plantagenet, Duke of York 1409–10	1,127	8.1
Edward Stafford, Duke of Buckingham 1503–4	1,168	6

Sources

PRO E101/505/26–7; DL28/1/14; E101/372/4, E101/505/17, E101/510/17; 'Ralph of Shrewsbury';
CUL EDR D5/2, 6; BL Add. Roll 64,803; *HAME* i, pp. 264–430; Northants RO Westmorland
(Apethorpe) 4. xx. 4; Staffs. RO D641/1/3/8.

Notes

This table is based on gross household expenses, including all those charged on the household,
whether in receipt of wages or eating within it. Within each household some individuals would
have received much more per day, others less.

1. Based on gross expense of £414 and daily attendance of 135; the expense probably under-
    values the amount of produce taken directly from demesnes without valuation.
2. Gross expense from Maddicott, *Thomas of Lancaster*, p. 27.
3. A part of the household was detached from time to time to look after horses, but the size of
    this portion, in grooms and pages, is uncertain and has not been included in the calculation.
    The average per person is therefore more generous than it probably was.
4. Some expenses in this household may have been borne by the receiver general (e.g. Devon
    RO CR 488, CR 500 and BL Add. Ch. 13,972), which would undervalue the daily expense
    per person given here.

guests, averaged 157 individuals, while the foreign household, which accompanied the Duke to London, was much smaller, averaging 57 people including guests
(Table 3). The riding household of the Earl of Northumberland, *c.* 1511–12,
comprised 36 individuals, accompanying him whenever he travelled. His secret
household, with his wife, children and those servants deemed necessary,
amounted to 42.[27]

What did all these servants do? The key to much activity lay in what was not
immediately functional, in religion, display, extravagance, courtesy, gesture and
movement, indeed in anything that underpinned status and magnificence. It was
for this reason that separate households were maintained, as necessary, for
wives, children and even babies. Everything was conducted to maintain the
estate, or status, of the individual (Plate 3). From a functional point of view,

Table 3. The household of Edward Stafford, third Duke of Buckingham, in 1507–8

Place/meal	Gentle servants (gentiles)	Valets (valecti)	Grooms (garciones)	Visitors (extranii)	Total
Thornbury: lunch (*prandium*)	53 34%	58	46	69 44%	157
Thornbury: supper (*cena*)	52 33%	60	45	78 50%	157
London: lunch	23 35%	22	20	25 38%	65
London: supper	18 37%	17	14	15 31%	49

Source

Staffs. RO D1721/1/5.

Notes

The table gives average daily attendances. The visitors are included in the preceding three categories. The Duke resided at Thornbury from 6 November to 27 January and again from 28 February to 22 March. The London figures represent Buckingham's journey to London, his stay there and at Richmond, followed by his return journey to Thornbury in January and February 1508.

however, the great household needed considerable organisation to achieve its ends. It had a departmental structure, at its most basic a pantry, responsible for bread and napery (table linen); a buttery, for looking after wine and ale; a kitchen; and a marshalsea. To these four departments others, usually specialised offshoots, were added as needed. In this way, the kitchen might have some functions hived off into sauceries and confectionaries, sculleries, poultries and larders. In the household of Bishop Mitford of Salisbury in 1406–7, there was a cellar, responsible for wine, as well as a buttery, which looked after the ale; there was also a chandlery for candles.[28] Most households had a financial department – called a wardrobe or chamber – for the lord's treasure. To our confusion, but not that of contemporaries, items of considerable value, particularly cloth and spices, were sometimes the province of another department, also called the wardrobe (or Great Wardrobe in the English royal household). And there were other departments responsible for looking after specific areas of the household, such as the hall. These departments were administrative entities. At the same time, there were rooms associated with these functions which bore the same names but which may or may not have been directly associated with the department as an organisation.

The work of the departments and their staffs will be examined in more detail later, but some aspects of their personnel and duties should be mentioned at this stage. The range of personnel can be seen in an ordinance for the Willoughby of Eresby household, *c.* 1319 or *c.* 1339. The household was in the charge of a steward, who had two coadjutors who might act in his absence, jointly with the

3. The birth of Henry VI at Windsor. The status of the infant is indicated by his coroneted cap of estate; his mother wears her crown in bed. At the chamber door, the news is given to a male messenger by one of the all-female staff attending the birth. The women's clothing, particularly the deep fur border on the gown of the lady holding the baby, marks them out as gentle servants. From the Beauchamp Pageant, *c.* 1483–7.

wardrober. There was a clerk of the offices – known elsewhere as the clerk of the household – who was the deputy of the wardrober, and a marshal. Together with other senior financial officials, a treasurer or controller (one who kept a counter-roll, or duplicate record of finances), they were later known as the head or chief officers. The Eresby household had a chaplain and almoner, who wrote letters or other documents as the need arose, as well as keeping a counter-roll of expenses in the absence of the wardrober. There was a chief caterer, or purchaser, and then a group of individuals who worked in the departments: two pantlers (who looked after the bread) and two butlers, with two grooms; two cooks and two larderers with two grooms; two ushers and two chandlers; a porter, a baker and a brewer, with a groom; two farriers and one groom; a saucerer and a poulterer; and a female laundress with a female assistant.[29]

The household was imbued with a sense of hierarchy that was only in part related to function. It reflected more widely the stratification in the rest of society, from the peerage down to the unfree villein. It might be expected that within the household the perception of difference was sharper than elsewhere – it was here, after all, that the groups were set alongside each other all the time – but the position was not without ambiguity and was subject to change. There were three facets that defined status: rank, precedence (relative within rank) and the possession of gentility, a quality which characterised a group of ranks.

The 'Rules' of Robert Grosseteste, *c.* 1240–2, drawn up for the Countess of Lincoln, envisaged that the household would include 'your knights and your gentlemen (*gentis hommes*) who take your robes'. In the Latin version of the text, *gentis hommes* appeared as *armigeri vestri sive valetti et alii* – 'esquires, or valets and others'; and in another part of the French text, the knights, chaplains, those who headed the household departments (*seriaunz de mester*) and the gentlemen were spoken of as a group. They constituted the free household (*fraunche maynee* or *libera familia*). The free household excluded another group, the grooms (*garcuns*) who, at one point, were said to eat as a body in hall, but some may have been at wages, without a right to food within the household, as there was a danger that they would eat what had been set aside for alms. It was a group of three valets – gentle servants – who were to be selected each day to serve drink at the high table and at the two side-tables. The 'Rules' also noted a division between servants whose domain was inside the house and those whose business was outside (*dedenz u dehors*).[30]

Some of these distinctions manifested themselves as economic gradations. In the household of Joan de Valence in 1295–7, all those valets who received footwear or a payment in lieu (*calciamentum*) when on business outside the household had a daily wage of 2d.; the grooms, on the other hand, formed a body that were paid a wage all the time (rather than eating in the household), at a daily rate of 1½d. Other groups were paid more in wages than the valets, ranging from 4d. to 10d. a day, but it is not possible to say how their rank was defined, or whether the level of payment depended on expertise and responsibility.[31] The 23 allowances for valets listed at Michaelmas 1296 covered individuals performing a range of functions: the clerk of the chapel, Humphrey of Joan's chamber, John of Joan's wardrobe, Richard the Usher, Joan's washerwoman, John of Beatrice de Nesle's chamber, Walter the Farrier, Richard the Saucerer, Isaac of the Kitchen, John the Baker, John the Palfreyman of Joan de Valence, Hec the Coachman, John the Palfreyman of Beatrice, Adam the Carter, the huntsman and John the groom of Edward Burnel. The list itself suggests a lack of precision, perhaps that the word valet referred to a rate of allowance for a grade of job, which others who nominally had a different rank, such as the groom of Edward Burnel, received in particular circumstances.[32] The household ordinances of Walter de Wenlok, Abbot of Westminster, of the late 1290s, setting out liveries of clothing, broke the establishment into four groups: senior officials and distinguished individuals; esquires, including the head butler, a master cook, a marshal, a farrier and a body-servant – *un vadlet pur nostre cors*; a third group, the valets of the offices (*vadlez de mesters*), who included a chamberlain, larderer, under-butler, under-pantler, porter, baker and brewer, carter and barber; and, fourthly, grooms, including a palfreyman, a groom for the chaplain and two grooms for the cart. Here, again, there was an individual who might be thought to be placed in one group as a valet, but was in fact considered as an esquire.[33]

In society in general, the categorisation of these terms sharpened, especially from the middle third of the fourteenth century. There was equally a transformation of terms that had been largely synonymous from a military point of view, such as esquire (*armiger, esquier*) and valet (*vallettus*), into ones that were differentiated militarily, socially and economically. At this time the rank of esquire, originally a servant of a knight who looked after his horse and arms, became solidly associated with a territorial and economic formulation of status, rather than a military designation. Household service was an important denominator in the categorisation of estates in general.[34]

In the schedule setting out the groups who were to pay the poll tax granted in 1379, knights bachelor and those esquires whose estates were sufficient to support knighthood were to pay 20s.; an esquire with less land was to pay 6s. 8d.; and the esquire who was without land but in service or had borne arms was to pay 3s. 4d. Valets were not noted in the tax, but a little later were equated with yeomen. In the late fourteenth and early fifteenth centuries, there was a downward movement of the term 'valet' to this end: it was no longer considered a gentle rank.

At the same time 'gentleman' came to be used to define the lowest rank of gentle society – knights, esquires, gentlemen – as opposed to members of the gentle classes in general.[35] In 1406–7, in the household of Bishop Mitford of Salisbury, the meals each day were divided between the members of the household of gentle rank (*gentiles*) on the one hand, and valets and grooms on the other.[36] In 1423–4 and 1425–6, Sir Hugh Luttrell of Dunster purchased livery for groups of gentlemen (*generosi*), valets and grooms.[37] In 1467, Sir John Howard's household had seven gentlewomen, 16 gentlemen, 49 yeomen and 27 grooms.[38]

Howard's household represented a common balance between the two groups, some 23% being of gentle rank. In the household of Thomas Arundel, Bishop of Ely, in 1381 and 1383, the proportion was 22%;[39] and in the household of Archbishop Bourgchier, in 1459, it was slightly higher, at 28%.[40] By the start of the sixteenth century, this proportion had risen further: in the household of the Duke of Buckingham, in 1507–8, it was between 33% and 37%, the higher percentage coming from Buckingham's foreign household, in London (Table 3).

The household depended on the character of its individual members, whether gentry or lesser servants, to establish its quality: it is against this that the movement towards gentility should be set.[41] There were several reflections of this transition. The cost of wages for household servants typically consumed about 10% of the budget of the great household; but in the households of the greatest magnates through the fifteenth and early sixteenth centuries, the proportion rose to between 15% and 20%.[42] Gentle servants also looked different: their garments were of a better quality (the liveries they were given were of more expensive cloth) and it was not uncommon, for example, for them to wear swords while carrying out their waiting duties (Plates 4, 5 and 6; compare Plates 52 and 53). In the fourteenth century, the development of a courtly concept of

knighthood, as opposed to a largely military one, accompanied changes in heraldry, the attachment of heralds to some aristocratic households, tournaments
and jousting. This process played a part in the growth of courtesy and ceremon-
ious practices, for which appropriate servants were needed.[43] But servants of
any rank were necessary to underpin status. Elizabeth Stonor wrote to her
husband in March 1478: 'And I pray you that ye wylle sende me som off your
sarvantys and myne to wayte upone me, for now I ame ryght bare off sarvantys.'[44]

Besides servants, guests formed an important element in the household.
Hospitality was a Christian duty and the guest had special status. Entertainment
was also an occasion for the display of generosity and magnificence.[45] From the
middle of the fourteenth century onwards, there is a good deal of information
about those visiting the great household. At this date, the great household
received individual visitors: rarely by the fourteenth century did it accept the
entire household of another magnate at its own charge. This had been the practice earlier. In 1207, Hugh de Neville of Essex had all his household costs at
Southoe, Hunts., borne by Saher de Quincy; those at Salisbury, by the Bishop;
and at Abingdon, by the Abbot.[46] Joan de Valence probably bore the entire cost
of the visit of the Countess of Gloucester and her son in February 1297; the costs
of her own household, with the exception of the wages of 12 grooms, were
covered by her son, Aymer, when she visited Newton Valence on 28 May 1297.[47]
When Hugh Audley the Younger visited the Archbishop of Canterbury at
Sturry on 10 June 1320, he incurred no household charges for his pantry,
buttery, kitchen, poultry, scullery or saucery, but he did pay for food for 23 of
his own servants and three grooms of others who had accompanied his household – and this development was probably indicative of the way hospitality was
rationed.[48] Monasteries, in particular, increasingly in the thirteenth century,
separated the entertainment of the lord (for which they might pay) from that of
his household. They subsequently resisted the right of all but the patron of the
monastery to hospitality, in which they were confirmed by statute in 1275.[49]

The English royal household, where both the potential charge and benefit
were much greater, may have maintained longer the practice of subsisting at the
expense of others. The detail of the royal visit – how much and who would be
supported on a hospitable basis – was, however, negotiable from at least the
1280s.[50] Thomas Arundel, as Bishop of Ely, entertained Richard II, Queen
Anne, John Holand and the Duchess of Brittany, the dowager Countess of
Pembroke and other magnates, ladies and men in great number (*viribus in mag-
nitudine copiosa*) on 6 July 1383 at a cost of nearly £140, as well as investing more
than £22 in napery and spices for the occasion.[51] His daily charges were normally between £3 and £4, about the same level as those of William of Wykeham,
Bishop of Winchester, whom Richard visited in 1393. Although Wykeham provided hospitality for the King on three occasions, on one of which the King
brought more than 180 people with him, the charge did not exceed £26 on any
of them.[52] When Henry IV used Wolvesey Castle at the time of his wedding to
Joan of Navarre, the Bishop of Winchester may have confined his expenditure

4. Arthur, Lancelot and Guinevere proceed to table. The King, Queen and others, seated along one side of the table, drinking, are attended by a gentle servant, with a sword, who brings food to the table and delivers it on bent knee. The table is covered with a cloth, with loose folds down one side, a rich selection of dishes, some covered, and a covered cup. There are trenchers of metal or wood in front of the diners and slices of bread on the table. A repainted illumination of the Bohun school, *c.* 1360–*c.* 1380, in a French romance of *c.* 1300.

5. A king, dining alone, not jostled on either side by fellow diners, from Walter de Milemete's manuscript of *De secretis secretorum*, presented to the future Edward III, *c.* 1326–7. The king is served by three kneeling attendants, one cutting bread, another opening a covered dish, the third with a flagon. On the table is a gold ship (*nef*), probably for alms – its only depiction on a table in medieval England – and covered cup, with a white cloth, with folds at the front.

6. The men of Sir Baltirdam, the Sultan's lieutenant in Jerusalem, given dinner by Richard Beauchamp. The guests are seated on carved wooden chests or bankers, round both sides of the table. One of Beauchamp's servants, with his device (a ragged staff) on his clothing and a sword, walks with Sir Baltirdam, who is carrying the marshal's wand. Beauchamp, wearing a jewelled collar, stands at the board-end, with his hand in that of Sir Baltirdam. From the Beauchamp Pageant, *c.* 1483–7.

to repairing racks and mangers in the stable, putting the house in order gener-ally, mending the glass in all the windows in the great hall, cleaning up after-wards and doing the repairs in consequence of the visit.[53]

From the mid-fourteenth century, more detailed listings in accounts permit a closer analysis of hospitality. At the same time, they give it a broad definition, embracing both the social visitor and those who were present on business, for example the carpenter eating in hall as part of the remuneration for his work. The proportion of guests to members of the household varied from establish-ment to establishment, depending on location, age of the head of the household and style of living; likewise the length of stay. In the household of Thomas Arundel, as Bishop of Ely, there were between 76 and 79 officials and servants paid fees in the early 1380s.[54] The diet accounts for 1380–1 show an average of 23 guests per day, 28% of those present. The numbers suggest 25% of those paid fees were not usually in residence.[55] In 1383–4, visitors averaged 17 per day (21% of those present), or 22% of those paid fees.[56]

Hospitality was not necessarily at its greatest among the episcopate. In the household of the Duke of Buckingham at Thornbury in 1507–8, between 44% and 50% of those present were not members of the household. The Duke's foreign household in London in 1508 had a smaller proportion of visitors, between 31% and 38%. At Thornbury, more guests came to supper than to lunch; in London, lunch was more popular (Table 3). The household in London, however, had proportionately more gentle servants and would consequently have seemed the more impressive to refined, metropolitan taste from the point of view of quality; but in terms of absolute numbers, the scale of entertainment was at its greatest at Thornbury, with 519 dining at lunch (319 of them guests) and 400 (279 guests) at supper at Epiphany 1508.[57]

A concentration of guests on particular feast days was not unusual. It is possible, though harder to establish, that there were focuses to entertainment within the week. In terms of the poor who came to the household of Eleanor of Castile in 1289–90, the emphasis was placed on Fridays; in Joan de Valence's household in 1295–7, their numbers were always greatest on Saturdays. Beyond this, Joan's household may have placed weight on Sunday as a day for entertainment, particularly for tenants and ceremonies with a religious connection.[58] For the household of the third Duke of Buckingham in 1507–8, at Thornbury, one of the few establishments for which there are sufficiently detailed figures to make calculations, it is possible to analyse the numbers of guests present at 124 meals. Most guests were present on Mondays (an average of 80), followed by Sundays (78), Wednesdays (76), Thursdays (75), Fridays (69), Tuesdays (65) and Saturdays (54). This household account, however, lacks the entry for Saturday, 1 January. If allowance is made for this, by adding an average of the guests at meals on the day before and the day after, Saturdays ranked equal with Wednesdays.[59]

What might a guest expect? Robert Grosseteste, *c.* 1240–2, enjoined the porters, ushers and marshals to attend to all guests without delay, courteously and honestly to make them welcome. The stewards and the rest of the household were to call them courteously, to arrange their lodgings and food and drink. At meal times, they were to be seated with the free household. Special regard was to be given to any whom the lord wished to be favoured.[60]

In the late fourteenth-century text *Sir Gawain and the Green Knight*, Gawain's arrival at the castle of Sir Bertilak was a model of courteous reception: he was greeted by the porter in a most pleasant manner, his business was asked and the porter promptly went to take the message to the master of the house. The drawbridge was then lowered and he was greeted by servants who went out, kneeling down to welcome him. Once inside the castle, several men held his horse and saddle while he dismounted, and led his horse off to the stable. Gawain was brought to the hall by a group of knights and esquires, amid further courteous greetings. Sir Bertilak himself came down from his chamber to greet Gawain in the hall and make him welcome. Bertilak took him to a chamber and assigned a servant to look after him; others were also ready to serve him and took him to a resplendent room. Here Gawain was brought a choice of rich clothes to replace the attire in which he had arrived. His room was then arranged with a chair before the charcoal fire that burned in the chimney; he was brought a furred mantle and he warmed himself in front of the fire. A table was set on trestles in his room, it was laid, and he was served with food – a meal of fish, it being Christmas Eve (that is, a day of abstinence), but with double portions (out of courtesy).[61] The contrast with the actual reception of Margery Kempe and her husband on a summer's afternoon in 1413 in the hall of Archbishop Arundel at Lambeth cannot have been greater: 'Ther wer many of the Erchebysshoppys clerkys & other rekles [reckless] men bothe swyers [esquires] & yemen whech sworyn many gret othis & spokyn many rekles wordys.' Nor did these lovers of courtesy appreciate Margery's bold remonstrances.[62]

A treatise of the late fifteenth century sets out what was to happen if a stranger of rank arrived at the gate at lunch or supper time. The porter was to go straight-away to the head officers and, if the guest was of sufficient standing, they would go to the gate to receive him, bringing him through the hall (which was full of seated diners) to the chamber that had been prepared as soon as his arrival was known. At his entry into the hall, the marshal and ushers were to greet him cour-teously, the usher taking his servants to drink at the bar of the buttery and showing them where their master's chamber was (but by a back way, if possible, rather than passing through the hall). The head officers then went back to their dinner, the guest being conducted to his chamber by a gentleman usher. Bread, beer and wine were then taken to the chamber and the guest's meal was pre-pared, unless the head of the household asked him to come to dinner with him. This was the usual practice if the second course had not been served at that stage and the guest was not of a status greater than the lord. Different arrangements obtained if he was of greater rank, or the guest was a woman, requiring two of the chief gentlewomen to attend her as well as the head officers of the house-hold.[63] Aside from their own servants, guests were accompanied by – and expected hospitality for – their horses, dogs and other animals. When Hulcot and his wife visited Bishop Mitford on New Year's Eve 1406, they brought with them five greyhounds, which boosted the consumption of bread by dogs from a handful of loaves to 26.[64]

There was another class of guest, the permanent or semi-permanent resident, or 'sojourner', who used the household, often with the lord's formal agreement, as a hotel, in the modern sense of the word. Those who did so were often related to the head of the household. There were also different tariffs, for what a present-day French hotel might call *pension*, as well as charges for visitors to the residents. This practice is apparent from the fifteenth century onwards, but may represent a formalisation of earlier custom: from at least the 1240s, the peasantry employed agreements, which were very similar in purpose, for the maintenance of individuals in their retirement.[65]

Staying in this way with Dame Milicent Fastolf at Caister in 1430–1 were two gentlewomen and their servants. Margaret Braunch was resident throughout the year at a charge of 20d. per week; her maid, Christiana Cook, was resident for four weeks at a weekly rate of 14d. In addition there was a bill for 20 meals for friends who had visited, charged at 2d. a meal, a modest total of £4. 14s. 8d., which allowed Margaret to live in some style without maintaining any significant establishment of her own. Alice Fastolf, who was only present for six weeks and five days, but had her maid with her the whole time, paid a weekly rate of 40d. for them both together. An additional 10 meals for friends were charged to her account, again at 2d. a meal, but with an extra 2½d. on the final bill.[66] Isabella,

Lady Morley, paid £80 for her stay in the household of her son-in-law, John Hastings, in 1463–4, with a further £1 for a meal given to the Duke of Suffolk and his followers;[67] but when a later Lord Morley suggested a similar possibility, *c.* 1470, lodging with the household of Thomas Stonor, Stonor's wife, Jane, was indignant, both at her husband's continued absence and at the proposed arrangement: 'Raythere breke up housallde [household] þan take sugiornantes, for servantes be not so delygent as þei were wonto bee.'[68]

Hospitality had other customs associated with it. Tipping of servants was not uncommon, nor were other gifts, if visits were regular. The Earl of March, at New Year 1414, with the royal household at Eltham, gave £26. 13s. 4d. to the officers of the King's hall, as well as cash sums to other servants of the King, the Bishop of Norwich, the Duke of York and the Earls of Arundel, Huntingdon and Salisbury.[69] A gift to an innkeeper or his servants on departure, known as *bel chere* ('good cheer', later corrupted in English to *belly-cheer*), was traditional. The clerks of Henry, Earl of Derby, travelling through Europe and the eastern Mediterranean to Jerusalem in 1392–3, recorded this payment whenever he departed.[70] Richard, Earl of Arundel (d. 1397), bequeathed to his wife her own hanap, or cup, called 'Bealchier', possibly the gift of a grateful guest.[71]

Gifts, tips and courtesies, however, could undermine the good order of the household. Bishop Grosseteste forbade the acceptance of gifts, except moderate quantities of food and drink, by his servants.[72] By the reign of Edward IV, the custom was countenanced but controlled. The esquires of the royal household were not to receive a share in the general gifts to the household, either given to the chamber or the hall, except 'if the gever geve them specially a part by expresse name or wordez'.[73]

Entertainment, in the broadest sense of the word, was an integral part of hospitality. On the one hand, the household had its own operational rituals, set up to control space, to enhance dramatic effect and pageantry, ceremony and magnificence in general. These ranged from trumpets to mark the arrival of food or individuals, or singing, to the use of lighting.[74] At York, in the Archbishop's household in the first part of the fifteenth century, it was the custom for ministers from the church to sing as the assay was taken of each course and after the concluding grace.[75] On the other hand, there were literary and musical entertainments and celebrations – which filled or succeeded the long hours devoted to eating – to which members of the household and visiting minstrels contributed. These might have included, in the thirteenth and early fourteenth centuries, material directly related to the household, in the form of household romance, poems celebrating the history of a particular family or dynasty and its lands. Such were the origins of *Waldef* (the Bigod household) and *Bevis of Hamtun* (associated with the D'Aubigny Earls of Arundel). The rhymes of Robin Hood may have a connection with the Lacy household or that of Thomas of Lancaster.[76] Musical entertainment was to be distinguished from the daily liturgical round of the household chapels; but the chapel personnel, some of whom were outstanding musicians, made a major contribution to household ceremony.[77]

By the end of the thirteenth century, some households had their own entertainers – or at least that was their function a part of the time and it was by that name that they were known. While the trumpeters of Thomas of Lancaster may not have been engaged in musical business the whole time, in that household, more than most, it may have been largely their occupation. Two of his trumpeters and his vielle-player were present at the feast to mark the knighting of Edward of Caernarvon at Whitsun 1306. That they were regarded as servants of high status can be seen by the purchase, in 1318–19, of five cloths for Lancaster's minstrels for the large sum of £13. In the same year, with the visit of Queen Isabella to Lancaster's household at Pontefract impending, Roger Trumpour made preparations for hanging pensels (or streamers) from the trumpets.[78] There is no evidence whether the complement of Joan de Valence's household included minstrels. The only occasion on which minstrels were noted in her accounts was at the knighting of John de Tany at Moreton Valence on 18 August 1297, when nine assisted at the celebrations – but the suspicion must be that these were additional to the household's own resources.[79]

Minstrels had a looser tie to the household than many servants: they were frequently most clearly identified when they were away from their parent establishment.[80] When Abbot Wenlok of Westminster, in the 1290s, envisaged that minstrels would be seated together in hall, he was probably referring to visiting minstrels.[81] The minstrels of Sir Ralph de Monthermer went away from Beverston with Sir John Mauduyt to the celebration of Walter de Langford, *c.* 1312–14, for which they were paid 6s. 8d. Three minstrels of Sir Ralph, with their three horses, also visited the household of Hugh Audley the Younger on 4 and 5 May 1320.[82] The identification of minstrels with a household (later probably matched by wearing the livery of that establishment, once that had become fixed) and their appearance at events away from the household, rather than being recorded in it, is a pattern that persists through the later medieval period.[83]

The looseness of the connection can also be seen in the nature of the payments given to minstrels. They were generously rewarded by their hosts, but drew comparatively few of the rewards available to other servants of their parent household except when they were present. There was an expectation that they would be in residence in their own households at the main feasts. According to the Black Book, the household of Edward IV contained 13 minstrels, playing trumpets, shawms, other wind instruments and strings, with one to direct them, who were to be present at the five principal feasts only. Two minstrels alone were to be present all the time when the King rode out, largely, it seems, so that the rest of the household could keep track of where they were, by their music. Another two string-players might be kept at the King's convenience.[84] The household watchmen, whose duty it was to sound the hours at night, were also musicians of distinction.[85]

The concentration of the need for minstrels on a few feasts created competition for the best. Edward I managed to secure, through the offices of his Queen, the continued attendance of Janyn, the minstrel of the Count of Aumale,

7. Salome tumbling before Herodias, then consulting her mother, who suggests she should ask for the head of St John the Baptist as her reward. The table is laid with a short tablecloth, probably covering a board on trestles, a covered cup and an ordinary cup, round loaves, knives and dishes with fowl or other meats, less heads and feet. From the Holkham Bible picture book, *c.* 1320–30.

Richard, the harper of the Earl of Gloucester, and Inglet, minstrel of the marshal of Champagne, at the feast of the Nativity of St John the Baptist in 1290. They were paid a bonus of 9s. as they remained with the King rather than going to the feast of the Earl Marshal the same day.[86]

Aside from those with a household connection, entertainment was provided by supernumeraries, hired for the event or brought by guests. The profession of minstrelsy was an honoured one and the injunctions of 1315, in time of dearth, against pretenders, effectively in search of food, were severe.[87] It could be a successful profession: those who were occasionally in royal service acquired modest amounts of property in London and elsewhere.[88] Substantial rewards were available to those at the top of the profession: the gifts given as a result of performance before King Edward I in 1286–7 ranged from more than £53 to be divided between 125 minstrels for playing on Christmas Day 1286, 2s. to a groom playing bagpipes, 7d. to a female acrobat tumbling before the King at Bordeaux, to 50s. each to two minstrels of the Duke of Burgundy.[89]

'Minstrel' encompassed all entertainers: female acrobats, such as Matilda Makejoy, who appeared in the English royal household between 1296 and 1311, entertaining the King and his children on an occasional basis (Plate 7);[90] actors or mummers, such as Philip the *istrio* (or player) of Edmund Crouchback, Edward I's brother;[91] harpers, gitterners (Plate 8), drummers, jesters and jugglers and fools. These last, however, had a firmer link with most households and were more akin to its servants in general. Edward II's Queen, Isabella, had a fool called Michael, supplied with shoes and other necessaries at York on 20 March

8. A brilliantly carved gittern, English, early fourteenth century, converted to a bowed instrument after the Middle Ages.

1312.[92] One of the valets of the household of Thomas, Duke of Clarence, was Master John Fool. He crossed to France in company with the Duchess of Clarence in November 1419. Along with four children of the chapel and three henchmen of Thomas Beaufort, he was given a red cloak of the Duke's livery. Unlike the children's, the fool's gown was not lined, nor did he have the hood given to the henchmen. The Duke's wardrobe provided him with a hood of his own, which had seven small spangles around its fringe, together with a silk fringe for each spangle.[93]

The purpose of these entertainers was little different from that of the other groups within the household: they added to the honour, status, profit and well-being of the lord. Despite variations in household size, in the quality of its members and the presence of external groups, be they military retinue, councillors or guests, in maintaining a household the aim of a lord in 1200 was broadly the same as that three centuries later. The changing balances, some matching general social developments, others peculiar to the institution itself, did create the potential for an establishment distinctive from other households. Further evidence of these differences and changes and their overall importance will come from looking at the largest group in the household, the servants.

CHAPTER 3
The Servants

In the early years of the fourteenth century, there can have been few who did not consider service in the great household a position of privilege. Outsiders, particularly the peasantry, could feel great resentment at the lifestyle of the rich, the arrogance of household servants and the contemptuous quality of their hospitality.[1] How were servants employed and what recompense did they enjoy that caused such antagonism? In the thirteenth century, there remained few vestiges of serjeanty tenure – land held in return for service – by which some of the principal domestic offices of magnates had been held.[2] As early as 1265, the servants of the Countess of Leicester were normally employed by a formal agreement, a *conventio*. At the same time, there seems to have been a system of giving servants leave and assistance to go home.[3] This was an evolution from the 'Rules' of Robert Grosseteste, *c.* 1240–2, where it was the intention that as little leave as possible should be allowed to domestic servants and that absences should be of short duration.[4] Once leave was established, the household was organised to use deputies for principal officers. In the household of Joan de Valence, the effects can be seen: the deputies might have no particular departmental specialisation and one man might be set in charge of various departments on different occasions. Roger Bluet, John Martyn and John Le Wariner acted as pantlers, the last also looking after the buttery; the kitchen was in the charge of Nicholas Gascelin and Master Roger the Cook on separate occasions; and the marshalsea was at various times in the charge of Adam Rimbaud, Hamo the Coachman and Walter the Farrier.[5] The duplication of household staff is also apparent from wills. Humphrey de Bohun, Earl of Hereford (d. 1322), left bequests of £10 to Master Walter, his cook, and £5 to Roger the Cook.[6]

On entering service, the servant swore loyalty to the lord, often in front of the rest of the household.[7] In the household of Walter de Wenlok, Abbot of Westminster, in the 1290s, it was the duty of the porter at the time of going to bed to make sure that no one was present except those who had so sworn.[8] In the English royal household, it was usual for the principal servants to find pledges for the performance of their duties and to swear their loyalty at the nightly audit of the domestic accounts. On 27 May 1307, Simon de Holpelston, a valet and usher of the Queen's larder, was admitted to his office, swearing an oath to conduct himself faithfully. He was required to find two sureties for his conduct.[9] Servants were responsible for goods of considerable value and their probity was essential. Robert Grosseteste advised they should be loyal, diligent, chaste, clean, honest and useful; the unfaithful, idle, indecent and drunk were to be turned out.[10]

Aside from the status of his place, by the mid-fourteenth century there were probably no fewer than five types of emolument which a servant could receive. Many were eligible for wages, a daily cash payment, but sometimes this was made only when a household servant was away from the household, out of court. Secondly, there were allowances of food, fuel and other commodities, together with accommodation or lodgings and transport. A stipend formed a third element, cash payments, typically on a quarterly basis, in addition to any daily payment for wages. Fourthly, servants were given livery – cloth of a quality appropriate to their rank, sometimes made up into clothing, and sometimes also with shoes or a payment in lieu. And lastly, servants received perks – perquisites – payments or goods either given to them (or taken by them) on a customary basis particular to their household, or as part of a more general custom of household living.

In the mid-fourteenth century, before the Black Death, the wage of a skilled labourer was approximately 3d. per day, an unskilled labourer, 1½d.; by the 1390s, the rates had risen to about 5d. and 3d. respectively. Although these should not be taken at face value (a skilled worker may have been required to find his materials), they provide a base-line for comparison.[11] In the household of Henry de Lacy, Earl of Lincoln, in 1299, grooms were paid wages of 1½d. per day, pages 1d.[12] Just over a century later, Bishop Mitford paid wages to his household servants living away from the household. The highest daily payment was 6d. to the household's caterer. The farrier, the baker and one or two other individuals of significance were paid 3d. a day; the head carter received 2½d., valets and grooms 2d., and pages 1½d. As well as these daily rates away from the household, there were payments of stipends (or fees), ranging from 1s. 6d. per quarter to Michael of the Kitchen, to 41s. 8d. to John Stokes, dean of the Bishop's chapel, possibly for a longer period.[13] In addition, the servants in this household received livery;[14] and there are also traces of customary payments, for example to kitchen staff at Easter.[15] Taken together, this made household employment with the Bishop of Salisbury a not uncomfortable living.

Not all households paid the same rate. At the top of the scale were the royal households. Wage payments at a *per diem* rate are listed in the royal household ordinances. The household of Edward II was largely divided into five groups, headed by the chief officers – the steward, treasurer, chamberlain, controller and keeper of the privy seal – who all had servants, accommodation and chamberlains to look after their needs, rights to fuel and food, candles and other necessaries for their offices, together with substantial fees ranging from 8 marks to £20 a year in rent. Below them was placed a group of serjeants, who were divided into two pay groups. One group received 7½d. per day, two sets of clothes per annum or 46s. 8d., together with food, usually including one mess of 'gross' meat (the main dish served that day), along with one mess of roast. The second group received 4½d. per day, two sets of clothes per annum or 40s. The next rank down, the valets of the offices (*valets de mestier*), received no more than 2d. per day, one set of clothes or 1 mark a year, together with 4s. 8d. for shoes. Valets usually had the right to have their bed, or their share in one, conveyed with the goods of their department. Their food allowance was less, only one mess of the 'gross' meat for the day and no roast. Grooms in the royal household, as in many other households, received an allowance that was very close to that of valets, in some cases identical; in 1318, however, many were paid 1½d. per day. The only pages in the establishment belonged to the valets of the kitchen.[16] In 1468, George, Duke of Clarence, paid esquires 7½d. for every day they were at court; yeomen, 4d.; grooms, 2d.; and pages, such wages as it pleased him.[17] These rates obtained widely and were not very different from those of 150 years previously.[18]

The livery issued to servants varied in quality both according to their rank and the opulence of the house.[19] Bishop Swinfield of Hereford, in the winter of 1289–90, dressed in the same cloth as his clerks. He had a striped cloth for his esquires and bailiffs, 4 cloths and 6 ells of which cost £14. 17s. 6d. The striped cloth for the valets was of a lesser quality, with 3 cloths and 4 ells costing £7. 11s. 10d. The cloth for the grooms and pages was cheaper still and used for less ample garments: the total outlay was only £8. 15s. 9d. for 4½ cloths and one robe. Livery for valets and pages in this household was issued only once a year, the other members receiving a further distribution in the summer of 1290.[20]

Custom and perquisites provided an important complement to official domestic payments, just as they did in the manorial economy. Besides occasional payments, household officials were entitled to benefits directly connected with their departments, which household ordinances strove, probably in vain, to control. The 1445 ordinance for the household of Henry VI declared that officers of the kitchen were to have no fees in their offices except those of old time accustomed;[21] while the Black Book describing the household of Edward IV maintained (inventively) that no fees had been allowed for offices before the reign of Edward III.[22] In the household of the future Edward V, the pantlers were entitled to chippings of bread (the crusts that had been sliced off), together with broken bread, cut but not used or taken in alms; in that of George, Duke of Clarence, they had the chippings and cuttings of loaves used for trenchers. The cellarer of Prince Edward had the empty vessels of wine; the butlers, worn cups and broken ale; the master cook, 'fleetings of the lead and coney skins' – the former were skimmings from the surface of cooking pots; the larderers were entitled to the necks of mutton, two fingers from the head, and legs, two fingers from the hocks, and parings of the flanks of cattle and sheep.[23] Other arrangements were formalised by the consent of the lord. In the household of Margaret Luttrell, in 1431–2, the skins of calves and rabbits belonged to the cook 'by agreement with the lady'.[24]

Besides these perquisites, servants benefited from the high regard in which they were held by their masters. When Sir Geoffrey Luttrell of Irnham died in May 1345, he left a series of bequests to relatives and to members of his household. His chaplain received 20s. and his confessor, 5 marks for clothing. His pantler and butler, John of Colne, received 10 marks and a robe, together with all the vessels of the pantry and buttery. One of his cooks, John of Bridgford, also received 10 marks and a robe, together with the brass and wooden vessels of the kitchen; another, William the Cook (*Le Ku*), 40 marks. Two further kitchen servants, William Howet and Robert Baron, both received cash bequests, 20s. and 6s. 8d. Luttrell made bequests to three children – two of whom were his godsons – of kitchen staff. Five marks were left to Alice de Wadnowe, maidservant; Luttrell's chamberlain received 40 marks; and William the Porter received 10 marks, a robe and all the apparel of the hall (dorsers and bankers).[25]

While some legacies were very substantial indeed, indicative of the considera-tion servants could command, there was also something of custom in them. When inventories were made of the property of Richard Gravesend, Bishop of London (d. 1303), the goods in his kitchen were worth only 30s. as Jolanus, the Bishop's master cook (who received a bequest of 40s.), had taken the other uten-sils for his fee; the butler had done the same with the goods of the buttery.[26] John Martyn, one of the valets in the household of Joan de Valence, had probably transferred there on the death of her husband. On 9 September 1296, Joan pur-chased from him goods that were part of his fee on the death of William de Valence. These included packing cases for candles and silver vessels. A purchase from him a little more than a fortnight beforehand of tallow, colouring and wick (for candles), which may also have been a part of his fee, suggests he had duties in William's wardrobe or chandlery.[27] Servants had other occasional rewards. In 1285–6, Edward I gave 10s. to an esquire of the treasury who had come to him on the Isle of Wight with news of the death of the King of France.[28]

This pattern of emolument was not necessarily old by the mid-fourteenth century: thirteenth-century arrangements were more fluid, or had other founda-tions. The household of Joan de Valence provides evidence for these changes at a point at which serjeanty tenure had little functional importance. In this house-hold most servants were in receipt of food and drink. The valets also received *calciamentum*, or payment for footwear; the grooms associated with the mar-shalsea did not receive food, but a daily wage. Of particular interest is a group of payments which can generally be classed as fees. The household baker, until 24 January 1297, received a fee for the use of his equipment at each baking. At this date Joan bought out his equipment for 2s. On 24 April 1297, as he no longer received a fee, the baker was paid a stipend of 5s.; his groom received one of 2s. at the same time, for Easter term that year. But the baker was clearly a source of trouble and in the summer of 1297 he left the household, on the grounds that he would not hand over 4s. 4d. which it was alleged was owed to the pantler.[29] Here was an uneasy relationship, where a man and his equipment were hired to perform a job – but what was their relationship to the household (the baker was regarded as a household valet for the purposes of *calciamentum*) and how might it be regulated? Other fees, typically of 1d. or 2d., were paid to kitchen staff on days when meat was cooked, but never on fish days. The basis for the payment is unclear and it is not known whether the kitchen staff, for example, also provided their own utensils. In the century after 1300, there were more regular terms of employment, a more formal definition of service, leading by the fifteenth century to annual contracts or quarterly hiring for lesser servants. At the same time there was an increasing specialisation or professionalisation of particular parts of service in large households, as well as a clearer distinction between upper or gentle servants, household officers and other menials.[30]

Most servants and attendants in the great household were male, certainly in the thirteenth and fourteenth centuries. There was some blurring of the picture in the fifteenth century. A recent study of gentry wills in the period 1460 to 1530 has shown that twice as many male household servants as female received bequests.[31] This indicates a substantial change in balance. The picture in the sixteenth and seventeenth centuries was very different, moving to a female preponderance in domestic service. Although it is possible to identify 85 servants in the household of Joan de Valence, only one was a woman – the washerwoman – and it is not clear whether any others, now unknown, resided in it. The washerwoman received the allowance of a valet for footwear.[32] It is just possible that the maid escorted to Raglan by Roger the Tailor around 11 October 1296 was a member of the household and that John the Baker may have had a female assistant for a part of the time;[33] but the woman (or women) of Moreton Valence, who collected rushes for Joan while she stayed there in August and September 1297, was almost certainly local and external to the household.[34]

With the exception of a very few female attendants or companions for the lady of a house and her daughters, as well as nurses for young children, the lack of women was not untypical. The Duchess of Clarence, joining her husband in France, in November 1419, left her daughters at Dartford Priory and was accompanied by 143 men from her husband's household, but by no women.[35] The listing of the household of a later Duchess of Clarence, c. 1468, totalled 144 individuals. With her she had a baroness, a gentlewoman, with a further five gentlewomen and five women servants, together with two chamberers, who may have been female; the rest of the household was male.[36] In general, aside from this group, the only women were laundresses or connected with dairy work, but in both these cases the women were not usually resident in the household, remaining on its fringes. Other references to women are occasional and exceptional before the fifteenth century. Agnes, the maid at Bogo de Clare's establishment at Melton Mowbray, whose supertunic was consumed in the fire there in 1284–5, was recompensed 3s. 6d. for her loss, two or three times the value of the supertunics lost by servingmen in the same incident.[37] The Tickhill Psalter, illustrating the slaying of Ish-bosheth by Rechab and Baanah, depicts a woman as the gatekeeper or usher (*hostiaria*), as well as cleaning corn. To commit this murder, access was gained to the palace through the gate while the gatekeeper was asleep (Plate 9).

The absence of women was intended: to contemporaries they were a distraction and not to be trusted. The late thirteenth-century household ordinances of

9. The slaying of Ish-bosheth by Rechab and Baanah (2 Samuel 4: 5–7). They gain entrance to the palace through the gate: the female gatekeeper (*hostiaria*) is asleep. The illuminator was in something of a dilemma, as a female gatekeeper would have been unusual; but she has been doing typical women's work, winnowing or cleaning wheat, with the sack, sieve, rake and other implements. From the Tickhill Psalter, *c.* 1303–14.

Abbot Wenlok of Westminster had the laundress receive at the gate of the household the cloths she was to wash. She was to hand them back there to the household officers, the grooms of clerks and others in the household. Wenlok's marshal was to enquire in the vicinity of the household whether there were any women of ill repute (*foles femmes*). The porter who, like many household officers, was to be chaste, was to remove three scourges from the household – grooms, ribalds and women.[38] The pseudo-Aristotelian *De secretis secretorum* – copied for Edward III among others – advised the king against placing trust in women;[39] and the royal household was particularly cautious about them. The steward and the treasurer at the nightly audit, *c.* 1300, asked all the chief officers to enquire in their offices to see if any of their staff had wives or mistresses close at hand or following the court.[40] About the same date, *Fleta*, describing the duties of the office of the marshal of the royal household, enjoined him to keep it free from common prostitutes, a persistent problem to judge by the penalties, which included cutting off their hair for a third offence and genital mutilation for the fourth.[41] Different arrangements were enforced at other times and the royal court may have maintained what amounted to its own brothel for parts of the Middle Ages.[42]

The ambivalence of these arrangements was perhaps hardly unusual in an establishment constituted almost entirely of men. Although marriage was possible for servants – both male and female – in the thirteenth century those on duty were expected normally to live apart from their spouses and children. In the household of Eleanor of Castile in 1290, four of the damsels of the Queen's chamber, Joanna Wake, Clemence de Vesci, Alice de Montfort and Marie de St Amand, who were all related to the Queen, were married. Joanna Wake had young children, at King's Langley, whom she was permitted to visit in June 1290: Joanna's servants had gone to look after them there in April 1290.[43] In September 1355, Elizabeth de Burgh, Lady of Clare, bequeathed 5 marks to Nicholas the Ewerer and Isabel, his wife; but it is not known if they resided together in her household.[44]

The residence of married servants together in the great household appears in the fifteenth century in households of rank and it may have been accepted in lesser establishments earlier. Households were then considerably less peripatetic and the presence of many more women had become usual: the circumstances of marriage and prolonged residence in the same place were much more likely to coincide. In the household of Sir John Fastolf at Caister, in 1430–1, Janyn Baker was listed among the valets. He was still in the household 25 years later: in January 1455, when Sir John Fastolf gave him and his wife 2 ells of canvas for aprons, they were working side by side.[45] There is fifteenth-century evidence for family groups working together, both male and female. William Fuller, his wife Joanna, and their two children served John Howard at Stoke-by-Nayland together about 1455. About 1467, the household calendar for the same establishment shows three members of the Alpha family – John, Margery and her daughter – classed among the grooms; Howard was also served by Richard Alpha and his daughter. In 1467, Margery Alpha may be the individual, simply called Margery, who was to look after Howard's children, to cook for them and with the help of her husband to bake and brew for them.[46] Marriage patterns of servants were very different from those of their masters and mistresses. In late fourteenth- and fifteenth-century York, servants, both male and female, were often in their mid-twenties by the time they married, whereas the landed aristocracy continued at this date to arrange the betrothal of children and to conclude marriages much earlier.[47]

How were servants recruited and trained? They frequently came, at a relatively young age, from localities close to the main residences or estates of the household, remaining in the household and, in some instances, rising through posts. Others had family connections with the household, or were inherited from the households of spouses or relations.[48] In the households of Eleanor de Montfort and Joan de Valence – both Countess of Pembroke – there were members of the Gobion family, possibly associated with the Kent estates of the earldom.[49] In Joan de Valence's household others connected with the estates included Ralph of Castle Martin and Thomas of Bampton; W. de Munchensy was one of her relations or connected with her paternal family. There were three members of the Gascelin family in Joan's immediate service: Walter and Nicholas played major roles within her household. They were connected with the family of Geoffrey Gascelin, one of William de Valence's knights and a substantial landowner in Wiltshire. The link was one that continued to Joan's son Aymer, in whose retinue and household service other members of the Gascelin family were found.[50] On the death of her husband, Joan de Valence took over a group of his servants, probably increasing her household numbers by some 25% between June and September 1296 (Table 1).

While Richard II preferred men from the earldom of Cheshire for his household, his successor, Henry IV, preferred Lancastrians. Later fifteenth-century recruitment into the royal household may have been more even across the country: in many cases domestic service continued unbroken into Yorkist rule.[51] To judge from the long lines of servants who were clearly related, family connection and introduction played an important part.[52] A treatise on letter writing, copied in the 1380s, contains a specimen letter written from one brother to another. The first records his good fortune at being made steward of a household, but says, rather improbably, that he does not know how to write letters or how to account. He asks his brother to be diligent in his studies, to learn to write letters, to account and to audit 'in order that you can help me to enter our expenses and to write our letters'.[53]

The recruitment of servants, particularly those of higher rank, gentlemen and esquires with territorial associations, helped consolidate the lord's influence in his locality.[54] For individuals of high rank to enter into the service of another was in no way demeaning.[55] They were an ornament to the household, companions for the lord and lady: servants of gentle rank enhanced the quality of the establishment. Two of the Stonor women, with the household of the Duchess of Suffolk in 1476, were not sufficiently well attired for this purpose: 'And [the Duchess] seyth with owght they be otherwyse arayed, sche seyth, sche may not kep them.'[56] Also of potentially high rank were children from other households, learning the ways of courtesy, manners and service – a practical finishing school – as well as consolidating links with other families.[57] One further group that might delineate the high standing of the establishment comprised servants of continental origin. In 1431–2, the Earl of Oxford had two Frenchmen working in his kitchen – but the origins of many servants can now no longer be traced.[58]

While the upper servants of the household remained for many years, by the fifteenth century lesser servants might form a more transient group. The principal terms of a number of agreements for lesser servants and other staff are detailed in the accounts of John Howard, later Duke of Norfolk. A carpenter, 'yonge Copdoke', was engaged in October 1465. He was almost certainly related to two other carpenters working for Howard at this time. He was to serve for 12 months, to receive meat, drink and a gown, along with 36s. 8d. per annum, but was to find himself bedding. In November 1465, he probably received black cloth as part of the mourning livery distributed on the death of Catherine, Lady

Howard; and, in January 1467, he was listed among the grooms of the household, but his name does not thereafter occur.[59] Other servants in this household served considerably longer: John Mershe the Elder and John Mershe the Younger, one serving in the kitchen, the other in the buttery, can be traced through the accounts for more than a decade.[60]

Many servants had no formal training, but learned on the job. The sequence of appointments they held demonstrates their passage to more senior positions. In the household of Thomas Arundel, as Bishop of Ely, in the 1380s, there was considerable stability in the membership and functions of individuals. There were some internal promotions, particularly on the clerical side, with choristers becoming valets, from where, after due service and ordination, they might expect ecclesiastical patronage.[61] Specialists, such as cooks or administrators, might train elsewhere, but it is most probable they learned their work in other households.

For the training of servants in their crafts, there is now little evidence other than the fifteenth-century tracts setting out matters of courtesy. It does not seem likely that other treatises, for example cookery books, were used as didactic material, but more as *aides-mémoire*. Those who trained as clerks of the household may have attended courses at Oxford, or learned from accounting formularies, but there was not much up-to-date knowledge in these documents.[62] To the dismay of some contemporaries, these administrators were sometimes clerks in orders.[63] Specialists had the possibility to transfer to higher posts in related households. William de Manton, in 1340 the wardrober of Elizabeth de Burgh, one of the wealthiest women of the age, subsequently became the clerk of her chamber as well, then her executor, passing on to the household of her son-in-law, the Duke of Clarence, and, from 1361 to 1366, to the post of keeper of the wardrobe of Edward III.[64] Advancement to other noble households was also the aim of gentle servants. Geoffrey Chaucer served in a sequence of households, of Elizabeth, Countess of Ulster, possibly as a page; then in the household of her husband Lionel, Duke of Clarence; and subsequently in the household of Edward III.[65]

Household service was on the whole continuous throughout the year. While there were arrangements for leave of absence, not until the fifteenth century was there an expectation in the largest households that there would be periods of rotation in employment. As the proportion of gentle servants increased, they were organised into groups in waiting and out of waiting. In the household of the fifth Earl of Northumberland this arrangement was made on a quarterly basis, so that the magnificence of the lord could be appropriately served on all occasions by persons of rank.[66] Otherwise the lot of the household servant contrasted with that of those earning wages and villeins, who would expect relief on some saints' days and on Sundays, possibly not to work on Saturday afternoons, as well as holidays, amounting to a week or perhaps two at Christmas and a week at Easter.[67]

The different pattern of work outside the household can be seen in the accounts of Joan de Valence at Goodrich in the winter of 1296–7. The season was marked by a massive wood-cutting operation nearby at the Dowards and Bishop's Wood. The woodmen were at work six days a week, cutting wood, transporting it to Goodrich and making some charcoal. In the week of Christmas, only two days were worked, but the full six days were worked the following week (ending 5 January 1297). This was a short period of holiday for non-household servants and may have been related to the performance of work by contract, as the workers were occasionally penalised for making insufficient trips to the castle during the week.[68]

The length of the working day itself varied from servant to servant, according to their duties. That some, notably the chief officers of the household, were expected to work or be on duty very long hours is clear from household ordinances. The marshal in the household of Walter de Wenlok, in the 1290s, was expected to be the first to rise and the last to bed, 'as he must be like a husband to the household'.[69] By the sixteenth century, others, gentle servants, had periods of time off duty during the day.[70]

If the connection between the servant and the household ended with the death of the principal, the arrangements were generous. Accounts frequently record the arrangements for breaking up the household, for the final payments to servants after the funeral, for which they would customarily receive a separate set of mourning livery. Aside from those customary perquisites to which household office commonly entitled servants, there were frequently additional stipends. All the servants of Edward, Duke of York (d. 1415), who had been with him for a year prior to his journey to France, were to be paid their stipends for the following term. Cardinal Beaufort left £2,000 to be distributed among his servants having regard to the amount of time they had served with him and their qualities, both in terms of rank and merit. Margaret, Countess of Richmond (d. 1509), left instructions to her executors to pay all her household servants for six months after her death, in addition to keeping her household together for at least three months, supplied with food and drink as usual.[71]

Servants were also maintained at the end of their own working lives. On the one hand, they might be supported within the household itself, continuing to receive allowances of food and drink. The Earl of Salisbury made regular payments in 1367–8, as alms, to Jaket, formerly a valet of Lady E. de Montagu.[72] Some households had close connections with hospitals, the Hungerfords with that at Heytesbury, the Dukes of Suffolk with Ewelme, and the Bishops of Winchester with the hospital at St Cross, as endowed by Cardinal Beaufort: these all provided a dignified environment for aged servants.[73]

If most servants – and thus most of the household – were male, they were also overwhelmingly young. With a shorter life-expectancy, much of society was young compared to contemporary Britain. How young they were is more difficult to determine. While the great monasteries of late medieval England had, by the fifteenth century, many boys who were not formally on the establishment carrying out tasks,[74] the approach of secular households was different, with tighter controls. Robert Grosseteste, *c.* 1240–2, identified the grooms – probably adolescent boys – as a potentially unruly and rowdy element, seating 'all the tumult of grooms' (*tute la frape de garcuns*) together in hall, after the free household had arrived, forbidding undue noise at meals, and requiring the grooms to leave together as a body. The care given to alms of food taken from the table suggests a desire to avoid the scavenging attentions of voracious teenagers.[75] Walter de Wenlok used similar measures to control the grooms in his household. Once Wenlok was seated, they were to assemble at the entrance to the hall and enter as a group. When all had eaten, they were to serve the cheese. After the meal, they were not to loiter around the entrance to the hall or in the domestic offices, but to go, without creating a disturbance, to their horses.[76] The grooms in the household of Joan de Valence, however, were paid a daily wage rather than eating in hall, a common, pragmatic response, developed by the end of the thirteenth century, to the dynamics of this group.

The employment of children – rather than adolescents – is more difficult to pinpoint. It highlights one of the changes in domestic service which needs further examination. The increased stratification in the upper ranks of fourteenth-century society was mirrored in domestic service. New functions and new ranks of servants were added, expanding notably the tier of servants below grooms – pages. Pages were junior both in rank and in age, probably pre-adolescent: this is their likely significance in bishops' households, where some may have been choristers. There are few references to pages in the thirteenth century. Joan de Valence's accounts contain only one mention of a page, paid at ½d. per day for his wages while at Moreton Valence, looking after the coach-horses over Christmas 1296.[77] Walter de Wenlok's marshal was to exclude all pages from his household and to ensure the valets of his household offices kept none.[78] In the household of Edward II in 1318, the only pages in the establishment belonged to the valets of the kitchen, an enormous contrast to the household of Edward IV.[79] The later documentation may be more formal, but there is no reason to suggest that in its listing of all members of the establishment it is more comprehensive. There is a general pattern in documents of the early fourteenth century: where household membership can be ascertained, there were few pages.

Most of the earliest references to pages are associated with the marshalsea, but this is probably an accident, as the cash wages paid to the personnel of this department furnish a better record of its membership than that for other departments. After 1320, numbers of pages grew and it may be that an impetus was given by the Black Death and the diminishing availability of adult labour; but the use of children may also reflect a development of courtesy. By the 1340s, Elizabeth de Burgh had pages in many of her household departments. They were issued with livery and there were opportunities for them to be promoted to the rank of groom. In 1355, she left £10 for her executors to distribute among the pages who wore her livery.[80] There were eight or nine pages in the household of Thomas Arundel, Bishop of Ely, in the early 1380s. While one was responsible for the palfreys, another for the hackneys, others were connected with the poultry, the larder, the launderer and the doorkeeper.[81] In 1393, William of Wykeham had five, described as the Bishop's pages; Bishop Mitford of Salisbury, in 1406–7, had five, one serving the Bishop, the others serving the steward and three named individuals, besides at least three further pages in the kitchen.[82] Here, perhaps, is evidence for the use of pages to undertake something more akin to a personal or gentle service, rather than serving as the junior staff of a household department.

In his *Boke of Nurture* of the mid-fifteenth century, John Russell made a further distinction, enjoining the marshal of the household to treat anyone sent by the king one degree above his status. Among those he lists were a page and a child. The page was to be received as a 'grome goodly in fere', the child as a 'grome gentille lernere'.[83] The terminology of this distinction is hard to sustain in late fifteenth-century households. Servants were described as children, without distinction from pages, in the household of Sir William Stonor in 1478–9, where they served in his buttery, kitchen and his chamber.[84] At this stage, however, there was no question about the term 'child', which in the eighteenth-century English royal household referred to rank, not to age, in, for example, the expression 'child of the kitchen'.[85] It has been suggested that in the latter part of the fifteenth century individuals entered service probably around the age of twelve, continuing until their mid-twenties;[86] pages may have been younger. While some children in the household could be useful and gave status, there was force in the gibe made to Elizabeth Stonor in 1477 that she had kept her husband 'among a meany [household] of boyes'.[87]

Other innovations in domestic service also sprang from the sharper focus on display, magnificence and courtesy increasingly evident through the fourteenth century. These separated individuals who had otherwise performed generic functions into categories that performed more specialised service, usually directly associated with the lord, a form of service that was suitable for servants of gentle rank. At this time, there are the first references to two new types of servant associated with the marshalsea, footmen and henchmen, and changes in body-service.

Footmen – attending aristocratic riders, running to hold bridles and performing similar services, to add generally to the impression of magnificence accompanying the passage and arrival of a lord – are noted around 1400.[88] A footman called John was employed by the 23-year-old Earl of March in 1413–14;[89] the Duke of Buckingham had two footmen in 1501, both of whom attended him going to court at Richmond.[90] Henchmen, originally attendants for sumpter-horses, appeared earlier in the fourteenth century. Their status was transformed into servants of honour, similar to footmen, to enhance the train of the lord, especially when he travelled without his full household. Unlike footmen, henchmen were mounted, at least for a part of the Middle Ages. Henchmen are first known in the royal household. In 1347–8 there were three, distinguished from the other sumptermen, who numbered 34 in the 1318 ordinance and 60 or 70 later in the century.[91] Two henchmen, Bernard and Henry Tylman, accompanied Henry, Earl of Derby, on his journeys in 1392–3, one going with him to Jerusalem.[92] Edward, Duke of York (d. 1415), bequeathed the saddles and horse-harness for his personal use equally among his henchmen, except one, Rokell, who was to have the best.[93] The henchmen of Thomas

Beaufort and John Beaufort, Earl of Somerset, received additional and more costly livery to the coursermen and sumptermen with whom they crossed to France in company with the Duchess of Clarence in November 1419.[94] Henchmen, along with other ornaments of pageantry, heralds, pursuivants and swordbearers, were exempted from the sumptuary legislation of 1463.[95] They were to be found in the households of many magnates: Anthony Woodville and Edmund Berners, both probably of noble families, served the Duke of Buckingham in this capacity in 1501.[96] It was not only the very great who had henchmen: in 1405–6 Sir Hugh Luttrell of Dunster had one who, as well as his clothing, received an annual stipend at a modest level of 10s.[97] By the 1470s, there is no doubt henchmen were gentle servants, young men or adolescents to be trained in courtesy and urbanity.[98]

A change may also be seen in household body-service. Firstly, the evidence relates to washing, taking baths and the use of the lavatory. In all these cases, it was expected that attendants would be present (Plate 10). The quality of the individuals who assisted on these occasions became more sharply defined. They were not the lowest servants in the household, but of higher rank. In the 1290s, Abbot Wenlok of Westminster had a valet for his body who ranked among the esquires of his household.[99] By the fifteenth century, there was no doubt that body-service attendant on the lord required a servant of gentle rank. In the royal household the groom of the stole, in charge of the privy chamber, was a senior individual, yet liable to assist at the most basic of bodily functions – as his title suggests, taking charge of the close stool.[100]

Secondly, the chamberlain's functions may have expanded during the fourteenth century. A transformation occurred in the pattern of clothing common among the aristocracy in England from the 1340s, with the adoption of close-fitting garments. Whether or not an individual had dressed himself or herself before, the new fashions required assistance with dressing.[101] This process became more elaborate over the next 150 years, as fashions became more complex and, in the early modern period, more stiff and rigid.[102]

How were servants controlled? The tensions of household society, with personal service focused on one or a handful of individuals, were apparent to Robert Grosseteste in the 1240s. Reflecting on features commonly found in court society – the marks of favouritism and obsequiousness, the jealousies and petty discords, the gossip, the cliques and factions of a nearly all-male group – Grosseteste enjoined unity of purpose: 'Let there be one heart in one spirit' (*sit cor unum in anima una*).[103] In terms of discipline, the household constituted a legally separate entity and its head had a right, if not a duty, to control what went on in it. In the royal household the legal exclusivity extended over a wider area known as the verge (after the marshal's rod or wand of office), 12 leagues from where the household resided. That it was a personal jurisdiction can be seen from its continuance when the sovereign was abroad.[104] It applied equally to other households, to the exclusion of royal jurisdiction. A fifteenth-century courtesy book indicates that in a private household the marshal's general jurisdiction might encompass offences that would otherwise have fallen to the

10. Saul in the cave, using the garderobe (1 Samuel 24: 4). Although this is set in a cave, the illustrator had in mind a household context, in which the use of the garderobe was not a private affair. David can cut off part of Saul's cloak as it was not unusual for attendants to be present. Saul's underclothes are clearly visible. From the Tickhill Psalter, *c.* 1303–14.

royal courts: fighting, drawing knives, theft and general affrays.[105] Household jurisdiction was in many respects a relic of a personal jurisdiction, rather than a territorial one. There are traces of it in the *Leges Henrici Primi*, probably of 1113–18. Members of the household, servants and retainers were the responsibility of the lord and under his control,[106] just as they were at village or villein level. *Infiht* or *insocna*, an offence committed by those who were living in a community in a household, was compensated by the payment of a *wite* to the head of the household if he had jurisdiction over both the accuser and the accused.[107]

In many households daily accounting sessions acted as formal gatherings for dispensing justice. In the household of Walter de Wenlok, Abbot of Westminster, in the 1290s, two successive minor offences were dealt with by reprimand, the third offence resulting in dismissal. For a serious offence, not only was the individual dismissed by the steward, but the matter was to be dealt with by Wenlok. Anyone dismissed was not to go to Wenlok to seek reconciliation: the steward's authority was not to be undermined.[108]

From *c.* 1295 to 1313, there are records of the nightly audit for the royal households, setting out fines imposed on servants for not carrying out their duties or doing so badly. On 4 October in a year probably around 1300, Adam de Winton, the under-clerk of the King's kitchen, was fined 3s. 7d., the value of 14 portions (*fercula*), accounted as delivered to the King's almoner but lacking that day and the whereabouts of which he did not know.[109] On 19 January, probably in 1302, the clerk of the kitchen and Master John de Pontefract, the larderer, were surcharged with 12d., the value of herring misspent in the King's chamber the previous Saturday. By 'misspent' was meant an impropriety in the account: the royal household worked by allowing a sum per person for a meal and if, at the end of the day, more had been spent, those responsible were surcharged. On 19 April, Roger the Usher (who should have been at the door watching and recording the meals going into the room) had his wages stopped for a month because at the account he did not have the records of the portions of food brought into the chamber or the hall.[110]

In the household of Edward IV, the King's chamberlain had authority to deal with disciplinary matters relating to those belonging to the chamber, for all except offences relating to the counting-house.[111] In 1468, the steward, treasurer and controller of the Duke of Clarence were enjoined to restrain the Duke's servants from 'seditious language, varyaunces, discentions, debates and frayes, as well within the seide Duke's courte as withoute, wherethorough any disclaundre or misgovernaunce might growe' on pain, for the first offence, of losing a month's wages, with a month's imprisonment for the second offence and dismissal for the third. Those found playing dice, cards or other games of chance for money (except during the twelve days of Christmas) faced dismissal, likewise those swearing.[112] The injunctions for the household of the young Prince Edward, of September 1473, were aimed, *inter alia*, at late-comers to Matins (punished by a seat at the water-board – the ewery-board – where they were to have only bread and water for dinner) and those who missed it completely, against swearing (punished according to the status of the offender), creating a disturbance or drawing a weapon, attempting to advocate a cause, and going to law without the knowledge of the Queen's council.[113] Servants and family might be covered by the same discipline. The epitaph of Margaret, Countess of Shrewsbury (d. 1467), in Old St Paul's, recorded that she made a decree in her household, from which her own children were not excepted, that all found swearing 'should lak that day ale wyn and chochyn [kitchen, i.e. food] and only have but bred and watre'.[114]

While discipline continued to be enforced in the household on a personal basis, the nature of service in the great household differed markedly between

1200 and 1500. There were widespread changes in terms of employment and the growth of a labour market. For domestic service one might expect a range of regular emoluments, rather than land. Specialisms developed and, to some extent, professional training. There were new degrees of servant, particularly to cater for developments in courtesy associated with a growing emphasis on gentility and magnificence. Together with the increased presence of women, the use of children to fill the lowest ranks of service probably altered the character of the fifteenth-century household considerably from that of the thirteenth. Household servants enjoyed positions much different from the rest of medieval society, not only in terms of routine, but particularly in the security of their livelihood and the benefits that flowed from association with a lord. In no area is that privilege now so manifest as in the quality of their accommodation and it is to changes in this area that consideration will next be given.

CHAPTER 4

Space and Residences

The transition of the great household in late medieval England from a peripatetic institution to one based in ever fewer residences for longer periods was a most important change in its character. The spirit of movement can be seen in the English royal household. King John moved on average 12 times a month; Henry III made 80 moves a year; Edward I, 107 a year; and Edward II, even more.[1] Peregrination slowed with Edward III and later monarchs. At the same time, fewer royal residences were in regular use, largely in the south-east, around London, the number falling from perhaps 25 locations early in the reign of Edward III, to about 10 in the reign of Edward IV. The reasons for this, in the case of the Crown, may be related to the developing bureaucracy of government, centred on London, at the same time as the resources generally available to it decreased and the standards of magnificence appropriate to a residence of a monarch required more lavish funding.[2]

The royal household had its own, exceptional reasons for travel. For lay households, from the late thirteenth century, prolonged periods of residence at a small group of sites were not unusual. The itinerary of Joan de Valence in 1296–7 was based on family property, with a single visit to London. Her stays on her own estates or family properties were lengthy, including one of five and a half months at Goodrich Castle, with about two months at Swindon and the same period with her daughter, Agnes de Valence, at Hertingfordbury (Map 2; Table 4). From the beginning of October 1318 to mid-May 1319, Thomas of Lancaster resided at Pontefract, with only two short breaks away in York. Lancaster carried out a number of substantial building projects and there was probably a good deal of work at Pontefract completed around this time.[3] In 1320, Hugh Audley the Younger, with his wife Margaret, the sister and coheiress of Gilbert de Clare, Earl of Gloucester, resided at Tonbridge. Although Audley, with a small group of attendants, made some journeys away, his wife's stay was continuous through most of the 183 days of the surviving accounts.[4]

The pattern in ecclesiastical households was a little different, as bishops led a more mobile life in their own dioceses. In 1289–90, Bishop Swinfield of Hereford, who carried out a visitation of his diocese in this period, moved more than 80 times in nearly 300 days.[5] But even with triennial visitations, episcopal residence had concentrated on a few favoured manors and residences by the fourteenth century. Bishop Mitford of Salisbury spent 139 days at Potterne in 1403, 99 in 1405 and probably close to 200 between the start of 1406 and his death in late May 1407. At the start of the fourteenth century, Potterne had been even more popular as a residence with two bishops, Simon of Ghent and Roger Martival; it was one of a group of favoured Salisbury episcopal residences including Sonning, Ramsbury, Chardstock and, later, Sherborne.[6] Robert Braybrooke, Bishop of London, 1381–1404, had five main palaces: Fulham, Stepney, London, Wickham and Much Hadham;[7] his contemporary, William of Wykeham, at Winchester, a much richer see, had impressive residences at Wolvesey, Bishop's Waltham, Farnham, Esher, Southwark and elsewhere on his estates, as well as smaller establishments, such as that at East Meon, for accommodating select groups within his household.[8] Monastic prelates commonly stayed for long periods in a manor house very near their monastery. Thus John Fossour, Prior of Durham (d. 1376), resided at Beaurepaire (Bearpark), about 3 miles from Durham; the Priors of Christ Church, Canterbury, resided at Chartham, a little further away; and the Abbots of Westminster at La Neyte, about 3 miles from the Abbey.[9] In both secular and ecclesiastical establishments, the trend continued in the fifteenth century, with a few properties alone acting as the principal residences of the lord – and attracting the bulk of expenditure on building and refurbishment. In this way the household of the Duke of York spent at least 236 consecutive days at Hanley Castle in 1409–10; the first Duke of Buckingham spent much time at Writtle and Maxstoke; and the third Duke concentrated much of his expenditure on Thornbury.[10]

From the end of the thirteenth century, buildings were intended – and designed – for almost continuous residence. Accompanying this stability, other features of domestic accommodation developed, with less emphasis on defence, more on display, comfort and order within the household. Attention was also given to the setting of the house in its surrounding landscape, its parks and gardens. While a household might spend much of its time in the country, in the midst of its estates, not all business could be transacted there; and the necessity of conducting affairs in large towns, particularly in London, or Norwich or York, led to the development of town residences.

In general there was a common pattern to elements of domestic accommodation. At the start of the period, the hall was the focus of the household. Services – pantry, buttery, kitchen – were located at one end and living accommodation for the lord – a solar or chambers – at the other. This arrangement marked a coalescence of elements that had probably been separate until the start of the thirteenth century. The lord's accommodation had been in a building physically separate from the hall; and other domestic offices, particularly the kitchen, were in separate structures, linked by tresances (corridors or covered ways) or pentices (a lean-to covering a way alongside a building).[11] Other elements, not necessarily contiguous, in the thirteenth-century household would have been a chapel and stables. The whole would have been enclosed with a fence, wall or moat or several of these (Figure 1). Instructions for planning or laying out a

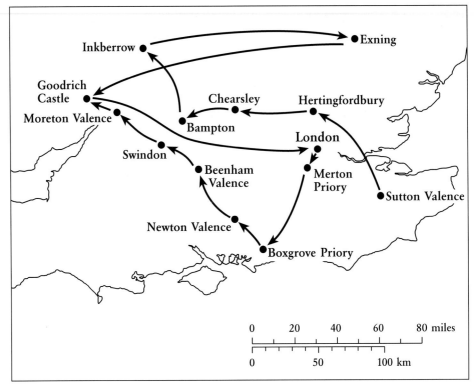

Map 2. The itinerary of the household of Joan de Valence, 1296–7.

house or castle, even one of considerable sophistication, could be sketchy, but a concept of overall architectural planning had taken root in some places before the end of the thirteenth century.[12] The royal palace at Clarendon, primarily the work of the monarchs up to and including Henry III, had all the standard elements, but organised piecemeal, added to here and there. By the middle of the fourteenth century, the royal palaces of Edward III, such as Windsor, were put together on the basis of a coherent plan.[13]

Various elements in this pattern changed through the late medieval period, especially chamber accommodation and the use of rooms for particular purposes. There was a remarkable transformation in domestic accommodation and the use of space between 1200 and 1500. Even in the royal household, there were comparatively few chambers in thirteenth-century buildings. Those there were, the king and queen usually occupied. At Marlborough Castle, works in the late 1230s were designed to improve the castle as a residence, particularly Henry III's chamber and that for his new Queen.[14] By the end of the fourteenth century, there were many more rooms. The names attached to them show that they were often inhabited by courtiers, as at Rotherhithe, *c.* 1370, or at Eltham in the 1380s.[15]

What was a chamber? In the thirteenth century, *camera* or *chaumbre* had a variety of meanings, from a set of hangings for a bed, a room or suite of rooms,

Table 4. The itinerary of the household of Joan de Valence, 1296–7

Sutton Valence, Kent (Valence estate)	22 May 1296–7 June 1296
Journey	
Hertingfordbury, Herts. (held by her daughter, Agnes de Valence: *VCH Herts.* iii, p. 463)	11 June 1296–7 August 1296
Journey via Chearsley, Bucks., a Valence estate (Phillips, *Aymer*, p. 241)	8 August 1296–12 August 1296
Bampton, Oxon. (Valence estate)	13 August 1296–1 September 1296
Inkberrow, Worcs. (Valence estate)	3 September 1296–28 October 1296
Exning, Suss. (Valence estate)	31 October 1296–18 November 1296
Journey	9 November 1296–18 November 1296
Goodrich Castle, Heref. (Valence estate)	18 November 1296–7 May 1297
Journey (itinerary including Joan's London house, Merton Priory, Newton Valence (held by Aymer de Valence, her son), Beenham Valence (own estate))	8 May 1297–31 May 1297
Swindon, Wilts. (Valence estate)	31 May 1297–7 August 1297
Moreton Valence, Glos. (Valence estate)	8 August 1297–11 September 1297
Goodrich Castle, Heref. (Valence estate)	12 September 1297–28 September 1297 and beyond

Source
PRO E101/505/25–7.

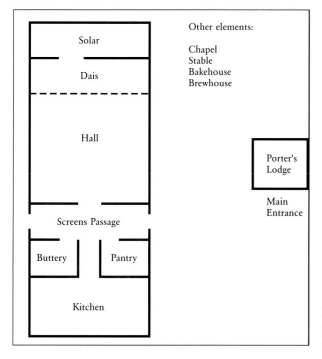

Figure 1. Schematic layout of a thirteenth-century manor house.

to the functions that were associated with them or, more generally, the area in which they took place. The chamber was usually entrusted to a chamberlain, though not always so called. Joan de Valence had her own servant, Humphrey of the Chamber, who performed these duties for her; her daughter-in-law, Beatrice, had a servant in a similar position. To see what happened in this room or suite of rooms, it is necessary to step aside from the modern view of a room as having, preponderantly, a single function. Space was used and reused and medieval furniture was designed to accommodate these changes. It would not have been out of the ordinary to find the chamber used for sleeping, dressing and washing, for living during the day, eating, receiving guests – in fact for anything that the occupant did not wish to do in front of the full glare of the household or preferred to perform in more intimate surroundings. This should not be confused with a modern notion of privacy, for this was still public living. Separation was a mark of status and honour, not of modesty.

By the late thirteenth century, more appointments were common. There was often a garderobe, or privy, attached to the suite of rooms, and the maintenance of this was one of the duties that John Russell in his mid-fifteenth-century *Boke of Nurture* expected of the chamberlain, along with looking after the bed, helping the lord dress and undress, and keeping the fire and lights in the room burning.[16] As well as the privy, there was a garderobe in another sense, now called a wardrobe, for keeping clothes and valuables. Among the works Bogo de Clare carried out in 1285 on his London residence was the construction of a wardrobe in his new chamber, with a lockable cupboard, as well as a doorway from the chamber to his private chapel.[17] Joan de Valence had another servant, John of the Wardrobe, who received the allowances of a valet, to look after her clothing. At the same time, there was a more senior official, Robert of the Wardrobe. He received wages at the rate of 8d. or 10d. a day when out of the household and made the purchases of cloth for clothing and livery, bought spices and carried out other household business.[18] There was also a household tailor, Roger.

The space required by the wardrobe for clothes could be more than would conveniently fit within the chamber. The wardrobe might then become more of a depot, as well as a workshop for the preparation of apparel. As so much of the purchasing for it was done in London, the wardrobe of the great household often established a base of its own there, sometimes separate from the accommodation used by the rest of the household. Thus, in 1501, the wardrobe of the third Duke of Buckingham was in Salisbury Alley, while his main residence was at Queenhithe.

How did households use space? An examination of the household of Joan de Valence shows in more detail the balance of the household's composition and operation.[19] In the late thirteenth century, the Valence properties included a number of impressive castles: Pembroke, Sutton Valence, Hertford and Goodrich. Today, Goodrich, with much work surviving from this period, is the most useful for further study (Plate 11). Sutton Valence is more ruinous; Pembroke Castle is largely earlier work; and Hertford reverted to the Crown on

11. Goodrich Castle, Herefordshire, from the east.

the death of William de Valence.[20] Joan de Valence resided at Goodrich from 18 November 1296 to early May 1297, returning there in September 1297. It remained in her possession until her death in 1307, when it passed to her son, Aymer; then on his death in 1324, it passed to Elizabeth Comyn, his niece.[21]

Goodrich was the site of major building works close to 1300, when the castle was almost entirely rebuilt, save for the twelfth-century keep. It has been argued, from the physical remains, that this was the work of Aymer de Valence.[22] It is more likely, however, that it was the work of Joan's husband, William de Valence, during the years between 1280 and his death in 1296, when it was complete – or at least substantially habitable – before Joan resided there. William de Valence received grants of timber for works on the castle in 1280 and 1282, with a further 12 oaks for repairs in June 1293.[23]

Valence had played a considerable part in Edward I's campaigns against the Welsh in 1277, leading, with Edmund of Lancaster, the forces of the army from south Wales and Pembrokeshire that confined Llywelyn to Snowdonia from the south. For some of 1278, William had oversight of the works on Aberystwyth Castle.[24] From then until the 1290s, he was involved in many operations against

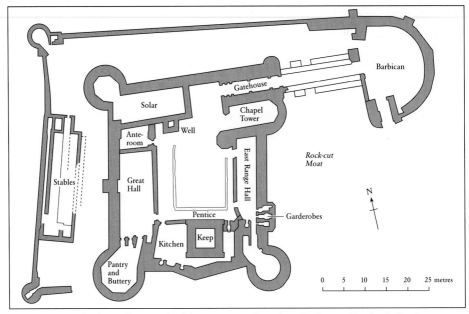

Figure 2. Goodrich Castle, Herefordshire, *c.* 1300 (based on D. Renn, *Goodrich Castle, Herefordshire* (1993) pp. 14–15, by permission of English Heritage).

the Welsh. In 1282, his son, William, was killed by them in a surprise attack at Llandeilo; Valence marched northwards in 1283 to counter Welsh unrest, capturing Castell-y-Bere in April. He accompanied Edward I on his progress through north Wales in 1284; and he also fought against the Welsh in their uprising of 1294. Valence already held an extremely strong castle at Pembroke; there is a suggestion that he may have had a hand in the work on the walls of the town there and at Tenby at about this time.[25] The rebuilding of Goodrich, one of a group of substantial castles in private hands – Caerphilly, Chepstow, Ludlow – essential for the security of south Wales and the Marches, shows the influence of royal work and should be seen as part of the broader pattern of fortifications constructed to effect the Edwardian settlement of Wales. The barbican at Goodrich has a resemblance to the design of the barbican at the Tower of London, a work of 1275–6. There is, in addition, firmer evidence that major work at Goodrich was under way in early 1296, possibly at royal expense, in an account for royal clerks and workmen lodged at Marstow, less than a mile from Goodrich.[26]

Goodrich Castle must be seen as much more than a fortification, as an up-to-date residence of the highest quality. During Joan de Valence's stay, from November 1296 onwards, there are few notes of works and no suggestion that her occupation was other than domestic. A lantern was bought for the kitchen window, on account of the wind, on 12 December 1296; six days later, a lock was bought for the door of the store-house where the fodder for the horses was kept.[27] In September 1297, the marshalsea mended the door of the chapel 'where the oats were kept', indicative of pressure on accommodation.[28] In terms of furnishings and equipment, Joan purchased a box for her messenger, for 1s. 6d., another box for alms, a bushel measure and trug for measuring corn, a mill for the saucery, an axe for cutting wood, knives and strainers for the kitchen, with repairs to a bag for her silver. At Christmas 1296, canvas was bought for making napkins.[29] Other objects associated with the Valence household indicate the extraordinary splendour and magnificence the establishment could command. These include a jewel box, known now as the Valence casket, which dates from *c.* 1290–1324 (Plate 12); the lid of a nautilus-shaped hanap, or cup, possibly associated with Beatrice de Nesle (Plates 13 and 14); and a lesser object, a pendant from horse harness (Plate 15).

What was the structure of this household and how, if at all, can it be related to the layout of the castle at Goodrich? In 1296–7, Joan's household was organised for administrative purposes into six departments: pantry, buttery, kitchen, saucery, lodgings (responsible for fuel and accommodation) and marshalsea. In addition, there were a chapel and clerks, and attendants for some chambers. A financial department, headed by a treasurer, based in London, oversaw the estates. A number of other groups can be identified within the household, which averaged 135 individuals per day in 1296–7, with 12 grooms for 31 horses. Joan's daughter-in-law, Beatrice, shared a chamber or suite of rooms with her until she departed with her husband Aymer, around 9 January 1297. The young Edward Burnel, a minor whose wardship had been purchased by William de Valence, was in Joan's charge throughout the year.

Joan's principal visitors were her son Aymer, who spent 67 days with her, frequently accompanied by Roger de Inkpen (probably the Elder: 25 days) and either of the two Thomases de Berkeley (22 days). Isabella de Hastings, her daughter, who was fetched in Joan's coach, stayed with her at Hertingfordbury from 9 to 15 July 1296, but not at Goodrich.[30] Agnes de Valence, another daughter, visited her at Exning on 8 November 1296.[31] A third daughter, Joan Comyn, brought her young son, John, to stay with his grandmother at Moreton Valence on 14 August 1297. They stayed at least until 11 September and, if the continued level of payments for cressets which burned in the chambers of the two women is a guide, they may have accompanied Joan de Valence back to Goodrich in mid-September and continued their stay there.[32]

Others visited for shorter periods of time. John de Tany spent 16 days with Joan, including 18 August 1297, when, at Moreton Valence, he was made a knight; Thomas de la Roche spent 15 days and Thomas de Breybeof, 13. Her son-in-law, John de Hastings, was with her for nine days. For female company, Joan had the Prioress of Aconbury (15 days) and the Lady of Raglan (14 days). Brief stays were made by other named visitors. The most notable among them were the young Gilbert de Clare, who stayed for one night on two separate occasions; his mother, Joan of Acre, who stayed for three days on another occasion and whose pack came to hunt the Dowards on 9 and 10 April 1297; and the new Earl of Oxford, who came to do homage on 18 April. Others, such as Nicholas de Carew and John de la Ryvere, had served William de Valence; Stackpole, who visited on 14 July 1297, was probably one of two of that name later retained by Aymer.

12. The Valence casket: made of sheet metal, riveted together, and decorated in enamel, possibly at Limoges or in England. The armorial decoration links it to the Valence family, either to William de Valence (after 1290) or his son, Aymer (d. 1324). It was probably a jewel casket and would have been lined with wood and fabric.

Guests also included neighbours and tenants from around Goodrich; they were particularly numerous on three Sundays towards the end of Lent 1297. Others came from Pembroke later, with John de Tany. A further body maintained in Joan's household – and possibly lodged there – throughout the year was a group of poor, never fewer than 20 and rising to 27 on many Saturdays, with a maximum of 61 present on the feast of St Katherine (25 November) at Goodrich in 1296. Joan was served in her household by a small number of friars, whose regime of abstinence is recorded alongside the fare eaten by the rest of her household.[33] Another group who came and went were the falconers, at least one of whom was present most of the time.

The main knightly visitors – Roger de Inkpen and Thomas de Berkeley, as well as a number of others – had formal connections with the Valence family, as members of the retinues of either William de Valence or Aymer, his son. Accompanying Aymer, they probably rode with that part of the retinue they had agreed to provide. An agreement between Aymer and Sir Thomas de Berkeley, made on 2 July 1297, committed the latter to service with Aymer in peace and

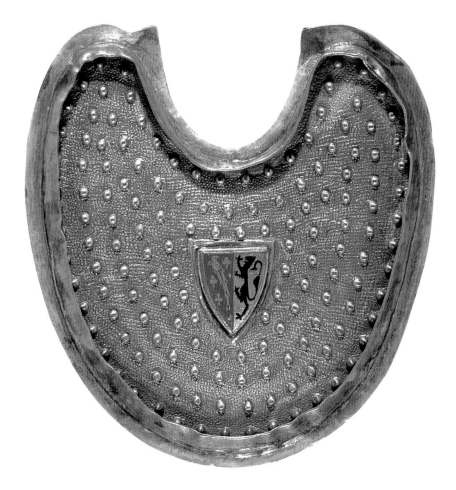

13 (*top*) and 14. The interior and exterior of the lid of a nautilus-shaped hanap, or cup, probably made in Paris around 1300 for Beatrice de Nesle, the wife of Aymer de Valence, enamelled with her arms on gold-plated silver.

15. Valence family pendant, for horse harness, before 1324, made of copper alloy, with enamel.

war, in England, Wales and Scotland, with five knights (including himself). Thomas was to have the right to eat in the household of Aymer, along with his four knights, two esquires serving him and four esquires serving the other four knights, and three valets for domestic business (*de meyster*) who were to bring the baggage of Thomas and the knights, making a party of 14 in all, with horses (Plate 16). He was to have for this service £50 annually and robes for himself and the knights, although this was to be modified if his son, Maurice, was one of them. Thomas and Maurice were each entitled to a *chaumbre de liveree* – a furnished chamber, bed or suite of rooms – in Aymer's household, both for themselves and for their knights if there should be room for them as well as Aymer's household; and the chamber was to be ready for them both day and night. In addition, if they went on business at Aymer's bidding anywhere in England and they and their followers and horses could not find food, they were to be at his charge for the first night only.[34]

The rebuilt Goodrich Castle, *c.* 1296, with its new defensive wall, round corner towers and connecting ranges, was divided into suites of rooms (Figure 2). The principal suite of accommodation was in the north-west tower and a great chamber or solar along the north side, with further rooms under it, an ante-room and stone bench, private chapel and garderobes. The great hall lay to the south of the lord's accommodation, with services, probably pantry and buttery, to the south of it, on the first floor and possibly in the basement of the south-west tower, and the kitchen adjacent to them (Plate 17). Other suites of rooms were the chamber, with garderobe, in the south-west tower; the group of chambers located in the south-east tower (Plate 18); a second – or east – hall, with access at the south end to the south-east tower and its chambers, to a block of three garderobes to the east, and to the chapel to the north; and the chapel and gatehouse tower, with a small group of chambers, one with a garderobe.

The chambers at Goodrich are interesting, firstly because of their number which was quite unusual at this date; and secondly because of their consistent quality, in terms of architectural appointment, most with fireplaces and sanitation: all were of the same high standard, not in a sequence of increasing quality. The appearance of a second hall in the east range and of the area under the principal chamber in the north range, which may have had a similar function, invites speculation about who might have used them. Were they used by esquires and valets of the military retainers or, for example, by the resident group of poor? But aside from the principal suite of rooms and the service areas and chapel, it is not possible to allocate ownership to any group of individuals.

Goodrich today contains much evidence of later domestic rearrangements, partitions and divisions, but its stone fabric is largely of the period immediately prior to Joan's stay. For all its military features, in 1296–7 it was principally a domestic residence. Although the accounts do not provide a detailed listing of all guests, the visits of military retainers were only one of the features of Joan's household. Rather, the accommodation provided separate suites of rooms that allowed individuals to maintain the rank and magnificence appropriate to them

16. Sir Richard Stapledon, accompanied by the now defaced effigies probably of an esquire, groom and horse, the faithful accompaniments of the military retainer, even in death. Exeter Cathedral, *c.* 1320.

17. Goodrich Castle, Herefordshire: the great hall, looking south to the south-west tower, where there was probably a pantry and buttery on the first floor and possibly also in the basement.

18. Goodrich Castle, Herefordshire: the fireplaces of the chambers in the south-east tower.

without interference. As far as Joan de Valence's great household was concerned, the separate groupings that lodged at Goodrich included resident establishments of others, her relations and wards; visiting households of other magnates; the poor; casual guests, as well as her own visiting servants; and lastly, in terms of quantity, military retainers.

The development of chambers is perhaps the most significant part of the work at Goodrich, inviting comparison with Roger Bigod III's contemporary work at Chepstow. There Marten's Tower (*c.* 1285–93) was constructed as the principal accommodation for the lord, with chambers with sanitation, surmounted by a chapel, in the south-east corner of the lower bailey (Plate 19). Chepstow Castle also had a new great hall, kitchen and service rooms and a well-appointed chamber block on the north side of the same bailey (Plate 20). This replaced the domestic accommodation and hall in the Norman Great Tower, a building that was also heightened and modified between 1292 and 1300 (Plate 21).[35] At Ludlow, a similar pattern of chambers can be seen in the construction between 1283 and 1292 of a new solar block and great hall, followed by a great chamber block and garderobe tower, probably around 1320, for Roger Mortimer (Plate 22). Contemporaneously with the dawning of an expectation that castles and residences would be occupied almost continuously, the quality of domestic accommodation in those of the greatest changed considerably, with a tendency to more (and smaller) rooms, with sanitation and other features. This develop-

19. Marten's Tower, Chepstow Castle, Mon., constructed *c.* 1285–93, as the principal accommodation for the lord, with chambers with sanitation. There was a chapel on the top floor.

20. Chepstow Castle, Mon.: the new great hall (*left*), kitchen and service rooms and chamber block on the north side of the lower bailey, late thirteenth century.

21. Chepstow Castle, Mon.: the Norman Great Tower, heightened and modified between 1292 and 1300.

ment is coincident with the rise of the use of formal indentures of retainer for military purposes, but reflects in general a pattern of domestic usage emphasising status and magnificence.

In the fourteenth and fifteenth centuries, the number of chambers in many residences grew. At the same time, the use of these rooms was increasingly assigned to individuals and their servants. At Bishop's Waltham, aside from the accommodation for the Bishop of Winchester, only a handful of individuals had rooms that were designated as their own on a personal basis. Most were housed in a series of communal chambers, designated by rank, for knights, esquires and clerks. Between 1438 and 1443, Cardinal Beaufort had the palace remodelled, providing a range of cellular lodgings at the north end of the inner court, as well as what was probably dormitory accommodation over the bakehouse and brewhouse (Figure 3 and Plate 23).[36] Cellular lodgings were not new. The remodelling of Windsor Castle between 1350 and 1368, with the provision of two great ranges of lodgings on the east and south sides of the upper ward, provides one of the earliest examples of their use.[37] But their wider adoption marks an important change in the design of the great household's residences. What is more difficult to establish, however, is how the household was accommodated and who used the lodgings. Some evidence for this comes from Caister Castle, where it is possible to identify the locations and uses of some of the rooms held by individuals.

22. Ludlow Castle, Shropshire: the solar block (*left*) and great hall (*centre*) were built between 1283 and 1292, followed by a great chamber block and garderobe tower (*right*), probably around 1320, for Roger Mortimer.

23. Bishop's Waltham Palace, Hants: the bakehouse and brewhouse, adapted between 1438 and 1443 to provide dormitory accommodation over the domestic offices.

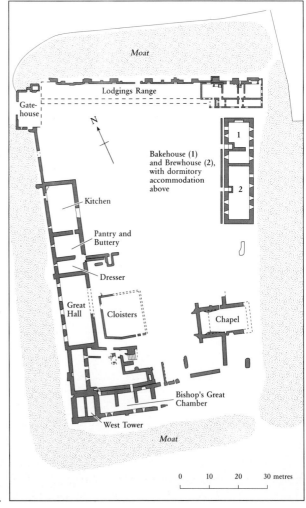

Figure 3. Bishop's Waltham, Hampshire, after the alterations of William of Wykeham and Cardinal Beaufort (based on J. N. Hare, *Bishop's Waltham Palace, Hampshire* (2nd edition, 1990) pp. 14–15, 20, by permission of English Heritage).

Sir John Fastolf started to build Caister Castle, Norfolk (Plate 24), replacing an earlier structure there, probably *c.* 1431. Construction continued for over 30 years at a cost of a little over £6,000. For this sum (which was modest compared with the building programmes of contemporaries such as Ralph, Lord Cromwell), Fastolf built a rectangular structure with a striking, tall, slender tower at its north-west angle, within a moat, with a base court with further buildings, probably some lodgings (on the site of the former manor), as well as other works in advance of the castle, in the area of the barge gate, possibly connected with artillery. The castle, which is largely of brick, would have recalled ones he had seen in France and possibly in Germany and the Low Countries – or, indeed, the palace of the Duke of Clarence at Woking, in whose household Fastolf had served, where substantial work was carried out in this material in 1420–1.[38]

Two detailed inventories of Caister show how far arrangements for residence had changed.[39] About 50 rooms and chambers are described, in a fashion that allows some of them to be fixed in relation to each other (Figure 4 and Table 5). The principal rooms were two halls – the summer hall, which had the great chamber (a bedroom) over it, and the nether, or winter, hall, which also had a chamber over it and was close to the accommodation of Fastolf's wife, Dame Milicent, and to a parlour in the tower. The nether hall had tapestry hangings, as did the room over it and the great chamber over the summer hall, but little mention is made of hangings elsewhere, although there were some unallocated in the wardrobe and some, hanging in other rooms in 1462, are not described in detail.[40] Some of the windows were glazed with armorial glass, bearing the Fastolf motto 'Me fault feire'; some of the walls were painted, with mixtures of vermilion, red lead and oil.[41]

In terms of sleeping accommodation, 28 rooms had a total of 39 beds, of which 27 were feather-beds, one a removing (or folding) bed, three pallets and four mattresses by themselves, one hanging-bed, and two others. Eighteen rooms were identified with individuals or officials of the household, accounting for 22 beds. The rooms with more than one bed were those of Sir John Fastolf (three), the chamber formerly belonging to his wife (three), and the chamber of Stephen Scrope, his wife's son by her first marriage (two). One of Dame Milicent's gentlewomen, Margaret Hodesson, had slept in a room adjacent to her.[42]

The base court contained chambers occupied by Fastolf's officials and relations – one of his lawyers, one of his gentle servants (Robert Fitzrauf), his cook, stablemen and gardeners. The chambers that were designated for guests – the yeomen's chamber and the chamber over the buttery – were within the principal court. Some servants at Caister were accommodated in their offices. In the bakehouse, there was a mattress, a blanket, a sheet and a coverlet. Somebody, probably a groom, slept in the great stable; the sumpterman's stable was similarly endowed with bedding. The gardeners' chamber had two mattresses, two bolsters, one pair of sheets, two blankets, one old carpet, three coverings or coverlets and a celure (albeit a worn one) of blue. Although the castle had two

halls, the inventory provides no evidence that they were slept in. The overwhelming majority of inhabitants was accommodated in chambers, although
some – valets and guests – may have slept together in rooms generally designated
for them. It was comparatively unusual for individuals in this household, except
those of the highest rank, to share their sleeping accommodation. Some furnished their own rooms and some rooms were for sojourners, or paying guests.

The furnishings of the rooms suggest that only a handful could have been
used for business, which was now mainly conducted away from areas where
most people slept. There was a chamber assigned to two of Fastolf's auditors,
Cole and Watkin Shipdam. As well as a bed, it contained a chair and a piece of
cloth for an accounting board.[43] It was in withdraughts or withdrawing chambers, that is, inner rooms of suites, that most business was done. Margaret
Paston wrote to her husband, *c.* 1454, about the arrival of four dormant tables
and the siting of at least one of them in his withdraught:

> I have take the mesure in the draute chamer þer as ye wold your coforys and
> your cowntewery [accounting equipment] shuld be sette for the whyle, and þer
> is no space besyde the bedd, thow the bed were remevyd to the dore, for to
> sette bothe your bord and your koforys there and to have space to go and sitte
> be syde. Wherfore I have purveyd [arranged] that ye shall have the same
> drawte chamer that ye had before, there as ye shall ly to yourself . . .[44]

Fastolf's chamber at Caister was a suite of three rooms: a bedchamber, with a
withdraught and a stew- (or bath-) house. His chamber had a folding table and
two chairs, besides a feather-bed and a little pallet-bed; and his withdraught also
had a feather-bed and a large astrolabe. The bath-house had about two dozen
books: from similar arrangements, by the start of the sixteenth century, separate rooms in secular residences evolved for libraries.[45]

At Caister the location of the parlour distinguishes its use from the withdraughts. It was in the tower, close to the winter hall, while the withdraughts
were all associated with the chambers of individuals. A similar distinction can
be seen at Ralph, Lord Cromwell's palace at South Wingfield, where the hall led
onto the parlour in the east range; but the withdraught – Cromwell's private
rooms – was accessed from a corner of the great chamber, above the other end
of the hall.[46] Parlours and withdraughts were different in function. The latter
were retiring rooms, whose use was reserved; the former were public.

Increasing evidence for rooms with these names and functions is found from
the latter part of the fourteenth century. The Catesby family properties at Ashby
St Ledgers and Catesby Place in Coventry both underwent work in the late fourteenth century. At Ashby, in 1392–3, the work included making a parlour – a
separate, two-storey building of stone (just possibly of brick), with a chamber
over the parlour (which had four windows), connected to the main house by a

24. Caister Castle, Norfolk, from the south-west. The North-West Tower, with the Nether Hall
and chamber above it. Built for Sir John Fastolf, from *c.* 1431.

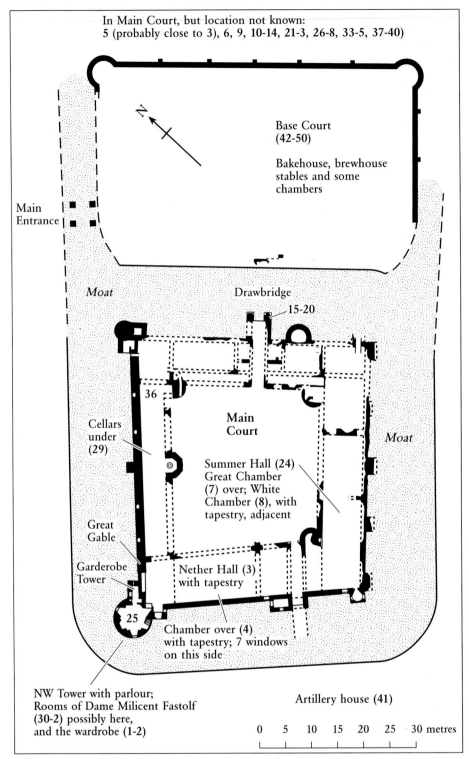

In Main Court, but location not known:
5 (probably close to 3), 6, 9, 10-14, 21-3, 26-8, 33-5, 37-40)

N

Base Court
(42-50)

Bakehouse, brewhouse
stables and some
chambers

Main
Entrance

Moat

Drawbridge

15-20

36

Cellars
under
(29)

Main
Court

Moat

Summer Hall (24)
Great Chamber
(7) over; White
Chamber (8), with
tapestry, adjacent

Great
Gable

Garderobe
Tower

Nether Hall (3)
with tapestry

25

Chamber over (4)
with tapestry; 7 windows
on this side

NW Tower with parlour;
Rooms of Dame Milicent Fastolf
(30-2) possibly here,
and the wardrobe (1-2)

Artillery house (41)

0   5   10   15   20   25   30 metres

Figure 4. Caister Castle, Norfolk, reconstructed by Sir John Fastolf between c. 1431 and 1459
(based on H. D. Barnes and W. D. Simpson, 'Caister Castle', AntJ 32 (1952) p. 39).

Table 5. Rooms at Caister Castle, in 1448, furnishings and functions

The locations of the rooms are given on Figure 4. Besides the 1448 inventory, further notes up to 1455 and the inventory of 1462 have been used.

1. Wardrobe, in the upper building (*in domo superiori*)
2. White Chamber (or white-hanged chamber) next the wardrobe: 1 bed, with white hangings, decorated with an escutcheon
3. Nether Hall (winter hall): arras of the morris dance; arras with a giant; arras for the dais in the hall, with a woodwose carrying a child; arras of the siege of Falaise for the west side of the hall; 2 chairs, fringed, 1 red chair; 6 cushions of tapestry; 1 banker of arras
4. Chamber over the Nether Hall: arras – 2 tapestries, of hunting and hawking
5. Buttery
6. Chamber over the buttery, for visitors: 1 bed
7. Great Chamber over the Summer Hall: 1 bed – gentlewoman in green taking a mallard in her hand – bolster, celure and tester; cover, a giant smiting a wild boar with a spear; arras (old) – the shepherds
8. White Chamber next the Great Chamber, sometime Nicholas Bokking's (Fastolf's receiver-general): 2 beds
9. The shovellers' chamber or the shepherds' chamber, sometime for Stephen Scrope: 2 beds (1 folding), hanging cloths with shepherds(?) or shovellers (spoon-bills, see Rafman's chamber, 10)
10. John Rafman's chamber (steward of the household): 1 bed, hanging cloth of popelers (spoon-bills), 2 tapets with clouds
11. The yeomen's chamber, for visitors: 3 beds
12. White Chamber (or white-hanged chamber) next Inglose's chamber: 2 beds, 1 with white hangings
13. Inglose's chamber: 1 bed
14. Chamber for Cole and Watkyn Shipdam, auditors: 3 beds; 1 chair, 3 forms, 1 folding stool, cloth counting-board
15. Porter's chamber: 1 bed
16. Chamber against the porter's chamber: 1 bed
17. Chamber of E. Fastolf, next to the gate (1455)
18. The inner chamber over the gates: 1 bed, 1 folding stool
19. The middle chamber: 1 bed
20. The withdraught over the drawbridge: 1 bed
21. Sir John Fastolf's chamber and the withdraught with the bath-house: 2 beds, 1 folding table, 1 long chair, 1 green chair; in the withdraught, 1 bed and 1 large astrolabe; bath-house – the library
22. Chapel
23. Chapel chamber (in 1455, occupied by William Worcester)
24. Summer Hall: crossbows and spears; pieces of red worsted and green worsted, 2 bankers and 6 cushions of tapestry; had tapestry on the walls in 1462
25. Tower: 5 storeys of hexagonal rooms; all floors except the top have a fireplace; adjoining rectangular projections on 2 sides for 4 storeys, of which the northern has the garderobes; tower parlour: 1 piece of red worsted
26. Kitchen
27. Larder (contains fish only)
28. Buttery
29. Cellar: silver vessels, 2 pipes of wine

Chamber and wardrobe lately Dame Milicent Fastolf (30–2).

30. Chamber where Margaret Hodesson lay (a gentlewoman in 1430–1): 1 bed
31. Chamber of Dame Milicent Fastolf: 3 beds
32. Outermost chamber next the winter hall: 1 bed, 1 chair

One of the chambers in notes 33–5 is the withdraught chamber for Lewys and William Worcester.

33. Chamber of John Boteler (his property only)
34. Chamber of Brother Carleton
35. Chamber of the rector of St G. (his property only)
36. Chamber of William Lynde and Geoffrey the Chaplain, leading out onto the cloister at the north corner
37. Chamber of John Bossherde, leading out onto the high gallery
38. Chamber of Robert Carpenter
39. Chamber of the rector of Castle Combe
40. Chamber where Dame Margaret Braunch sleeps

The rooms named in notes 41–50 are probably outside the Main Court.

41. Artillery-house: armour and arms
42. Bakehouse: a horse-mill, with bedding
43. Brewhouse
44. Bokking's chamber (probably John Bokking, lawyer) in the Base Court: 1 bed, coverlet of popelers
45. Fitzrauf's chamber: 1 bed, celure and tester of blue clouded
46. Thomas Fastolf's chamber: 1 bed, tester of red say with the Fastolf arms
47. The cook's chamber: 1 bed, 1 red coverlet of roses and bloodhounds' heads
48. Great stable: 1 mattress, coverlet of blue and red
49. Sumperman's stable: 1 mattress, coverlet of blue and red
50. The gardeners' chamber: 2 mattresses and assorted bedding

Sources MCO Fastolf paper 43; Amyot, 'Transcript', pp. 254–79; *PL* i, pp. 111–13.

tresance. The roof of the building and tresance required 4,000 tiles and 26 crests.[47] At Catesby Place there was also a parlour.[48] Among the buildings constructed at Eltham by Henry IV were two storeys of 'drawyngchambers', each 30 feet long and 22½ feet wide. Their presence then continues in royal houses.[49]

Parlours could be sufficient in size to fulfil a number of functions. At Writtle, at one stage a favourite residence of Anne Stafford, dowager Duchess of Buckingham, a survey of 1521 noted that the principal lodgings were arranged in two storeys around a courtyard, within a moat, with a base court which contained, in two storeys, a further 28 sets of lodgings, the porter's lodge, 'every oon of thaym having for the mooste parte booth draught and chymney'. Beyond the base court were the stables and a barn. In the main court were the buttery, pantry, kitchen, great chamber, chapel and a large parlour. The hall at Writtle had burned down some years before and had never been replaced: 'and for sowyth as in the said maner there is noe hall, therefore the hall was kept in a goodly and a large parlor'.[50]

There was an increasing diversity of function ascribed to rooms. It was no longer enough, for example, that the furniture of the hall might be cleared away after a meal in order to provide a space for dancing. Dancing chambers appeared at Windsor under Edward III, at Eltham under Richard II and at Leicester Castle in the fifteenth century.[51] Accompanying this was a sharpening definition of function. A bedchamber was, increasingly, just that, but could have an ante-chamber.[52]

By the fifteenth century the great household was lodged in a complex of buildings that had many more rooms than its thirteenth-century equivalent. The buildings were more organised and planned, with more invested in them financially – a concentration of resources to make the most of magnificence. Part of these resources was transferred from defensive measures. Much fortification, even from the late thirteenth century, as at Acton Burnell, was for show: the lightly fortified manor house was an appropriate successor to many castles. By the fifteenth century, warfare in England was not, for various reasons, about sieges, but about conflict in the open. Fortification did have a place, offering refuge and perhaps sufficient deterrence or delay to move the seat of a conflict. A siege, employing artillery, was unusual. Caister, besieged and badly damaged in 1469, was one of the few castles where there may have been an attempt to provide defensive artillery.[53]

Expenditure on magnificence was apparent in terms of the building, as an architectural or political statement. Lords set out to impress through the design of their houses, be it in the courts and high tower of Ralph, Lord Cromwell's manor at South Wingfield, the brick-built tower of his castle at Tattershall (Plate 75), the tall, slender tower of Fastolf's Caister, or the halls of innumerable manors and castles. Their setting, in parks, or surrounded by moats and walls, added to their splendour. The first sight Gawain had of Sir Bertilak's castle was of

A castel þe comlokest þat ever knyȝt aȝte [owned],
Pyched on a prayere [meadow], a park al aboute

with a palisade, running for more than 2 miles enclosing many trees.[54] Just as much as the palaces of Flanders or Burgundy, the residence of the Bishops of Ely at Somersham was set out with a view to the effect on the visitor of the totality of buildings and landscape features, enclosures, water and parkland.[55] The delights of the Thornbury of the third Duke of Buckingham included well-made gardens, with a gallery, an orchard and a new park, recently enclosed to the chagrin of some of his tenants, uncompensated at the time of his death in 1521.[56]

Andrew Boorde's ideal house, visualised in the 1540s, was of two courtyards. The principal offices and accommodation were in the first courtyard, with the stables for riding horses and the privies in the outer courtyard. Stables for other horses, a slaughterhouse and dairy, bakehouse and brewhouse, were to be situated further away. Other essential elements were a clean moat, a garden for herbs, orchards, clean fishponds and a park with deer and rabbits.[57]

In the overall architectural composition, even the domestic offices had a proper place. At Henry VII's Richmond,

Undre and beside the halle is sett and ordred the housis of office – the pantry, buttry, selary, kechon and squylery – right poletikly conveyed, and wisely ther coles and fuell in the yardes without nyghe unto the seid offices.[58]

Secondly, by concentrating expenditure on comparatively few residences, it was possible to use high-quality or luxury materials, decoration and images, all

25. Herstmonceux Castle, Sussex, from the south. Built in brick for Sir Roger Fienes, *c.* 1441.

26. Bishop's Waltham Palace,
Hants: the south-west tower,
viewed across the remains of the
bishop's great chamber. Tiled
floors were laid in this area of the
palace between 1438 and 1442 as
part of Cardinal Beaufort's works.

of which enhanced the lord's standing and displayed his magnificence. This applied both to the fabric of the house and to the use of prestigious soft furnishings. The medium of construction had an impact: the effect of brick was markedly different from stone or wood. It gradually gained a place in the construction of some of the most impressive buildings, especially in eastern England, becoming more widespread in the fifteenth century (Plate 25), although it had been used on a large scale in royal buildings earlier, at the Tower in 1278, with imported bricks. The use of brick often involved craftsmen from the Low Countries, some of whom had exceptional skill in brick-making and brick-laying. Bricks and tiles were also used for paving floors, although both marble and plaster were sometimes used.[59]

The paving of floors, with both native-produced and imported glazed tiles, was a major improvement, in terms of potential cleanliness and decorative effect. In 1438–9, Cardinal Beaufort's works at Bishop's Waltham included the purchase for £6 of 2,000 paving tiles, which were imported through Southampton and laid in his parlour and in the alley leading towards his chamber; a further 1,000 were laid outside his chamber in 1441 and another 5,400 purchased for £18, some of which were laid in the chapel. In 1442, the tiling progressed to the newly built galleries and the tower (Plates 26, 27 and 28).[60] Specially patterned tiles were made for other magnates, such as those produced for the third Duke of Buckingham showing Stafford family badges and

27. The birth of Richard Beauchamp. The chamber has a tiled floor (with a tiled or a paved corridor adjacent) and fireplace; and an elaborate bed with a fringed celure and embroidered tester. The chest probably contains birthday gifts – standing cups and spoons – a mark of the estate of the child. Beauchamp's mother is naked in bed, as was the custom; the swaddled baby is held by a gentlewoman and there are three other female attendants. From the Beauchamp Pageant, *c.* 1483–7.

28. Richard Beauchamp at dinner with Sir Baltirdam, the Sultan's lieutenant in Jerusalem. Sir Baltirdam, out of courtesy, acts as his own household marshal, carrying the rod, with his hand on Beauchamp's shoulder. He is at the end of the table (the board-end), where the principal servant would have been expected to stand. Next to Beauchamp (who has a jewelled collar round his neck) is his personal chaplain, who is seated in the place of honour (as a tribute to his regard for Christianity). There are fowl on dishes on the table; and a covered cup. Three servants in the foreground are bringing more food: one may be a carver. Sir Baltirdam's swordbearer is in the background. The floor of the chamber is paved or tiled. From the Beauchamp Pageant, *c.* 1483–7.

29. Floor tiles from Thornbury Castle, showing a four-tile pattern with the English royal arms and Garter, with the badges of the third Duke of Buckingham in the corners. Early sixteenth century.

the Garter (Plate 29).[61] Once an investment like this had been made in a floor, older forms of floor covering might be discarded. A tiled floor was to be seen, although some rooms continued to be strewn with rushes or covered with rush matting.[62] Tiles were, however, cold to the feet, and by the mid-fifteenth century some carpets were used on floors in chambers, especially around beds. When dressing, the lord would stand on a footsheet.[63] Once textiles were laid on the floor, they were vulnerable to outdoor footwear. Indoor footwear, in the form of corks or sandals, appeared in the fourteenth century, openwork indoor shoes about the same time, and slippers in the fifteenth century.[64]

Glass was used in royal houses and palaces before the end of the twelfth century, but it was not until the end of Henry III's reign that glazing extended to most of the windows of his principal rooms; some were only partially glazed, having wooden shutters to cover the remainder of the opening.[65] Although glass became much more widespread in the fourteenth century, it was still a luxury item. The works to Castle Hedingham carried out by the Earl of Oxford in 1431–2 included a payment of 12s. to a glazier for repairing the windows in a room strikingly called the 'Glaschambre'.[66] Decorated glass was more expensive. Linen cloth was used for some windows of lesser buildings: around 1420 it was purchased by Dame Alice de Bryene for use in the kitchen windows at Acton Hall, Suffolk.[67]

Tapestries and cloth hangings played an important role in interior decoration during the fourteenth and fifteenth centuries, as indeed they may have done earlier. Abbot Baudri of Bourgeuil, in his fabulous description of the chamber of Adela of Blois, *c.* 1100, detailed tapestries with scenes from the Old Testament, Greek mythology and the history of Rome, concluding, around her bed, with the expedition to England by her father, William the Conqueror. The floor included an inlaid world map.[68] As part of the preparations for the visit of Queen Isabella to Pontefract, Thomas of Lancaster's household put up hangings (tapets) in the hall.[69] Behind the Luttrell family at dinner is what may be an edged hanging, decorated with the martlets of the Luttrell arms (Plate 53).

The royal collection of tapestries – or arras, an indication of both quality and continental manufacture – did not become substantial until the reign of Richard II. Other members of the royal family, including the Black Prince, who left his son an arras showing Saladin, had an interest in this form of decoration. By the start of the reign of Henry VI, there were a little under 100 pieces of arras in the royal collection. Magnates had smaller collections. Although many may not have been specially commissioned, some designs exhibited clear connections with the owner – Fastolf's tapestry of the siege of Falaise (hung in the winter hall at Caister), or the Guy of Warwick tapestries owned by the Earl of Warwick – and were designed to celebrate his achievements.[70] To a world that was largely unlettered, images were powerful means of communication. A series of magnificent tapestries imported from the Low Countries made an impressive addition to Edward IV's collection. By the middle of the fifteenth century rich collections also belonged to others, such as that of William de la Pole, Duke of Suffolk, inventoried at Ewelme in 1466 (Plate 30).[71]

Tapestry could be moved with considerable ease: decoration could be varied comparatively easily or placed in store. The *Destruction of Troy*, purchased by Henry VII from Pasquier Grenier, who had made a similar set for Charles the Bold of Burgundy, normally hung in the hall at Richmond. When Henry VII met Archduke Philip at Calais in 1500, this tapestry was among his accompaniments.[72] In August 1501, the Duke of Buckingham had arras from his wardrobe in Salisbury Alley in London taken to Penshurst.[73]

Painted decoration was used extensively – and famously by Henry III. As well as religious and secular subjects, ranging from the Crucifixion, the Evangelists, the Last Supper, Dives and Lazarus and images of saints, to the world maps at Winchester and Westminster, paint could be applied to almost any surface in the room as patterned decoration, or to imitate drapery or stone-courses.[74]

30. The Devonshire hunting tapestries: the boar and bear. Probably dating from *c.* 1435–45, this is an important example of the highest quality of tapestry that was available in the Low Countries and which would have attracted English aristocratic purchasers. This tapestry may have been imported into England during the fifteenth century, although it is not recorded before 1601, when it was at Hardwick Hall.

Painting, other than patterned decoration, was less prominent from the fourteenth century onwards. At the same time, sculpture had a substantial position in some royal buildings, for example the statues of the Kings of England at Westminster Hall and in the hall at Richmond Palace,[75] and at least a more general decorative presence elsewhere. In the gateway to the episcopal palace at Norwich, Bishop Alnwick marked his devotion to the Virgin Mary with crowned 'M's.[76]

The buildings of the household were the stage for pageant and drama, equally intended to increase the standing of the head of the house. A proportionately greater investment in ceremonial arrangements could be made at a few locations than in many. Continuous residence itself may have permitted an elaboration of ceremony, developing routines that used space in a fixed pattern, rather than shifting residences necessitating changes in the basic arrangements for service.

Prolonged periods of residence had other consequences. The household required more space. Goodrich covers no more than 0.5 hectares, while Caister

extends to some 2.4 hectares. At Bishop's Waltham, the main palace site is about 0.9 hectares, perhaps three times as much with the outer court and the bishop's garden but excluding the ponds and park. Here, what was spacious in the twelfth century became cramped as accommodation expanded in the fourteenth and fifteenth centuries. A common requirement was more room for storage – a peripatetic household had its resources distributed across the estates and residences, a static one needed concentration. Underground or basement storage rooms had the advantage of stable, relatively cool temperatures. The use of sand may have helped both to bed in large containers and to stabilise further the environment, and other smaller containers or cupboards – gardeviandes – were frequently used.[77] At Goodrich, the cellar accommodation covers about 35 m². With increased consumption of wine in the households of the great, by the greater number of gentle servants, more cellarage was needed (storage for ale, with a much shorter shelf-life, was a lesser problem). The culmination of this development can be seen at Hampton Court, where the vaulted cellars cover approximately 135 m².[78]

For continuous occupation, sanitation and water supply arrangements had to be sufficient. There had to be effective drainage and clearance of wastes – the smell from the kitchen wastes at Westminster in 1259 distracted the life of the royal household.[79] Bathing in a tub in a chamber, although outlined in the mid-fifteenth-century *Boke of Nurture*, was increasingly superseded by bathrooms or stews. In the reign of Edward III, many of the royal houses, both small and large, from Eltham and King's Langley to smaller establishments such as Easthampstead, had elaborate arrangements.[80] The stews attached to Sir John Fastolf's chambers at Caister in the 1440s were normally expected in a residence.[81] Cleaning the house had to be adapted to a continuing regime rather than a concentrated period of activity immediately prior to the arrival of the household.

Separate suites of accommodation and a growth in the area covered by the site of the household entailed changes to arrangements for heating and lighting. A great hall, heated by a central hearth or brazier, filled with wood or charcoal, instead of being one of the few sources of warmth and light, became one among many. Fireplaces proliferated as chambers grew in number (Plates 18 and 31). Those at Goodrich in 1296–7 were supplied by a substantial campaign of wood-cutting that continued throughout the period of Joan de Valence's residence there. A century later, arrangements were different, relying on supplies in wood-

31. Preserving fire in the household: Moses, who has thrown Pharaoh's crown into the open fire, has been condemned to death. He proposes to eat a burning coal, taken out of an earthenware vessel. From the Queen Mary Psalter, early fourteenth century.

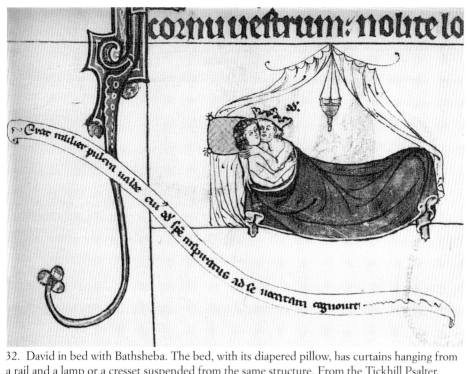

32. David in bed with Bathsheba. The bed, with its diapered pillow, has curtains hanging from a rail and a lamp or a cresset suspended from the same structure. From the Tickhill Psalter, *c.* 1303–14.

yards or storage rooms. At Hanley Castle, over the winter of 1409–10, fuel was obtained in bulk on only a handful of occasions. In December, 184 men were hired for a day to fell and trim wood, which 164 men, also hired for one day, made into faggots, composing the 276 cartloads of fuel that were brought in. Six cartloads of stakes were acquired at the same time to make a fence for the wood-yard. The supply lasted until March when another 228 men were hired to fell and cut fuel for faggots. Charcoal needed more preparation, with the hire of three charcoal-burners for a period of nearly a month before All Saints.[82] By the early sixteenth century, prudent household management kept some degree of heating even in largely unoccupied houses;[83] and households similarly defined allowances for lighting various chambers.

A further consequence of the peripatetic nature of the household can be seen in furniture and other equipment. Much had to be portable, especially the most important parts, the costly soft furnishings, at least in the thirteenth and four-teenth centuries. The woodwork itself was of little consequence, as it was mainly covered by textiles and it was not generally moved from place to place. As resi-dences became more favoured, there was less impetus to move all the household goods and more investment was made in pieces of furniture that it would have been unusual to move. This process was still under way at the end of the fifteenth century: for many types of furniture, it is the items made in the sixteenth century, as permanent or semi-permanent pieces, that are the earliest to survive.

Something of the changes that took place can be seen by looking at beds and sleeping arrangements. The bed of a lord or lady was of particular importance: it has a prominent place in many wills. The bed was used, not only for sleeping, but as the principal seating throughout the day for most activities within the chamber. It was the most important piece of furniture (possibly the only furniture) in the room. At its most developed, it was a state bed, such as the bed of King Henry III which was in the Painted Chamber at Westminster, with posts coloured green, powdered with gold stars, with a canopy, or tabernacle, over it.[84] While there is evidence for framed, or standard, beds (which could not easily be moved), the main features recorded from the thirteenth century onwards were the hangings, designated together with accompanying cushions and coverings as a 'bed'. A canopy, called a celure, which could be either rectangular or shaped like a conical tent, known sometimes as a sparver, was prominent among these.[85] Joan de Valence's bed had the latter type. The bed was transported with her, in its own bag, by sumpter-horse. In August 1296, 80 rings and cords for curtains, and a pavilion (a loose, tent-like arrangement, placed above and probably around the bed) were purchased. In November of the same year, five crooks were bought as part of this structure, either to support it or to impart shape to the hangings. In May 1297, 7s. 8d. was spent by Roger the Tailor, dyeing the covering, possibly of the bed itself or the pavilion.[86] The bed was set up in Joan's chamber. Within the chamber, there was a cresset light that burned each night: it may have been suspended within the bed itself (Plate 32). There is much that this account does not tell us about the bed, about its frame, mattress or linen; but there is sufficient to indicate that it was an elaborate affair.

The textiles used for the beds of the nobility were appropriate to the most prominent piece of furniture in the chamber. The bedding made for Bogo de Clare in 1285 included a quilt embroidered with red-haired sirens, a mattress of lined red sindon (a fine linen) stuffed with wool, and a pound of wool for stuffing an unlined mattress, also of red sindon.[87] In 1348, among the goods drawn from the private wardrobe of the King's chamber for Princess Joan, in preparation for her intended marriage to Pedro of Castile, was a bed of red sindon, double-lined, worked with fighting dragons, embroidered in silk, powdered with gold besants, and with a vine-leaf decoration in the border. The bed contained one quilt, one dorser (the hanging at the head of the bed, also known as a tester), one celure, a mattress (stuffed with 18 lb. of cotton, which would have made it quite thin), two pairs of sheets of linen of Rheims (but glossed as Aylesham), six cushions, eight tapets; four pillows, worked, of camoca (a silk), stuffed with 6 lb. of down; a cover of coloured cloth and a coverchief of camoca (Plate 33).[88]

Litter, straw or rushes, even furze or broom, was used for bedding, to stuff canvas palliasses, for pallet-beds, and to line beds.[89] The valets of the household of Edward II had the right to have beds of this sort – which they were expected to share – carried on the departmental carts.[90] A courtesy book from the first part of the fifteenth century directed pallets for grooms to be made 9 feet long and 7 feet wide, ample enough for several grooms to use at once. The lord's bed,

33. The death bed of
Richard Beauchamp, while
Regent of France, at Rouen.
He is shown worn out,
naked in bed; with a mitred
cleric, holding a socketed
cross (one that could be
used in processions on a
staff), attended by another
clerk holding a chrismatory,
with the oils for anointing
the Earl. The gentle
servants in the room show
their grief. Beside the bed is
a close stool with a cushion.
The textiles on the bed are
plain. From the Beauchamp
Pageant, *c.* 1483–7.

on the other hand, was an elaborate, curtained construction, for him alone.[91] These materials reflect a division of status, the elaborate textile beds of the lord remaining in position, while the pallets were moved away during the day. In 1501, at the same time as the servants of the third Duke of Buckingham had straw purchased for their beds, their master had his feather-beds transferred from his wardrobe in Salisbury Alley to Barnes, where he was staying.[92] The lord's bed was accompanied by an impressive round of care and attention. The linen was elaborate and regularly laundered; beds were made with spices – probably like pot-pourri, in bags.[93] Bed-making rituals became expansive: in the household of Henry VII, assays were made of the litter for the King's bed and the feather-bed; and it was sprinkled with holy water after it had been made.[94] Sleeping arrangements on military campaigns might be different: in 1318–19, the bedding of Thomas of Lancaster was stuffed with hay.[95]

If the lord slept in his chamber, where did his servants sleep? In the thirteenth and the first half of the fourteenth centuries, servants slept scattered around the house, almost anywhere that could be found that was warm and comfortable, in the kitchen, in the hall, in corridors, but not in the household offices, which were kept locked. That this was, in part, still the case under Henry VIII can be seen from the Eltham ordinances of 1526, which attempted to stop the practice.[96] Others slept close to their posts. The serjeants at arms in the household of Edward II slept close to the usher of the chamber[97] and John Russell's chamberlain was to be within calling distance of his master at all hours.[98] By the fifteenth century, more beds were made – by carpenters who carried out other general building work about the house – as fixed pieces of furniture, as provision for servants.[99] At the Stonor manor of Horton, Kent, in about 1425, besides the bed in the principal chamber, there were seven wooden beds in other chambers.[100] In 1437–8, at Bishop's Waltham, Thomas Mychell, a carpenter, was paid for felling timber and making nine forms for the hall and chambers, as well as making new beds in the chambers.[101] The provision of chambers for many servants, as at Caister, transformed their accommodation.

Access to a residence in London was essential for a lord of distinction, lay or secular, for the conduct of business, for purchasing, for attending Parliament and for innumerable other reasons. Some maintained houses in other towns – Dame Katherine de Norwich kept a town house in Norwich, the Percies and the Nevilles had residences in York – but most had to have access to London for some purposes.[102] Around 1520 there were probably 75 aristocratic residences in London: they had been a feature of life in the capital since the twelfth century.[103] They were not needed permanently by their owners and they were, accordingly, rented out or lent.

Joan de Valence, visiting London in May 1297, to mark the first anniversary of her husband's death, stayed in her own house, in company with her son, Aymer, and his wife. The house had been put in order over the previous six days, with repairs to the stables and her own chamber. As well as her own property, she had an arrangement with the Bishop of Winchester for the use of his palace in Southwark, where some of her household goods were lodged.[104] When Aymer de Valence visited London for Parliament in March 1300, a part of his household paid for lodgings.[105] The loan of a bishop's residence and the general insufficiency of accommodation within London for the household were recurring features. In the latter part of 1465, when Anne Stafford visited London, although she started out in her own house in Bread Street, she moved to the house of the Bishop of Worcester, one of a group of episcopal residences in the Strand; but neither was sufficient to accommodate all her servants.[106]

When the Duke of Buckingham visited London in 1501, his household stayed principally at his house in Queenhithe. The Duke spent a good deal of this time at Barnes: he stayed, possibly in lodgings on a bed and breakfast basis, while visiting the court at Richmond, where he had his lunch and supper. While the accommodation at Barnes was furnished from Buckingham's wardrobe in London, he did not need to bring all his household goods with him. London tradesmen were ready to supply his household with many necessities. His horses were stabled at livery in Lambeth, at the sign of the bear. Laurence Baker supplied fuel for the Duke's chamber and kitchen, he hired out pewter dishes, his wife loaned napery and washed it; and casual labour was hired for the kitchen.[107]

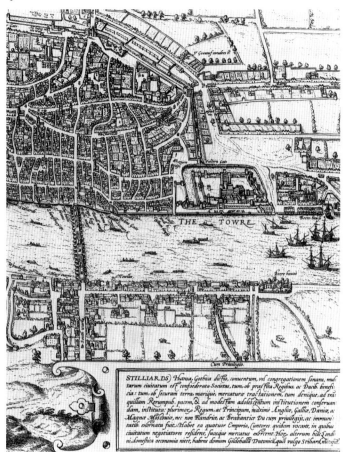

34. Fastolf Place, Sir John Fastolf's moated London mansion, opposite the Tower of London, captioned as a 'beere howse'. From Braun and Hogenberg's map of London, first published in their *Civitates Orbis Terrarum*, in 1572, here taken from the 1574 German edition, but based on survey work carried out between 1547 and 1559.

Some lords may have considered their London properties as hotels in the modern sense. Sir Walter de Brugge used the London house of Thomas Mortimer in this way around 1400.[108] The property had a large, enclosed garden, its own resident gardener, store-house and wood-house. The gates to the house had a chamber over them. There was a principal chamber; a free-standing larder, with a chamber on top; a kitchen; and a common latrine over the stables. The property was in the charge of a janitor, one Thomas Marshal. He had in his possession two chargers and a dozen each of plates, dishes and saucers, an indication of the scale of use the property might expect.[109] As well as a base from which to conduct business, property in the capital could be particularly important for the standing of the lord. The investment Sir John Fastolf made in his magnificent Fastolf Place, in Southwark, replete with garden, walls, moat and drawbridge, was designed both for comfort and to impress (Plate 34).[110] It was perhaps also for this reason that the expenditure of a household in London was commensurately greater: although the cost of living in the capital was higher, it was here that display could be made to greatest effect.[111]

This examination of households and their accommodation points to major changes between 1200 and 1500. It contrasts with the physical remains we now have, which can be poorly dated and often look rather inflexible. There were considerable shifts in the way that rooms were used or designated. The results of the investment that accompanied prolonged residence are apparent in the provision of more chambers, with increasing comfort and luxury, heat and light, and in advances in sanitation. The residence itself was planned as a coherent entity, rather than growing piecemeal. At the same time, space was defined more rigidly in terms of function. In response to changes in the balance of the groups composing the household, the social use of accommodation altered markedly. A diminishing military element gave way to gentle servants and visitors who required appropriate lodgings. Equally, the sharpening of the division between gentle and non-gentle household members was to find its expression in the reservation of space for exclusive use. A deeper understanding of this can be gained by looking in more detail at the routines of life in the household.

CHAPTER 5
The Rhythms of the Household

When the Earl of Northumberland, with the advice of his council, took an over-view of his household in 1511, he did not fail to isolate the different patterns of activity, the daily routine, the events of the week, month and quarter, to provide a framework for its management.[1] These patterns are now no longer clear for secular life for much of the Middle Ages: when, precisely, an event occurred within a day can be difficult to determine, although it may be placed in sequence with other events. Before the latter part of the fifteenth century, much in this routine has to be inferred. The bequest of Richard, Earl of Arundel, in his will of 1393, to his wife Philippa, of two silver candelabra, decorated with armorial escutcheons, for use at supper in winter, indicates something of the timing of that meal.[2] On 30 October 1459, when 110 were present for supper at Lambeth Palace, use of tallow candles, usually around 7 lb. per day, rose to 16 lb.; and we need not doubt that the house was well lit for guests who stayed into the evening.[3] Two changes make an overall pattern easier to discern. The first is a new sense of time, with the advent of mechanical clocks; and the second, the development of ceremonial and the habit of ceremoniousness, which made it more important to document the detail of domestic events.

How was time measured in the household? There were three systems in common use in England in the later Middle Ages. The first rested on a division of daylight into 12 hours of equal duration – the 'artificial day' – with the length of the hour varying from summer to winter and from day to night. Available to all was a second system, the time announced by church bells to denote the canonical hours, from Prime through to Vespers or Compline. While the parish church in the countryside may have relied on the sun to measure the day, monas-tic institutions had more sophisticated methods, employing water clocks. It was in these institutions, at the end of the thirteenth century, that mechanical clocks came into use, dividing the day into 24 hours of equal duration.[4]

In England, the spread of clocks into a domestic context dates from the second half of the fourteenth century. At the palaces of Edward III, at Windsor in 1351–4, at Westminster in 1367–9, at Queenborough and King's Langley at about the same time, at Sheen by 1377, the clocks were bells, with associated mechanisms, mounted in towers,[5] although there was a small clock in the chapel at Queenborough in 1393–6.[6] Chamber clocks in cases are recorded not long after. A silver-gilt clock was repaired by John Orlegemaker for the imprisoned Queen Joan of Navarre in 1419–21.[7] Clocks from at least six household departments remained in London among the goods of John, Duke of Bedford, when he went to France in 1434. These last included instruments which probably struck more frequently than the hour, together with one which had some registration of saints' days, on a wheel or a ring, throughout the year.[8] Clocks reached the households of the nobility at about the same time. In June 1367, latten wire was bought for the clock of the Earl of Salisbury; a clockmaker visited Hanley Castle in October 1409 to work on the Duke of York's clock; and one belonged to the Earl of March in 1413–14 (Plate 35).[9]

The household ordinances and regulations which survive from the 1440s onwards used clock time to outline a schedule for the day. Although these were generally cast in terms of whole hours alone, further precision was possible. A household marshal, overseeing the service of food in hall, might be expected to reckon when the food had been on the tables for three-quarters of an hour.[10] The ordinances doubtless project more regularity than they effected, but they offer an insight into the commonplace which no other source provides. Cicely, Duchess of York, the mother of both Edward IV and Richard III, was said to rise at 7 a.m., to say Matins with her chaplain, then hear Low Mass in her chamber, after which she 'takethe somethinge to recreate nature'. This was followed by divine service in chapel and two Low Masses. Next came lunch, with reading. After lunch there was a period of one hour in which she gave audiences, followed by a quarter of an hour's sleep. Then there was prayer until the first bell for Evensong, at which she had a drink of wine or ale. Her chaplain said Evensong with her; at the final bell for Evensong, she went to her chapel to hear it sung. Evensong was followed by supper with further discussion or recitation of the text heard at lunch-time. The period after supper she passed with her gentlewomen, 'to the fecacion of honest myrthe'. Wine was served an hour before bed, after which she went to her privy closet, with her final prayers for the day, retiring to bed by 8 p.m.[11]

The household day was dominated by liturgical celebration, the desire of the head of the household to participate and the intention that some, at least, of the domestic officers and servants should also do so. In the household of the Duke of Clarence, in 1468,

> . . . Every holy-day the clerke of the seid Duke's closett shalle ringe a bell, at places convenient, to Matyns, Masse, and Evensonge; and one of the chapleyns shall be redy to saye Matyns and Masse to the housholde, and also Evensonge; and that every gentylman, yeoman and groome, not having resonable impediment, be at the seid dyvine service . . .[12]

While this promoted good rule in the household, liturgical celebration also tended to magnify the status of the lord.[13] There was frequently more than one location in the household for the service, from the intimacy of observance in the

Table 6. The daily routine of the household

	George, Duke of Clarence, 1468[1]	Prince Edward, September 1473[2]	Cicely, Duchess of York, 1470s[3]	Edward IV, draft ordinance of 1478[4]	Henry Algernon Percy, Earl of Northumberland, 1512[5]	Henry Algernon Percy, Earl of Northumberland, summer routine[6]	Henry VIII, ordinances of Eltham, 1526[7]
4 a.m.	–	–	–	–	–	Cooks up	–
5	Gates open (summer)	Gates open (summer)	–	–	–	Head officers up. Food struck out	–
6	–	Gates open (winter). Mass for hall officers	–	–	Food struck out. Mass for officers	Breving in counting-house	–
7	Gates open (winter)	Matins in chapel	Arise, Matins and Low Mass in chamber	Breving	1st waiting shift. Breving in counting-house	–	Pages of King's chamber arise. Privy Chamber waiting
8	–	–	Breakfasts	–	1st waiting shift. Breakfasts	Breakfasts	King's chamber ready
9	First lunch (winter)	Mass (sung)	–	First lunch (meat)	1st waiting shift	–	–
10	First lunch (summer)	First lunch (meat)	–	First lunch (fish)	Lunch	Lunch (meat)	First lunch (in hall)
11	–	First lunch (fish)	First lunch (meat)	–	–	Lunch (fish)	Lunch (hall not kept)
12	–	–	First lunch (fish)	–	–	–	–
1 p.m.	–	–	–	–	2nd waiting shift. Breving (caterer et al.)	Breving	–
2	Household officers meeting	–	–	–	2nd waiting shift. Drinking	Drinking	–
3	–	–	–	–	2nd waiting shift. Evensong	–	–
4	First supper (winter)	First supper	First supper	First supper	Supper	–	First supper (in hall, on workdays)
5	First supper (summer)	First supper (summer)	Duchess's supper	–	–	–	–
6	–	–	–	–	–	–	Supper (hall not kept)
7	All night	–	–	All night (winter)	3rd waiting shift	–	–
8	–	Bed	Bed	–	3rd waiting shift	All night	–
9	Gates shut (winter)	Gates shut (winter)	–	–	All night	Gates shut	–
10	Gates shut (summer)	Gates shut (summer)	–	–	–	–	–

Note This table omits activity which is not related to timings or is not sequenced.

Sources 1. HO, pp. 89–94. 2. HO, pp. *27–33. 3. HO, pp. *37–9. 4. BB, pp. 203–10. 5. NHB, passim. 6. NHB, pp. 391–4. 7. HO, pp. 135–240.

35. The earliest domestic
clock in England still
unaltered and in its original
position, at Cotehele,
Cornwall, was installed in
1485–9 for Sir Richard
Edgcumbe, controller of
Henry VII's household. The
clock has no face, but
operates one of two bells (the
other was used for ringing for
services) in the chapel
bellcote.

lord's closet, to the elaborate service of the household chapel, with its fine vestments and music. Portable altars gave further flexibility. In the household of the fifth Earl of Northumberland there were at least five services during the day – Matins, Lady Mass, High Mass, Evensong and Compline. There were rotas for 11 priests and the members of the choir to serve at these occasions; and the main feasts called for further observance.[14]

Timetables, derived from a group of fifteenth- and sixteenth-century ordinances (Table 6), show that the household ran on parallel tracks through the day, with the lord pursuing one route, and his household, servants, wife and children, others. The beginning of the day was marked by the opening of the gates. Those involved in essential household tasks, such as the preparation of food – the cooks and those officers who were to supervise them – were the earliest risers. Accounting (breving) was carried out first thing in the morning at this date. In the thirteenth and fourteenth centuries it had generally been conducted at an evening meeting.[15] The change reflected the growth in administrative business: by the fifteenth century, the work of the accounting clerks in the great household was continuous. The first services of the day, a Mass for the principal officers of the household and other servants who were able to attend, took place early in the morning, freeing them from attendance when business needed their attention.

The lord or lady, on rising, heard Matins or Mass, or both. Only after this service did the select few proceed to the first meal of the day, breakfast. Its timing was probably influenced by monastic routine, where it was an 'irregular' meal, not taken until after High Mass.[16] It was a meal often eaten by travellers.

This is helpful, as far as timing is concerned, demonstrating that it was not taken immediately on rising. On 8 August 1296, Joan de Valence went from Hertingfordbury to Tring, at least 28 miles. Breakfast was provided for Joan and those with her, at St Albans, after the household had travelled 10 to 12 miles.[17] The household of Edward I, perhaps one of the most itinerant in late medieval England, had, in 1305, a cook specifically designated to prepare the King's breakfast;[18] and most servants travelling on business or with the royal household would have been entitled to breakfast or an allowance in lieu.[19] Otherwise, before the fifteenth century, breakfasts have the mark of douceurs, typified by those given by Sir John Dinham, in 1393–4, for Chancery clerks and officials of other courts at Westminster, to aid his business.[20]

From the early fifteenth century, in some households, breakfast was taken by a small group most days.[21] In the household of Dame Alice de Bryene, in 1412–13, six to eight portions were served at this time, as opposed to 18, 20 or more at both lunch and supper.[22] At Epiphany 1508, a day of very considerable hospitality in the household of the Duke of Buckingham, breakfast was provided for him, his wife, his sister, his son and more than 30 others, including his treasurer, his auditor, eight gentlemen of his chapel and visiting knights and gentlemen.[23] In Buckingham's residence at Queenhithe breakfast was served in a special room, for which a small number of benches was made in 1501.[24] The meal was regarded by some as an extravagance. The austere Duchess Cicely was quite determined: 'Breakfastes be there none, savinge onely the head officers when they be present; to the ladyes and gentlewomen, to the deane and to the chappell, to the almoner, to the gentlemen ushers, to the cofferer, to the clerke of the kitchin, and to the marshall.' Other officers who had to be present at the account at that time were also allowed breakfast.[25] Breakfasts before the fifteenth century were primarily bread, possibly with cheese, and some ale, although in the royal household there may have been a cooked meal, at least for the king. By the end of the fifteenth century, the content was different. In the summer of 1501, Buckingham ate pike, plaice, roach, butter and eggs at breakfast.[26] The Earl of Northumberland, a decade later, expected for himself and his wife, in Lent, bread, beer, wine, two pieces of salt fish, six smoked herring, four white (salted) herring or a dish of sprats; out of Lent, half a chine of mutton or boiled chine of beef was substituted for fish.[27]

After breakfast there were further religious services, typically High Mass, which was sung in some households.[28] Between breakfast and lunch the lord had leisure and would expect to be attended by his servants of gentle rank. This was the first of three periods in the day when his time was not bespoken by the domestic regime, the others being between lunch and Evensong, and between supper and all night. The service of the principal (and for many in the household, the first) meal, lunch (*prandium*), started between 9 a.m. and 12 noon, in most households occurring either at 10 or 11 a.m., but later in summer. It was also served later on days of abstinence, with the intention that it succeed Evensong. This practice derived from the early Christian custom of fasting until nightfall on these days: once the liturgical celebration for the day had been completed (it was advanced considerably from its time on other days), food might be taken.[29] About three hours were therefore available for the preparation of each of the main meals on meat days, with usually an hour longer on days of abstinence. The food allocated for the day, at least in the household of the fifth Earl of Northumberland, was set out for the whole day at its start, so a longer period would have been available for preparing items for the second meal.

The silence of the ordinances for the period immediately after the designated meal-time signifies the duration of the meal. Two hours for lunch would not have seemed unusual in an aristocratic household; indeed, longer may have been required, perhaps as much as three hours, for the meal of the lord and his colleagues. The length of time devoted to meals – between four and six hours to the consumption of the two principal meals, perhaps a third of the day if breakfast is included – is a very striking feature. This was partly (except at breakfast) because of the numbers to be fed. In the largest households two sittings in hall were employed. When hall was not kept, meals could start later. The time taken, however, was also a function of the elaborate nature of ceremonial attached to eating by the fifteenth century. The meal periods of servants were shorter, as it was the intention that servants' meals in hall, perhaps both sittings if there were two, should be completed within the compass of the lord's meal. Robert Fitzrauf, one of Sir John Fastolf's gentle servants, relating events in November 1459 shortly before his master's death, had in an hour, between 11 a.m. and 12 noon, ample time for lunch.[30]

Lunch time in some establishments may have concluded with a period of rest or sleep for the master or mistress of the house. The Duchess Cicely's quarter of an hour's nap was matched in expectation by John Russell, whose *Boke of Nurture* enjoined the chamberlain both to expect it, to be ready with kerchief, comb, pillow and headsheet and, if possible, to keep it brief, 'For moche slepe is not medcynable in myddis of þe day.' The lord was then expected to wash and visit the lavatory.[31] After lunch there was a period of comparatively free time, concluded with drinking. This was a formal activity, immediately prior to Evensong. Drinks were usually accompanied by bread. It was a popular time for guests, offering an opportunity for a briefer visit than a meal.[32] In the household of the Duke of Buckingham, in 1501, there may also have been a time for formal drinking in the morning, between breakfast and lunch.[33]

After Evensong, the household proceeded to supper (*cena*), in the largest households, in two shifts. Supper had an accompanying ritual similar to lunch, with the addition that, in winter, arrangements had to be made for lighting, adding an extra touch to any ceremonial passage.[34] Lighting had also to encompass the whole household where business was still to be conducted. Most would have been tallow candle (paris candle), frequently manufactured within the household from the products of animals slaughtered for the larder. In the household of the Bishop of Bath and Wells 6 lb. of tallow candles were used each day on average while the household was in Somerset, from November 1337 to January 1338. Aside from the lights for the hall, on many days 1 lb. went to the Bishop's chamber, with a further 1 lb. going to the chamber of the Bishop's official and commissary. Activities continued in other household departments in the evenings: on 14 November, 1 lb. was issued for the bakehouse and, two days later, a similar amount for the brewhouse.[35] Thornbury Castle, in 1507–8, must equally have had some areas of darkness, but was comparatively much better lit. On Sunday, 2 January 1508, 39 lb. of paris candle were consumed, together with 81 lights called sisers and three prickets. The last two categories were allocated for the use of the Duke of Buckingham, his wife, his sister, Lord Stafford and two other individuals, the great chamber at supper and the hall at supper, the pantry, the cellar and the buttery, with 60 sisers for the chapel.[36]

After supper was a time of recreation and relaxation, for entertainment by household musicians and others.[37] The lord's day came to a formal conclusion after further prayers, perhaps in his closet, with a ceremony known as 'all night'. Beds were made by this time and at this point rations of bread, ale and sometimes wine were brought to the lord's chamber for the night.[38] The lord's chamber was lit throughout the night either by a mortar or cresset, a wick floating in a reservoir of fat or wax, delivered at this time, or by tall candles, known as perchers, or by other lights (Plate 32).[39] The only other parts of the household illuminated at night were stables where great horses were kept and possibly areas where falcons were located. A cresset was usually employed, as in the stables at Hertford when Joan de Valence stayed there in October 1295, but sometimes there were candles, a serious fire risk.[40]

After all night, the household was made secure, with the gates barred and the household offices shut up for the night. Security was a constant: throughout the day a porter, or sometimes more than one, attended the gate, to control admission and to stop the pilfering of household goods and food (Plate 9).[41] The household offices, that is the pantry, buttery, kitchens, larders and other stores, were also kept secure to avoid the poisoning of food, of which there was a particular fear. The ceremonial assays of food and drink, publicly taken, were in earnest.[42] Watch was kept at night. In the household of Edward IV, there was a wait (or watchman) to pipe the watch four times a night in winter, three times in summer, with 'bon gayte', who was to check every chamber and office door, as well as look out for fire, thieves and other perils.[43]

From the opening to the closing of the gates, the household day in summer lasted 17 hours. In winter, the day was up to three hours shorter. For Prince Edward, not quite three years old at the time of the 1473 ordinance for his household, the daily routine spanned 13 hours. At a similar period a monk may have been expected to be active 13 or 14 hours during the day, from about 7 a.m. to 8 p.m., excluding a midnight service.[44] The timetable for a household servant was not dissimilar to that of a skilled craftsman. The masons at Calais, in 1474, were to start work in summer (25 March to 29 September) at 5.30 a.m. at the latest, and continue until 8, when they had an hour for breakfast. They were then to work from 9 until 11, when they broke for lunch, returning to their labours at 1 o'clock. They were allowed to stop for drinking at 3, but were to be back at work by 4, after which they continued until 7 p.m. The winter schedule was similar, except that it was circumscribed by dawn and dusk.[45] The timings present some problems of generalisation. There may have been an earlier bedtime in the country than in London;[46] and in some merchant households meals may have taken place at different times.[47]

In the weekly cycle, one of the most prominent features was the impact of religious observance on diet. By *c.* 1200, it was common in the great household for there to be three days each week when flesh was not normally eaten. This pattern of abstinence on Wednesdays, Fridays and Saturdays, when the great household largely ate fish, persisted throughout the Middle Ages, with some important variations. Closely linked to it was a pattern of eating which postponed lunch on fast days until a later hour and which, by the end of the fourteenth century (there is circumstantial evidence for it earlier), restricted consumption on days of fasting to lunch alone. This was most common on Fridays, but was employed on other days as well, to intensify the regime of abstinence.

Abstinence at its most straightforward can be seen at Bristol Castle in the household of Eleanor of Brittany. She had been captured by King John in France in 1202 and spent the rest of her life imprisoned, but in some style, befitting a granddaughter of Henry II. On Saturday, 16 August 1225, besides bread and ale, there were purchased sole, almonds, butter and eggs; on Sunday, mutton, pork, chicken (or pullet) and eggs; on Monday, beef, pork, honey and vinegar; on Tuesday, pork, eggs and egret; on Wednesday, herring, conger, sole, eels, almonds and eggs; on Thursday, pork, eggs, pepper and honey; concluding on Friday, a fish day, with conger, sole, eels, herring and almonds.[48] The household of Joan de Valence presents some distinctive variations from this pattern. If the year from Michaelmas 1296 had followed the pattern of three non-meat days per week, with the addition of Lent, it would have had a balance of 183 days when meat was eaten and 182 of abstinence. In practice, many Wednesdays – 34 in the course of the year – were treated as days when some meats could be eaten.[49] The mitigation of the regime of abstinence required special licence. It persisted throughout the Middle Ages. In the 1470s, in a specimen budget for the household of a knight, the projected costs were based on 167 days of abstinence and 198 days of meat consumption.[50] Fourteenth-century evidence suggests the practice on Wednesdays involved eating meat at one meal and fish at another. In the Valence household, there was no distinction in the sort of meat eaten on Wednesdays. Other households restricted consumption to the lighter meats – to poultry in the household of the Duke and Duchess of Brittany in 1377–8.[51]

The annual course of the household was charted against the Christian year, its great festivals and fasts. To the weekly pattern of abstinence, additional days were added when fasting could take one of two forms, either the eating of fish instead of meat, or near-complete abstention from food. The extra fish days concentrated on the vigils of major feasts, delineating those of especial popularity, to be relieved on the feast itself by celebration. Christmas might be observed with a day of abstinence on the vigil, with a pattern of celebration and abstinence also marking St Stephen, Holy Innocents, the Circumcision, through to Epiphany. Typically the Lenten fast was preceded by Collop Monday and

Shrove Tuesday, to consume surplus meat and eggs (in which combination may lie the origin of the so-called English breakfast). Easter week included a feast for the poor on Maundy Thursday, followed by a complete fast (perhaps with the exception of bread and ale) on Good Friday. Easter itself was marked by a feast of meats, in some households including a little lamb as Paschal symbol, and a customary payment to the cooks.[52] Ascension week commenced with additional days of fasting (or abstinence) on the Rogation days, Monday and Tuesday, as well as the abstinence already provided for Wednesday, with a celebratory feast on the Thursday.

The great Marian feasts – the Purification (2 February), the Annunciation (25 March), the Assumption (15 August) and the Nativity (8 September) – were marked by abstinence on their eve in nearly all households. To these occasions were frequently added Corpus Christi (in the later Middle Ages), the Nativity of St John the Baptist (midsummer, 24 June), All Saints (1 November) and sometimes All Souls (2 November), and St Katherine (25 November). In 1296–7, the household of Joan de Valence supplemented the days of abstinence with 25 April (St Mark); 28 June (vigil of SS Peter and Paul); 24 July (vigil of SS James and John); 9 August (vigil of St Lawrence); 23 August (vigil of St Bartholomew); 20 September (vigil of St Matthew); 29 November (vigil of St Andrew); and 20 December (vigil of St Thomas the Apostle). If a major feast day, or its vigil, fell on a day of abstinence, a further degree of abstention might be observed, either absolute fasting (except for bread or ale), or avoidance of dairy products. Friday, 7 September 1296, the vigil of the Nativity of the Virgin, was already a fish day: the household of Joan de Valence therefore consumed little (only herring, eggs and pottage, and no butter) and some individuals may have fasted absolutely. Similarly on Friday, 14 September 1296, the Exaltation of St Cross, only herring and eggs were consumed. In an interesting reversal, on some fish days at festival time, an exception was made for the poor within Joan's household, who were treated to mutton.[53]

The weekly routine could vary in another way. The household of Joan de Valence was not untypical in containing a group within it that followed a stricter regime. Some of these individuals were friars. They abstained from meat – usually eating a fish diet – on some Mondays and Tuesdays.[54] The friars also fasted throughout Advent in 1296, up to and including 9 January 1297, with the sole exception of 27 December. On Christmas Day itself, the friars were joined in their fast (on a Tuesday) by Aymer de Valence, who also fasted with them on 8 January.[55]

With the appearance of a record of the portions (*fercula*) served at the day's meals, in the second half of the fourteenth century, comes further evidence of the regime of abstinence. In the household of William of Wykeham, Bishop of Winchester, in 1393, lunch was the only meal taken on Fridays. In addition, in Holy Week, on Wednesday, 2 April and Saturday, 5 April, lunch was the only meal. On the Monday of Ascension week, there was only one meal – of fish; on the eve of Whitsun and the three Ember Days in the following week, equally, only one meal was taken.[56] As well as Fridays, Ash Wednesday and the other

Wednesdays in Lent, there were a further 26 days in 1412–13 on which Dame Alice de Bryene confined supper to a small group of individuals.[57]

While there was a degree of consonance in the observation of the main festivals, the pattern was subject to personal variation. The practice diverged from the theory of liturgical observance: not all households marked the Ember Days, or the vigils of the feasts of all the apostles. The degree of abstinence practised was flexible and many observed fasts on dates that were not obligatory.[58] There were further changes and mitigations to the weekly dietary regime in the fifteenth century. The dispensations for individuals, themselves matters of status, and the refinements of aristocratic piety were gradually followed at large. In Anne Stafford's household, by mid-August of 1465, the fish content of Wednesday's meals was diminishing, replaced by lighter meats such as piglets and poultry. At the same time, fish appeared on Mondays on a regular basis, but only as a part of the foodstuffs, suggesting a pattern of one meal of meat and one of fish on that day.[59]

In 1501, for that part of the household of the Duke of Buckingham in London, at Queenhithe and at Barnes and Richmond, the transformation of Wednesday from a day of abstinence had almost been completed; there is also evidence that on Monday one meal was of fish. On six days of the week, the usual pattern was to provide both lunch and supper (the Duke and a few others had breakfast as well); but on Fridays there was only one meal – lunch. On other days, abstinence might be enhanced by restricting food to a single meal.[60] In another account for the Duke, for 1507–8, covering the great household at Thornbury, a slightly different pattern occurs. Here the consumption of fish on Wednesdays had a stronger presence – and this may indicate that it was those of a lesser status in the household who continued to eat more fish on this day. During Lent, the household employed a stricter regime on Fridays and other celebratory days by withdrawing dairy items and eggs (which had previously been completely excluded in Lent as a matter of course). The pattern of two main meals per day for the whole household continued, for six days a week, with a much smaller group at breakfast. On Fridays, however, most people had one meal only, lunch; a small group of *gentiles* had both lunch and supper, but on that day no breakfast. There was a genuine reduction in the quantity of food consumed: about twice as much was consumed on Saturdays as on Fridays.[61] On the other hand, Archbishop Bourgchier's household, in 1459, although it had the same pattern of one meal on a Friday and two on a Saturday, consumed as much at Friday's single meal as at both Saturday meals combined.[62]

Feast days were marked by an especial round of religious services. The consumption of wax candles, overwhelmingly employed in ecclesiastical use rather than for light elsewhere in the household, rose markedly on these days. On 16 December 1296, 114 lb. of wax was bought at Monmouth for the household of Joan de Valence, sufficient for the Christmas season and after. It was being made into candles as late as 7 February, when wicks were bought for 50 wax candles.[63] Eleanor of Castile had her candles coloured green and vermilion;[64] and in 1406–7, the purchases, made by Bishop Mitford, of wax, wick and candles, including a Paschal candle, all from John Payntour of Devizes, suggest decoration.[65] The Purification – or Candlemas – was marked by the purchase of wax candles and offerings to the Virgin.[66] At the end of Lent, in the week immediately before Easter, religious celebrations intensified. Maundy Thursday was marked by gifts to the poor: in 1406, Margaret Beauchamp, Countess of Warwick, gave 65 gallons of ale and a cade of red herrings.[67] For the services of Tenebrae, the clerk of Queen Isabella's chapel acquired a wooden Judas to hold the 12 candles that would be snuffed out one by one, symbolising the disciples deserting Jesus.[68] On Good Friday (and after the celebration of the Resurrection on Easter Sunday), the fifth Earl of Northumberland and his family crept to the Cross; the family took communion on the eve of Easter.[69]

These religious occasions were also celebrated in the household outwith the chapel and many had customs attached to them.[70] That some were closely associated with the cycle of agricultural life is unsurprising, given that at least 90% of the population were engaged in employment connected with the land, and the wealth that funded the great household derived overwhelmingly from that source. Entertainment within the great household at Christmas, Easter and Whitsun was common.[71] A celebration of the resumption of tillage coincided with Candlemas. Harvest was well marked: in the household of Dame Alice de Bryene, in 1413, the boon workers were entertained in the household from 1 August to 26 August, consuming specially baked loaves, about twice the size of the normal household white loaf, but shared between two.[72]

To start the yearly cycle at Christmas, there was a group of events celebrated between the beginning of Advent (the Sunday nearest to the feast of St Andrew, 30 November) and Epiphany (6 January), which may best be treated together, although some were distinct devotions. The feast of St Nicholas, the patron of children, celebrated on 6 December, brought with it to the household the figure of the boy bishop. In an inversion of traditional roles, the ambitions of the young clerical impersonator did not rest with the gifts he might receive, but extended to a parody of most aspects of ecclesiastical activity and dignity. Thomas Arundel, Bishop of Ely, in December 1383, gave 6s. 8d. to the boy bishop of Hatfield on 6 December, and a further 40s. to the bishop among the choristers of his own chapel at Holy Innocents.[73] The scale of the celebration at St Nicholas can be seen in the household of Henry de Grey, Lord Grey of Codnor, in 1304–5. There was a distribution to the poor of 4 bushels of wheat, a further 4 bushels of rye, and herrings. The gathering that day was much larger than any over the period of Christmas itself: there were 88 horses in the stable on 6 December, but only 25 on 25 December, with 55 on New Year's Eve being otherwise the largest number. The accounts also show typical preparations for a large feast, with purchases of bowls, a boar, large amounts of food, 52 lb. of paris candle and 7s. 4d. for minstrels.[74]

Before Christmas itself, days of abstinence could be observed on 20 December, the eve of the feast of St Thomas the Apostle, and Christmas Eve. In some households, if Christmas Day fell on a day of abstinence, the fasting might be transferred to the day before; others kept the fast on the day. Christmas was marked by a special Mass and by many other customs, by domestic entertainment and visiting minstrels and players. The household of Edward III, celebrating Christmas at Guildford in 1347, had costumes made for a dramatic per- formance, with 14 each of female masks, masks of bearded men, angels' heads, dragons, peacocks and swans supplied by the Great Wardrobe. The following Christmas, at Otford, there were masks for men, with heads of lions, elephants and phantoms (*vespertiliones*) mounted on top, and separate masks of wood- woses and virgins. A few days later, at Epiphany, at Merton, there were 13 cos- tumes for dragons and men with diadems.[75] These events were a precursor of productions such as John Lydgate's mummings, prepared for Henry VI, and the pageants and revels typical of Christmas, New Year and Twelfth Night celebrations in the late fifteenth- and early sixteenth-century royal household. By *c.* 1500, these works consumed the bulk of the royal funds expended on entertainment at this time of year: although there were performances by players, those of both the King and visitors, the amounts paid for them were not substantial.[76]

There are more references to entertainment in households at this time of year than at any other point. Sir Hugh Luttrell, at Dunster Castle, at Christmas 1405, was entertained by two sets of players, one comprising six of his tenants from Dunster, as well as by many small children from Minehead who came to dance before him.[77] In the Christmas season of 1406–7, Bishop Mitford received a spate of entertainment, with a host of visiting players – seven men from Seend on 27 December, three tenants from Potterne and three tenants of the Bishop of Winchester performing one interlude on 28 December, a minstrel from Lavington at Christmas, various players on 4 January, separate groups of men from Sherborne, Devizes and Urchfont, four of Lord Lovel's minstrels at Epiphany and two of the Duke of York's on 12 January, a drummer for 10 days and a gitterner at Epiphany. Of particular note were the preparations made by Mitford's own household for writing out interludes and playing at Christmas, along with red lead and other colours bought for the *disgisinges*. During the remainder of the period from October 1406 until the Bishop's death in late May 1407, there was less entertainment: three boys performed in front of the Bishop at a date between 16 and 20 February, three men gave a Lent interlude at Potterne on 3 April and there was dancing on 10 May at Salisbury.[78] The play produced within the household is a reminder of the impact that a resident chapel might occasion.[79]

The character of these events was different from performances a century later. There were still visiting players – the fifth Earl of Northumberland budgeted 20d. a play, allowing a total of 32s. for 'playes playd in Christynmas by strane- gers' – but the arrangements for Epiphany in this household, *c.* 1515, were shot through with formality and ceremony, embodying a political message in the display of courtesy and magnificence, organised by the staff of the household.[80] The 'pageant' performed in the household of John de Vere, thirteenth Earl of Oxford, at Christmas 1490, was probably of a similar nature.[81] At the same time, there was a growth in the number of minstrels whose function was ceremonial:[82]

among the minstrels in the household of the Duke of Buckingham, on Christmas Eve 1507, were 18 members of the choir from the household chapel, nine boy choristers, six trumpeters and two other minstrels.[83]

New Year's Eve and New Year's Day were both marked by further celebration. Henry VII gave 10s. 'to my lorde princes players that played in the hall upon New Yeres Even'.[84] Music was an essential accompaniment to the start of New Year's Day, with musicians playing at the door of the chamber of the fifth Earl of Northumberland and his wife, and then at those of his sons.[85] New Year was marked by the giving of gifts. The gold pitcher, with enamel-work and precious stones, given by Edward I to his Queen at New Year 1286 was, at nearly £50, by some way the most expensive object in the account for jewels that year.[86] The recipient, Eleanor of Castile, at Christmas 1289, also had a goldsmith's bill, which encompassed 72 paternosters (rosaries), probably intended as New Year's gifts.[87] Richard Mitford, Bishop of Salisbury, began 1407 with a gift of 4d. to each of the pages in his household, with eight knives for the boys and others of his chapel, and 24 purses. In November 1406 he had purchased in London 72 rings, all for New Year. Two brooches, one set of gold beads and 14 of jet, the last with paternosters, completed the gifts.[88] Rings were a popular token at this time of year. The Earl of March, spending the start of 1414 at Eltham with Henry V, acquired six rings, with sapphires, at a mark apiece on New Year's Day, doubtless to give away, as they are listed along with the gifts of cash he made that day. He also received gifts – two falcons, one from Sir Robert Corbet, the other from Robert Morton – and the falconers who brought the birds were rewarded handsomely for their pains.[89] The household ordinances of Henry VII noted the reward of those who brought the King's gift to the Queen, and vice versa, at their footsheets on the morning of 1 January.[90] The round of celebrations concluded on Twelfth Night, with frequently the largest celebration of the season. Misrule and alternative authority were marked by Isabel of Lancaster (a nun of Amesbury, though little cloistered) with a gift of 2 gallons of wine at Epiphany to the king of the bean, who presided over the celebrations presumably having found the bean concealed in the traditional Twelfth Night baking.[91]

The feast of St George (23 April) usually fell after Easter. Besides the celebrations at Windsor, the feast was marked, particularly in the houses of Garter knights, with both secular and religious celebration. In 1464, John Howard gave six of the Earl of Warwick's minstrels 6s. 8d. on the evening before the feast.[92] The fifth Earl of Northumberland held a Requiem Mass on the morrow of the feast, for the souls of former knights of the order.[93] The feast of St John the Baptist (midsummer) was widely celebrated: John Catesby gave 8d. on the eve of the feast to boys performing a play in his hall.[94] Secular celebration frequently included a bonfire, prepared in the household of Henry VII by the grooms and pages of the hall.[95] John Howard bought midsummer candles for the ecclesiastical celebration of the day in 1464.[96]

All Saints (1 November) held particular significance for the household. While liturgically the winter season ran from Michaelmas to the beginning of Lent,[97] within the household it had different limits. By the later fifteenth century, the winter season in the household was marked by fixed dates for the increased allowances of candles and fuel. These allowances either began, or increased significantly, at the feast of All Saints and ran through either to Easter, undiminished,[98] or to the Purification (2 February), with a further, reduced set of allowances to continue until around Easter.[99] Earlier events tend to confirm the view of All Saints as the start of the household's winter. At Hertford, on 23 October 1295, 30 men who had loaned their carts for carrying wood for Joan de Valence, in anticipation of the increased fuel consumption, were fed in the household.[100] In 1406, at precisely this time, fuel was brought by labour service to the household of Bishop Mitford at Potterne.[101] Calendrical differences mean that All Saints would have fallen a good week later than it does today. The feast was also marked by an exceptional distribution of meals to the poor in the household of Edward I.[102] The Earl of Oxford celebrated the occasion in 1490 with payments to the master of the children of his chapel, as well as to visiting minstrels.[103]

In counterpoint to the ostinato of the daily routine, the tasks of the week, month and calendar year, the Christian year and seasonal customs of the household, may be set the life cycle of the household, from birth to death, the patterns of life and the way in which the main events of its course were marked. These were of more general significance and celebrated widely in society, but they were frequently invested with a particular character in the great household. The peculiar demography of the household, a male institution, made some events comparatively unusual, others comparatively common. The few women were largely segregated, a group apart. The consequences were of enormous importance for the mentality of the Middle Ages, for the development of chivalry and courtly love, for behaviour within the household, the relationship between the many men and the few women in the establishment. This relationship was formalised by marriage.

Aristocratic marriage was driven by a sense of status, of suitable matches, of economics and dowries. Child betrothals and marriages – which had the effect of depriving the king of the profits of wardship and marriage – were favoured by the nobility. The presence of many male servants in the household must always have made the formation of an attachment – and potentially a disparaging one – outside an arranged marriage a possibility. Joan of Acre, daughter of Edward I and widow of Gilbert de Clare, married Ralph de Monthermer, a member of Gilbert's household, as her second husband, to the vexation of her father and other nobles. The household was also a scenario for illicit liaison, for courtly love: the visits of Sir Bertilak's wife to Gawain were all too plausible for the poet's audience.

Marriage established a household, or two separate bodies, for man and wife, but this did not need to happen immediately. Upper-class marriages frequently brought with them a considerable disparity in age and physical dislocation. They might take a young woman far from home, or bring a young man to a widow of some age. The economic detail of the marriage might be regulated by contract. Marriage at an early age did not entail a sexual relationship: canon law presumed the age for consummation as 12 for girls and 14 for boys. In practice, the ages may have been higher. By the fifteenth century, contracts sometimes specified that it was not the intention that the partners should sleep together until they were 16.[104] Arrangements had therefore to be made for accommodating the parties until they reached an appropriate age. John of Brabant married the 14-year-old Princess Margaret in 1290. Their betrothal preceded John's arrival in England in 1285. Until his marriage, he lived in the royal household, sometimes with Edward I's children. Beatrice de Nesle had married Aymer de Valence by October 1295. She lived with her mother-in-law probably continuously until January 1297, when she departed to live with her husband. In August 1297, she was given royal accommodation at Marlborough, while her husband was away on the King's business: she joined Aymer in Flanders at the end of the year.[105] The marriage of Thomas Betson, a trusted associate of Sir William Stonor, to Katherine Ryche, a daughter of Stonor's first wife, took place in 1478 when Katherine was probably 15 or 16, but after a period of at least two years of betrothal or courtship. Betson wrote to her in 1476, when she was no more than a child: 'And yff ye wold be a good etter off your mete allwaye, that ye myght waxe and grow fast to be a woman, ye shuld make me the gladdest man off the world ... I pray you grete well my horsse, and praye hym to gyffe yow iiii of his yeres to helpe you with all.'[106]

One of the consequences of early marriage by women was that they could have a succession of husbands, some much older than they, who might leave them young widows. Remarriage brought far fewer constraints for the widow than her first marriage: she was effectively beyond family control, although she might have to buy out royal interest in her marriage. Not all widows remarried. Marie de St Pol, who married Aymer de Valence in 1321, did not remarry after his death in 1324, when she was about 20: she died in 1377. Aymer's sister, Agnes, who died in 1310, had had three childless marriages by 1296. The three marriages of Elizabeth de Burgh had ended by 1321, and she then remained unmarried for nearly 40 years, enjoying the concentration in her hands of the dower from her successive husbands.[107] These events had important effects on the characteristics of the household, on its composition and resources.

What of the event of marriage itself? The pledging of faith between the parties was the most important element, after which they were considered legally married and the marriage might be consummated. The following morning, there was a celebration for the uprising (*levacio*) of the new wife. A church service might be a part of the ceremony, but it was not essential to the legitimacy of the marriage.[108] The bride was endowed at the church door with property, her dower, which might include goods, even fish, as well as land.[109] The exchange of rings was also a part of the recognition of marriage;[110] and rich clothing – cloth of gold wedding dresses for royalty, at least – was usual.[111]

How many children did the aristocracy and gentry have? A near-continuous sequence of pregnancies could be the lot of the aristocratic or royal woman. Eleanor of Castile married at the age of 14 or 15 in 1254. Over the next 30 years she had 15, possibly 16, children, of whom only six were living at the time of her death in 1290.[112] Joan de Valence married in 1247. She had at least seven children, four of whom were alive in 1295–7: Aymer de Valence was probably the youngest and was about 26 at the time of his father's death in 1296. Philippa of Hainault, Edward III's queen, had 12 children in 27 years. Gentry families may not have been as large: in 1343–4, John de Multon of Frampton had two brothers, Thomas and William; he had a single son, John.[113] John Catesby (d. *c.* 1405) had three sons, William, John and Robert, a daughter, Joan, and possibly another, Elizabeth.[114] Thomas Stonor (d. 1431) had eight children by Alice Kirby and she probably had more by her second husband, Richard Drayton. Stonor's son Thomas (d. 1474) had six children by his wife, Joan. His eldest son, William, had three marriages and children by the last, but his first wife, Elizabeth Ryche, had three daughters and a son by her first marriage.[115] These arrangements produced household and family groupings of some complexity. Large numbers of pregnancies suggest that birth control was unusual among the aristocracy, even if it was more widely used in society by the close of the thirteenth century.[116] Not all marriages were so fertile, although the reasons for this are far from clear; and perinatal and infant mortality were high, through disease and accident, even with constant care and attention in the households of the nobility.

Childbirth was marked in the household by a number of different customs. There is little trace of any special treatment marking pregnancy, at least in the early stages: nothing distinctive appears, for example, in the arrangements for the journey of Isabella of Angoulême around 21 March 1207, from Freemantle to Clarendon (the future Henry III was born on 1 October).[117] Although pregnancy is not alluded to directly, in May 1312 Queen Isabella, expecting the future Edward III (born 13 November), may have been spared the sea voyage that her husband took from Scarborough, while fleeing with Gaveston from Thomas of Lancaster.[118]

Arrangements for births, however, were more consequential. The birth of Prince Edmund at Woodstock in August 1301 disturbed the trade of the neighbourhood: the Bishop of Winchester received comparatively little in the way of tolls from the borough of Witney as the arrangements for the purveyance of the household of Queen Margaret deterred merchants from coming.[119] Elizabeth de Bohun, Countess of Hereford (and daughter of Edward I), was in the later stages of pregnancy when she left Linlithgow on 27 July 1304 for Knaresborough Castle. She reached there on 12 August and gave birth to a son, Humphrey, probably about 10 September. Considerable attention was given to her bathing arrangements over the next few weeks. She was also attended by clergy, including the confessor of the Prince of Wales, and two monks of Westminster, Robert de Bures and Guido de Asshewell, who brought one of the Abbey's most sacred relics, the girdle of the Virgin, which was believed to be of especial assistance to women in labour.[120]

Arrangements for royal births under Henry VII are documented in his household ordinances of 1493. The room where the Queen was to be delivered was decorated with rich hangings, sufficiently lit, and furnished with a royal bed, a carpet on the floor, and a pallet-bed; the cupboard in the room was to be hung with the same suite of hangings as the rest of the chamber. Prior to the Queen's confinement there was a formal ceremony of leave taking, with spices and wine, in the great chamber. After that, she was brought to the room where she was to be delivered, at which point all men were excluded. All the offices of the Queen's household normally filled by men – butlers, pantlers, servers, carvers, cupbearers – were undertaken by women, collecting the goods from the chamber door. The godparents were to be close at hand, for the christening, at which time gifts were given. The child was then handed over to a nursery nurse – and a separate household for the baby, including rockers and the usual household officers (Plate 36). The nurse's food was to be assayed while she suckled the child. Once the baby was weaned, a physician was to supervise the nurse, to oversee the infant's food. The baby was to have a 'great cradle of estate', suitably dressed in rich stuffs. Provisions for the nursery included further rich materials, but also more practical necessities, a great chafer, a basin of latten and two large pewter basins for the laundry (Plate 27).[121]

36. *Top*: the discovery of Moses, in a wicker vessel, by Pharaoh's daughter and Moses' sister, as they were going to bathe in the river. Moses is then handed over to a nurse on the instructions of Pharaoh's daughter. *Bottom*: Moses, in a children's game at a feast, strikes Pharaoh's son and he cries out. Pharaoh orders him to be put to death and the court begs for mercy. From the Queen Mary Psalter, early fourteenth century.

Part of the reason for equipping a young child with a household was to treat it with the dignity appropriate to its rank, through a great household in miniature – hence the caps of estate sometimes seen on babies (Plate 3), and the full panoply of domestic arrangements and rich stuffs. For the short-lived William of Windsor (the fifth son of Edward III, born in May 1348), whose funeral arrangements were recorded in the account of the Great Wardrobe before the necessities prepared for his life, there was a great bed of green taffeta embroidered with red roses, images, serpents and other work of gold and silk, comprising dorser, quilt, celure, curtains, cushions and woollen mats of various shapes.[122]

The news of a successful delivery was marked by gifts to those bringing the message. Joan de Valence, learning from a valet of her daughter, Isabella, that his mistress had a baby daughter, gave him 6s. 8d.[123] The mother was able to celebrate her uprising (*relevacio, purificacio*) a little while later. Elizabeth de Bohun celebrated at Knaresborough on 11 October, with the assistance of Robert, the King's minstrel and 15 other minstrels. There was also a Mass marking the occasion.[124] Queen Philippa's uprising in June 1348 was accompanied by jousting and the preparation of two suits of clothes for her, one for the vigil, containing four garments (mantle, cape, supertunic and tunic) of blue velvet worked with gold birds. The second suit, for the day of the uprising itself, contained five garments of red velvet (cape, mantle, tunic and two supertunics), embroidered with oaks and other trees, with a lion beneath each made of large pearls and the whole field powdered with small pearls and embroidery. The hangings for her chamber for the day were made from 78 pieces of silk, decorated with the letter S in gold paper.[125]

Despite his mother's offering at the tomb of St Robert of Knaresborough on 13 October, Humphrey de Bohun died probably at about six weeks old; and William of Windsor was buried on 5 September 1348, aged about three months. Humphrey's elder sister, Margaret, died in February 1305 and the two were buried together in Westminster Abbey in the chapel of St Nicholas. In the case of the two boys, there is a record of the funeral arrangements – and the status accorded on the basis of rank to these small children. Humphrey de Bohun was placed in a lead coffin at Fulham, with four candles around the body. On 8 November he was buried at Westminster and there were payments for 120 staves for candles and the hire of a hearse (a frame for candles), offerings for his soul at Mass, with 5s. to the Friars Preachers of London and 4s. for ringing bells to the same end.[126] The arrangements for the funeral of William were more lavish, with cloth of gold to cover the body, 60 silk pennons with gold, six mortars, 170 wax candles and torches and 50 poor people around the shrine dressed in black russet.[127]

In the household, birth itself was an unfamiliar experience. Few servants had their wives in close company and, even then, arrangements for childbirth were likely to be subordinate to the main activities of the household. In 1289, Isabella Poer was left at Condat, Gironde, with the wife of Peter the Waferer and other men and women under the direction of Martin Ferrand, one of Queen Eleanor's esquires, for 91 days, for the birth of her child as far as her uprising.[128] The household, however, did command resources, both medical and spiritual, which could assist at birth. While it may not have been until the later Middle Ages that lying-in hospitals became more generally available, those in the great household had the benefit both of physicians, with a knowledge of obstetrics, and probably of midwives.[129]

If childbirth was comparatively unusual in the household, so too were children. The number of children in their early years cannot have been great, confined to those of the lord or those committed to his care, for example as wards. Edward Burnel, probably born on 22 July 1286, whose wardship had been purchased from the Crown by William de Valence, was maintained in the household of Joan de Valence in 1296 and 1297. He was bought hose, shoes, gloves, belts and reins for his horse, and special provision was made for him to have milk and eggs in Lent.[130] From the end of the thirteenth century onwards, base-metal toys, ranging from knights to utensils, mechanical toys and toys requiring particular skills, such as tops and puppets, belonged to children of the wealthy (Plate 37).[131] As a child, Edward II and his brother Alfonso both had wooden castles. Alfonso also had a siege engine and one was made of wood for the young John of Brabant, in 1289, at a cost of 3s., along with swords for skirmishing. The games suggested by these toys would have been common to many children, but the cost of their manufacture placed them in the bespoke, aristocratic market.[132]

The boisterousness of the young is well reflected by the 7s. paid to Martinet the Taborer, in 1303, for the repair of his tabor, broken by Edward I's sons, Thomas and Edward, as well as for entertaining them and another inhabitant of the same nursery, the tiny Lady Margaret de Bohun. In 1305, Martinet repaired with parchment the little drums (or tambourines) of the King's sons.[133] The young Moses, found by Pharaoh's daughter and taken into the royal household, was condemned to death for striking Pharaoh's son, in what the illustrator of the first part of the Queen Mary Psalter must have considered similar rumbustiousness at a royal court (Plate 36). The behaviour of the very young was not markedly different from present-day children of similar age.[134]

Games and pastimes in the household included chess, backgammon, raffle, dice and cards, and ball games, such as tennis or palm. Money changed hands too. The 23-year-old Earl of March lost more than £157 on 45 occasions in 1413–14 at a whole host of games, including 10 marks betting on cock-fighting on Shrove Tuesday, the day on which it was traditionally organised by children.[135] Henry VII lost half a mark at cards to his son, the seven-year-old future Henry VIII, on 23 May 1498.[136] In an aristocratic context, bows and arrows, swords and riding – paramilitary play – led on to tournaments and jousting.[137]

Play was only a part of the education of the aristocratic child. As they became older, children, both male and female, were placed in other households to learn courtesy. The practice of service, on the one hand, emulating the example of Christ, serving his parents from the age of 12 to 29, fetching water, cooking and serving at table (Plate 38), provided an honourable training. At the same time, young persons of rank helped to promote the magnificence of the household in

37. A child's toy: a mounted knight of
c. 1300, in hollow, base metal.

which they lodged. While many servants were young, in their teens or early twenties, the employment of children as servants, either in specialist capacities or more generally, developed after about 1350. There might be a near equivalence of status between servants and children of the household, sharing many functions, such as carving.[138]

Within the great household, there were formal arrangements for the education of two groups of young servants, choristers and henchmen, both usually of well-connected backgrounds. Choristers, both in ecclesiastical households and in those of prominent members of the laity, formed a group of highly skilled and prized servants. Thomas Arundel, Bishop of Ely, had 10 in September 1381;[139] in the 1470s, Edward IV had eight children of the chapel, who would remain there until the age of 18 when, if there was no room at court or in the Chapel Royal, they were to proceed to Oxford or Cambridge.[140] The children of John Howard's chapel were under the control of his priest, William Davies, who organised the boarding arrangements for them in 1481.[141] In the household of Edward IV, both choristers and henchmen were looked after by the master of grammar.[142] There was a separate master of the henchmen to school them as courtiers, in jousting and riding, to teach them languages, music and dancing.[143]

There were opportunities for formal education within the household, with resident knights and household clerks, but the household was not always the chosen setting. By the mid-fourteenth century, the sons of the gentry were often educated in grammar schools.[144] At this date, in Lincolnshire, there were 11 such schools. In 1343, John de Multon of Frampton chose to send his brothers, William and Thomas, to the school in Lincoln, escorted there by boat by Steven, his household cook. Subsequently the schoolmaster was paid 4s. 8d. for their board and lodging.[145] In the early 1390s John Catesby sent his sons, William and John, away to what was probably a grammar school. Catesby also paid Margaret Yslepp 6s. 8d. for teaching his daughter, Joan, although she does not seem to have boarded out.[146] In 1432, following the death of Thomas Stonor, arrangements were made to secure the education of his daughter, Isabella.[147]

The events of the life cycle included some distinctive practices besides the celebration of name days and those of saints whose devotions were particularly supported by a household. Knighthood marked the culmination of chivalric training and an ideal that suffused upper-class society, giving a particular character to the household (Plate 39). Household knights were bound to serve their lord, be he the king or a lesser man, thus constituting a military element within the household – numerically not the greatest part, but culturally of great importance. By 1241, knighthood was enjoined on all those who had land worth £20 p.a., an obligation that might only be circumvented by payment to the Crown. The act of knighting was an event marked by considerable expense, with royal support from the mid-1240s for this act of display, as, for example, at the knighting of William de Valence in 1247.[148] Around 250 people celebrated, with Joan de Valence, the knighting of Sir John de Tany, at Moreton Valence on 18 August

38. Three scenes of Christ serving his parents: (i) fetching water from a spring beneath a tree; (ii) using bellows on a fire, over which is suspended a cauldron under a cowled, hooded chimney; (iii) serving his father and mother at a table, covered with a patterned tablecloth. Note also the stool, the striped pitcher and bowl. From the Holkham Bible picture book, *c.* 1320–30.

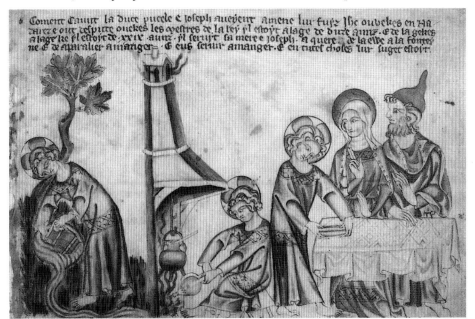

1297. In September of the same year 14 writs were obtained by Joan for assistance towards the knighting of Aymer de Valence, bringing a retinue of 49 to fight with Edward I in Flanders.[149] Aymer was in his mid- to late twenties at this time; but knighthood could be attained from the mid-teens.[150]

The military retinue in the household, particularly the royal household, was the foundation of contemporary armies; it was central to the manoeuvres of chivalry, tournaments and jousting. In November 1303, Aymer de Valence retained Sir Robert Fitzpayn for the tournament that Christmas, finding mounts for him, his son, if he was a knight, and two knights bachelor, as well as robes and saddles and bouche of court, not only for the knights but also for their attendants, in the town where the tournament was to be held.[151] The wife of John de Multon of Frampton, in January 1343, made an offering at Frampton on the day of the jousts at Windsor, at which her husband may have taken part; in 1348, the same household bought wine for Thomas, fourth Baron Furnivalle, and others at the jousts.[152] John died in 1352, but his son, John, then a minor, grew up to put his chivalry to the test. With a loan from Edward III's mistress, Alice Perrers, he set off for Prussia in 1367 – where he was to die the following year – in the retinue of his kinsman, Anthony de Lucy.[153] The elaboration of chivalric practice was an essential ingredient in the household in the fifteenth century – from the wearing of livery associated with the bearing of arms, to the pageantry that was a concomitant of tournaments.

The household accompanied the lord on journeys of piety and pilgrimage, both within England and abroad. William de Valence and his followers went on Crusade to the Holy Land, *c.* 1270;[154] Henry, Earl of Derby, went to Jerusalem in 1392–3;[155] and Richard Beauchamp, Earl of Warwick, made the journey early the next century (Plate 28). Robert de Vere, Earl of Oxford, travelled with his household in 1273 to the shrine of Simon de Montfort at Evesham, where he offered a candle of the same length as himself.[156] In early 1296, shortly before the departure of William de Valence and his son, Aymer, for Cambrai to meet French envoys, offerings were twice made before the relics in the church at Sutton Valence. Bradsole Abbey was visited on two occasions in January. William de Valence returned to Dover about 16 March, but shortly afterwards fell seriously ill; a candle was made to his measure on 22 April and he was dead within another month.[157]

The great household was exceptional in medieval society in terms of its access to and use of medical assistance. Whereas much of society made use of barbers for its general medical needs, the expenditure of the great household on specialised physicians and medicines could be very large. In February 1296, the Valence household in Kent twice had medical assistance from Master Thomas the Physician, who was brought from Canterbury.[158] The costs of Bishop Mitford's final illness in late 1406 to 1407 amounted to about £17, including purchases of medicines and fees to two doctors, Master Thomas Thirlwall, probably from Reading, who came on a number of occasions, and the more distinguished Master John Malvern, from Oxford.[159] During her final illness between September and November 1465, Catherine, the wife of John Howard, later Duke of Norfolk, was attended first by a local friar, who provided her with medicines, and subsequently by London physicians. As it became clear that she would not recover, the purchases of medicines abated in favour of sweets and waters, to provide comfort and relieve symptoms rather than effect a cure.[160] The most affluent retained physicians. Thomas Edmond served Humphrey Stafford, Duke of Buckingham, for an annual fee of £10, to be called whenever the Duke needed him, along with three horses, a yeoman and a page.[161] But casual payments seem to have been made to others, to barbers for blood-letting. The barber of the Bishop of Lincoln made medical preparations for Thomas Arundel, Bishop of Ely, in December 1383, and Arundel also paid John Garlekheth, a surgeon, 40s. for his services during the year. Another doctor was paid 2d. for examining his urine in September 1384.[162] The royal household had its own apothecaries to prepare medicines: in 1313–14, Odinet had a lead plate on which to mix up the ointments and make plasters for Queen Isabella, as well as a knife for cutting up the herbs which her surgeons required.[163] The fifth Earl of Northumberland ordered that his household have 30 sacks of charcoal a year for distilling flavoured waters for medicinal purposes – rose-water, borrage-water and water for the stone.[164]

Death, however it might be postponed, was marked by a series of rites and customs. In these the household had a role of importance, at the burial, in acts of commemoration and prayer to assist the soul through Purgatory, lasting years, and in some cases, centuries. Death was a public affair (Plate 33). The depositions relating to the nuncupative will of Sir John Fastolf, made – if it was made at all – two days before his death, show he was continuously attended. Between 8 and 11 o'clock on the morning of Saturday, 3 November 1459, Sir John probably had seven people with him: John Paston (who was to allege the new will was made), two friars, the vicar of Caister and three others. One of the friars, Clement, went in and out of the room, to see how Fastolf fared during his sickness. Other servants were on hand. Thomas Howes said Mass in his chamber and another of his chaplains, John Davy, read a book of devotions to him. His physician, Friar John Bernard, was present after he had said Mass in chapel; Fastolf's barber shaved him in his chamber; Nicholas Newman, the chief of his chamber servants, brought him spices and wine; the wine was brought up by John Marshall, his butler; and John Love, the yeoman of his chamber, was in attendance day and night. Here were servants, anxious for their master, concerned for their future, some possibly covetous of Fastolf's wealth. Shortly after his death, the advice of the Bishop of Winchester, one of his executors, was that his burial and month's mind should take place fittingly 'accordyng to hys degre and for the helth of hys soule', along with the distribution of alms to the poor and the saying of Mass to the amount of 100 marks, pending the meeting of his executors; and that Fastolf's servants should receive their rewards according to his will.[165]

Philippa, Countess of March (d. 1381), was not unusual in requesting that her household be kept together until she had been buried.[166] The maintenance of the household was a mark of the dignity of the deceased, aside from the practical

39. Sir Geoffrey Luttrell, on his war-horse, in full armour, being handed his helmet by his wife, Agnes Sutton, with his daughter-in-law, Beatrice Scrope, holding his shield. From the Luttrell Psalter, *c.* 1320–45.

benefits that accrued from the continuance of the organisation at a time when much needed to be arranged and hospitality and charity given. This role was complemented, at least in terms of commemorating the deceased and organising the obsequies, by the development of the role of heralds, particularly in the fifteenth century, stressing the chivalric achievements of the deceased.[167]

The choice of burial place gave emphasis to the connections of the deceased. The interment of members of the Valence family in Westminster Abbey underscored their relationship to the Plantagenet dynasty. In the Abbey there are four monuments to members of Joan de Valence's immediate family, three to her children and one to her husband. Margaret and John de Valence (d. 1276 and 1277) were buried partly at the expense of Edward I. Their resting places are marked by inlaid grave slabs to the east of Edward the Confessor's shrine. The tomb of Joan's husband, a remarkable effigy in Limoges enamel, on a wooden chest, itself on a heraldic stone base (Plate 40), is in St Edmund's Chapel, but was probably originally close to the shrine to the Confessor. It formed one of a group of tombs, including those of Henry III, Queen Eleanor, Aveline de Forz and Edmund Crouchback, set up around the shrine in the 1290s.[168]

On 15 May 1297 Joan de Valence commemorated the anniversary of her husband's death with a large feast in London, in the company of David Martin, the new Bishop of St David's. Those present included her son Aymer and his wife, her son-in-law John de Hastings, and many others. The pantry account for the day has 26s. 6d. worth of expenditure, sufficient for about 460 people. Two barges took Joan to Westminster, probably for the first time since William de Valence's death, where two silk cloths, bought for 50s., were hung above her husband's tomb. She went on to stay at Merton Priory, where there was a Mass for her husband on 21 May 1297.[169]

The events of a year earlier are less clear. William died probably on 18 May 1296 at Brabourne. His body was taken from there to London, but his wife almost certainly remained at Brabourne. On 8 June 1296, the clerks of the Archbishop of Canterbury were paid for proving his will, sealing and copying it; his seal was broken, probably in the presence of the Archbishop. The corpse was not buried immediately, but was embalmed. His heart was removed for separate burial (at a location now unknown) and placed in a special silver vessel. The custom of heart burial offered possibilities for multiple commemoration. William's brother, Aymer, Bishop of Winchester, was buried in Paris, but with his heart in Winchester Cathedral; the body of Eleanor of Castile was buried at Westminster, the viscera at Lincoln and her heart at the Friars Preachers in London. Theological objections to the practice came to the fore in the late thirteenth century and it was uncommon after this date. In terms of commemoration, the Valence household probably marked the first 40 days after William's death with a feast on 27 June 1296. The vigil of the Assumption (14 August), kept that year at Bampton, was observed as a day of abstinence, with Masses and ringing of bells for the soul of William de Valence. His obit roll was carried to dependent houses of Westminster in September.[170] Immediately upon her husband's death, the pattern of charity in Joan's household changed. She had

40. Tomb effigy of William de Valence, Westminster Abbey, *c*. 1296.

previously supported seven poor each day, with 14 on Saturdays; the number now rose to 20, with 27 on Saturdays.

Joan marked the twentieth anniversary of the death of her daughter, Margaret, while she was staying with another of her daughters, Agnes, at Hertingfordbury, on 6 July 1296. There was an offering of 8d., but apart from a note that the household started to consume, in the chapel, 50 wax candles on the same day the following year, nothing was recorded of further commemoration.[171] Her eldest son, William, killed by the Welsh in 1282, may have been buried at Dorchester Abbey. She stayed the night of 11/12 May 1297 at Dorchester on her way to London to celebrate the anniversary of her husband's death, but her accounts do not reveal anything in connection with her son's tomb.[172] Joan's third son, Aymer de Valence, was buried in Westminster Abbey in 1324. His second wife, the young Marie de St Pol, sought the advice of Edward II on his funeral. There were payments for black furs, part of the livery of the household at the time of the funeral; and there was a chantry established at Westminster to pray for his soul and that of his second wife. In 1377, Marie left the Abbey a cross, with a foot of gold and emeralds, which William de Valence had brought back from the Holy Land a century before. Her own interment at Denny Abbey, the foundation she had endowed and transferred, was to be modest, in the habit of a nun of the Sisters Minor, without excessive expenditure.[173]

The pattern of these observances – of delay in the burial, the use of a family burial site, of substantial arrangements for a funeral, with offerings, cloth of gold or rich silks to hang over tombs, the construction of effigies and tombs, and ongoing arrangements for liturgical celebration and distribution to the poor – is common to many households. The association of the household dwindled after its formal break-up and the task of commemoration was handed over to a perpetual arrangement in a religious house or church, although it might find a lasting link in tomb sculpture (Plate 16).[174]

There was a dichotomy in planning a funeral. On the one hand, it could be an event of magnificence, of large-scale charity; on the other, there was funerary austerity. At both, however, the household was present. In his will of 1319, Humphrey de Bohun, Earl of Hereford, envisaged burial in Walden Abbey, Essex, near the body of his wife Elizabeth, bequeathing 1,000 marks for the general expenses of his funeral, with the tombs of his father, mother and wife to be hung with cloths as rich as his own.[175] Bohun's son, Humphrey, Earl of Hereford (d. 1361), kept his funeral expenses to a minimum, dispensing with the feast on the day of the burial, the general distribution to the poor and the attendance of men of rank, save one bishop to bury him at the Austin Friars in London, in the presence of the friars and his household.[176] The corpse of Edward, Duke of York (d. 1415), on its passage to Fotheringay, was to be escorted by six of his esquires, six valets and two chaplains, appropriate magnificence even in death.[177] The funeral of Bishop Mitford at Salisbury in 1407 was a major occasion. More than £68 was spent on the day on the funeral feast, the hire of 39 cooks and the construction of temporary buildings, tents or

41. The tomb of Bishop Richard Mitford (d. 1407) in Salisbury Cathedral.

42. The funeral and burial of Richard Beauchamp. The coffin is lowered into the tomb chest by two of the Earl's men, possibly gentle servants of the household. Further men dressed like these can be seen in the left background. The service is conducted by the Bishop of Lichfield, here reading from a large service book. In the right background are hooded mourners, with cloaks and torches, and three weeping women. In the top left corner are ships and buildings which indicate that the body has been brought to Warwick over land and sea. From the Beauchamp Pageant, *c.* 1483–7.

marquees, for the spits and dressers. A customary payment – crook-penny – was collected from the Bishop's tenants on his death; and there was black cloth for livery at the funeral, amounting to a charge of more than £40. Mitford, an aged servant of a former king, was interred on 7 June, probably no more than a fortnight after his death following a long illness (Plate 41).[178] The arrangements on the sudden death of Thomas of Lancaster, Duke of Clarence, on 22 March 1421, fighting the French at the battle of Baugé, took longer and required more magnificence. The costs of the funeral, at Canterbury in September 1421, with anniversaries and continuing celebration over the next five years, amounted to more than £135.[179]

Elaboration in ceremonial accounted for a vast increase in funeral expenses in the fifteenth century. The tomb of Richard Beauchamp, Earl of Warwick (d. 1439), was contracted in 1453 to be made for a little under £180 (Plate 42).[180] The obsequies of the Earl of Northumberland in 1489 cost more than £1,000, excluding the making of the tomb.[181] There was a similar growth in the cost of funerals among the gentry.[182] In this pageantry, the role of the household was of the first importance. At the funeral of Prince Arthur, the eldest son of Henry VII, not only did his herald throw his coat of arms over the coffin as it was buried – symbolising that he was now a man without a master – but the officers of his household also brought to a formal conclusion the household's association with its lord, breaking their staffs of office and casting them into the grave.[183]

This pattern of the elaboration of routine in all aspects of the life of the great household is especially apparent in the fifteenth century. The best evidence we have for many of the practices comes itself from this period, the period of the greatest formalism, but with a careful reading of earlier sources it is possible to trace their more modest antecedents. The structures of the day, the week, the year, the round of liturgical celebration and the rites of passage of the life cycle, all were invested with special significance by the household. The set-piece opportunities for display involved huge amounts of planning and preparation by many of the large numbers of domestic servants. Nowhere can this be seen more vividly than in the supply of food and drink to the household and the routines for the service of the meal.

CHAPTER 6

Food and Drink

Given that eating might take up about a third of the day and that the meal was an occasion when a lord might show himself in his magnificence, courteously providing hospitality, alms and good lordship, rightly were food and drink prominent in the records of the medieval household. For large parts of the household, this was its *raison d'être*. The proportion of the household budget was commensurate: Joan de Valence spent at least two-thirds of her domestic outgoings and about 40% of her income on food and drink (Table 7).[1] Depending on the size of household, three or more separate departments were concerned with the acquisition, preparation and delivery of sustenance – the pantry, buttery and kitchen – to which may be added the cellar (if there was a significant quantity of wine), larder (sometimes with separate offices for fish and for hunting, as well as for meat), spicery (sometimes a part of the wardrobe), saucery and scullery. Each had its own staff. Out of 85 servants whose careers can, in part, be traced in Joan de Valence's household in 1295–7, at least 28 were involved at some stage in the provision of food and drink.[2]

How were households provisioned? Before the thirteenth century, the great household relied to varying degrees on a system of food farms, that is, renders in kind from its estates. In the thirteenth century, lords generally managed their estates directly, a system known as demesne farming, as opposed to leasing them out and living on rents, in cash or kind. Robert Grosseteste, *c.* 1240–2, therefore advised the Countess of Lincoln to establish how much corn her estates would produce and to plan the household itinerary a year at a time, taking account of the seasons and the relative abundance of properties in meat and fish, with the intention that no single place should be overburdened by her stay.[3] At any date in the thirteenth century, this was probably a simplification of practice, but there was considerable scope for providing for the household in this way. From the later fourteenth century onwards, when leasing was again common, it was not unusual for a home farm to be retained, to provide some of the household's needs without purchase.[4] Demesnes supplied corn, especially wheat for bread and mainly barley or oats for malt. They were also useful for some meatstock, but made little impact on the provision of fish and spices.

A household on the move did not usually carry stocks of food, but unless there was predictability in the pattern of movement, local markets were not able to make a significant impact on provisioning. The household's purchasing officials and manorial servants therefore often acquired goods in the country round about (*in patria*), away from markets, in a form of pre-emption, which allowed the household the first choice of goods.[5] It is important to distinguish between two sorts of acquisition, food for immediate use and food for consumption at a later date. The bulk purchase of the latter was frequently called a 'provision'. These foodstuffs were either preserved already, or the household had to make some arrangement to preserve them immediately, or, with livestock, poultry and some fish and shellfish, to keep them alive until needed.

Grosseteste envisaged a household economy in which the market had little place, except for specialised products or the disposal of surpluses. This was not a pattern that persisted. With increased stability of residence, the regular use of markets was important to all households from the fourteenth century onwards and is particularly evident in the smaller ones. The household of Hamon Le Strange of Hunstanton, in 1343–50, made its principal purchases of meat each week on Sunday at a local market.[6] Merchants sure of their market might come to the household. John Love supplied fish most days of abstinence while Anne Stafford's household was at Writtle in 1465.[7]

Not all goods required by the household and not available from the estate could be found in local markets. The advice of Robert Grosseteste was to make bulk purchases twice a year, for wine, wax and the wardrobe at the great fairs.[8] In September 1297, Joan de Valence sent Robert of the Wardrobe to the St Giles Fair at Winchester, to conduct business there on her behalf.[9] Although fairs continued in importance through the fourteenth century, they were eclipsed by the ability of large towns, particularly London, to supply these goods most of the year round.[10]

In common with other magnates, Joan de Valence made use of a mixture of the methods of supply. At the start of her stay at Goodrich, in the winter of 1296–7, 33 oxen were acquired for the larder, 10 drawn from the manors of Moreton Valence, Sopworth and Whaddon, the rest purchased.[11] Lord Grey of Codnor, on the other hand, over two months in 1304–5, drew most produce, with the exception of fish, from stock. Ale (probably about 130 gallons) was bought on two days in Nottingham and Codnor, in contrast to 50 quarters 5½ bushels of malt drawn from the estates, which would have produced about 98% of the ale consumed within the household.[12] This pattern was subject to infinite variation later in the Middle Ages. In London, great households often used their own supplies, giving them independence from the London corn market. In 1338, the Bishop of Bath and Wells had wheat brought to the capital from his Hampshire manor of Dogmersfield; in 1465, wheat for Anne Stafford came from her manor of Writtle.[13]

Feeding the great household with meat presented a number of different possibilities. The Martinmas slaughter of animals, salting down carcasses, continued as a method of ensuring a supply of preserved meat through the winter.

Table 7. Costs and proportions of expenditure on food and drink

	Joan de Valence 1296–7	John de Vere, Earl of Oxford 1431–2	Edward Stafford, Duke of Buckingham 1503–4
Total expenses	£414	£418	£2,061
Ale	£70 (17%)	£36 (9%)	£173 (8%)
Bread	£106 (26%)	£27 (6%)	£134 (7%)
Kitchen	£96 (23%)	£97 (23%)	£494 (24%)
Staple fish as percentage of kitchen expense	£37 (39%)	£38 (39%)	£61 (12%)
Herring numbers (red and white)	52,530 (£18)	26,640 (£13)	19,890 (£10)
Salt-fish: cod, ling, etc.	c. 450 (£11)	647 (£19)	2,735 (£43)
Stockfish, etc.	not known (£8)	463 (£6)	1,217 (£8)

Sources

PRO E101/505/26–7; *HAME* ii, pp. 522–48; Staffs. RO D641/1/3/8.

Notes

The total expenditure of Joan de Valence does not allow for items drawn directly from manors; nor does it include about £6 worth of salt-fish drawn from the Pembroke estate, or a value for wine or liveries of cloth. Building expenses have been excluded from all accounts. The Buckingham account represents the total cost of the establishments of the Duke, Duchess and their son, as well as the Duke's foreign household.

Staple fish are those listed above and which form the bulk of the fish provision. The figures for Joan de Valence have, in part, been extrapolated from cash sums paid for these articles elsewhere in the account. The value for stockfish assumes consumption on 107 days, the same number of days on which salt cod was consumed.

It was practised at Frampton in 1343, at Hunstanton in 1349 and in many other places. Throughout the period, fresh meat was available in winter, but it was more expensive and its consumption was restricted to those of the highest status.[14] By the mid-fifteenth century, a higher proportion of cattle may have been available as a consequence of the driving trade, bringing cattle from the north and west – and the availability of fresh meat increased. Sir Hugh Luttrell bought animals in south Wales to provide for his household at Dunster. Some were shipped across the Bristol Channel in November 1405 and salted down, and others were acquired immediately before Easter 1406, in anticipation of the conclusion of Lent.[15] In the autumn of 1409 and at Easter 1410, south Wales was also the source of animals driven to Hanley Castle for the household of Edward, Duke of York.[16] Livestock required feeding, however, and the most effective way of maintaining the household supply was to keep them dispersed until they were needed. There were localised arrangements to consolidate live-stock ready for consumption. Joan de Valence used her reeves to acquire animals on her behalf, either keeping them on manors, or assembling them from markets, ready for her household as it moved near. As she moved through

Wiltshire in the early summer of 1297, she acquired at Swindon on 2 June, from the reeve of her manor of Shrivenham, 13 pigs, together with 5 bushels of salt; a week later, she bought one ox, 24 sheep and four pigs from her reeves of Collingbourne and Swindon; and on 23 June 1297, one cow was bought from the reeve of her manor at Fernham.[17] In May to June 1393, in the household of the Bishop of Winchester, the butcher spent 13 days and his page 35, assembling and maintaining animals at Esher in preparation for the Bishop's arrival.[18]

Butchery or other preparation was carried out in, or close to, the household, by its own butchers.[19] Around London, there might be different arrangements. The household of Anne Stafford at Writtle accounted in April 1465 for the costs of over-wintering 10 oxen at Stafford and 10 at Kimbolton. When she moved to London, pasture close to the city for oxen and sheep was hired from one John Johnson, together with a building to act as a slaughterhouse, the operation of which he oversaw.[20] In 1501, the Duke of Buckingham hired a slaughterhouse and butcher in Southwark to turn his animals into a supply of fresh beef and mutton for his household at Queenhithe.[21] In practice, the outcome was similar to obtaining supplies of fresh meat from a butcher/grazier, but here all was controlled by the lord.

Poultry were commonly kept live in the household, sometimes with other fowl such as partridges,[22] and piglets.[23] When the household moved, cages were prepared to convey the poultry; and there were also nets, for enclosures or for catching the birds.[24] Dovecotes provided a ready source of fresh meat. The young birds – squabs – were eaten from spring through to November or early December.[25] More exotic birds were kept on estates until they were needed, or may have been maintained by specialist bird-catchers or falconers. The concentrations of larks, bitterns or cranes at great feasts could have been supplied in this way, although some households caught the birds themselves. In 1393–4, Sir John Dinham acquired a net, with latten wire, for catching larks;[26] but when the Duke of York needed larks, probably in anticipation of his Epiphany feast in 1410, a member of his household enquired in the countryside round about Hanley to provide 48 birds (Plate 43).[27] About a week before the funeral feast of Bishop Mitford, Ralph of the Buttery acquired at Wimborne Minster cranes, egrets and spoonbills.[28] Parks were a useful source of birds of this sort. On 3 July 1501, the Duke of Buckingham was sent 25 herons (17 of them alive) from his park at Newton Blossomville.[29] Anne Stafford kept pheasants and other birds within her own chamber in 1452–3, some of which may have found their way to the table.[30] Peacocks and peahens were kept on the estates: in 1337–8, Ralph of Shrewsbury had a bittern at Evercreech and a peacock at Fulham.[31] In the same way, swans and swanneries were carefully maintained.[32]

To these birds must be added the wildfowl and seabirds that could be taken in abundance in littoral areas.[33] Wildfowling was traditionally the occupation of autumn and winter, when the birds were at their best and, flocking together, more easily caught. It was part of a pattern of hunting and hawking, not just for sport, but to supply the necessities of the aristocratic table. Hawking was largely

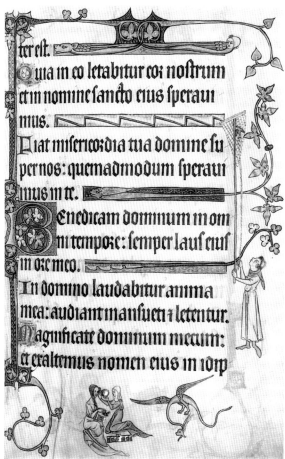

43. Marginal illustrations from the
Luttrell Psalter, *c.* 1320–45: a lady at
her toilet, plaiting her hair; with an
ivory comb, a mirror held by her
maid, and a jewel box, with gold
fastenings. Bird-catching, using a
net, closed by a wire or rope.

confined to the warmer months.[34] Gerfalcons were used to catch herons and
cranes; sparrowhawks to catch teal.[35] While Joan de Valence and her son,
Aymer, kept hawks and falcons, she also kept a pack of dogs, which was
employed on her estates – and other packs visited, that of the Countess of
Gloucester coming to Goodrich to hunt on 9 and 10 April 1297.[36] Members of
Joan's household were employed to catch partridges and rabbits,[37] but most of
the quarry was deer. Outside Lent, some venison was eaten most months and
there was a deliberate attempt to use it as a foodstuff, certainly after the death
of William de Valence, at which point Joan's household acquired a huntsman.
In 1296–7 there was hunting on Joan's estates in Ireland and in England, in
Kent, Worcestershire and around Goodrich. The meat was salted, put in barrels
and moved to the household.[38] Venison reflected high status: in 1406–7, for
maximum effect, Bishop Mitford concentrated his limited consumption on
major feasts.[39]

Joan de Valence's huntsmen were almost certainly not pursuing wild boar, of
which very little was used in the household.[40] Wild boar had been hunted almost
to the point of extinction by this time, but was more widely available on the

44. Calendar, from the Queen Mary Psalter, early fourteenth century, for December, a common time for the slaughter of pigs. A man kills a pig with the back of an axe; another butchers the animal that has been hung up.

Continent. In the western part of Essex, between 1198 and 1207, in the forest records noting legitimate hunting (but not illegal poaching), the most common quarry was roe deer, of which nearly 1,200 were taken, as well as 62 red deer, 25 wild boar and 12 feral cattle.[41] In the later Middle Ages, the deficiency in wild boar was made up by keeping boars in a domesticated context, fattening them up for consumption.[42]

How were meats prepared and conserved (Plate 44)? To take the example of pork, the flesh of boar was usually eaten fresh, but the pig was much valued for meat that preserved well. With the aim of keeping it sound for months rather than days, pork was kept in barrels in a solution of brine; or preserved, like modern ham or bacon (not readily distinguished in medieval accounts), with a combination of salt, air-drying and smoking. The salting of meat went on throughout the year, although there were peaks in autumn. When Joan de Valence arrived at Goodrich Castle in November 1296, 81 pigs were killed, gutted and salted at a rate of 1d. per eight pigs.[43] Two servants, Isaac of the Kitchen and John the Baker, preceded the main party to make preparations. Pork butchery must have started as soon as they arrived, for on its second day at Goodrich the household consumed four chines of pork and the entrails of four pigs. The butchery was aimed at conserving most of the meat: the chine (the backbone and immediately adjoining area) was what was left after the sides of meat had been cut off for preserving.

The presence of chines demonstrates the general seasonal chronology of butchery. In the household of the Bishop of Bath and Wells, in 1337, chines were consumed in November, starting on the 9th, running through into December, with as many as 28 on the feast of St Katherine (25 November). At the same time, the household used up the balance of an old stock of preserved pork from Banwell.[44] Elsewhere, the consumption of chines started a little earlier. The accounts of Anne Stafford, 1465, mention two chines of pork on 9 October; and from 23 October until Christmas they were a regular item.[45]

How long did preserved meat last? Daily accounts provide some pointers on this score but no absolutely clear answer, as it is difficult to establish the age of meat preserved from the previous accounting year. The household account of Dame Katherine de Norwich, which started at Michaelmas 1336, noted on 3 November that the household started to consume 12 hams remaining in the larder at Mettingham from the previous year, that is, laid in store prior to Michaelmas. On Easter Day (20 April) in 1337, a new *baco* (preserved pork) was started, the first of the year: the presumption is that this was killed before Lent and probably in the autumn.[46] This indicates a period of preservation of some five or six months and it must have been a common intention to preserve meat through Lent. The pattern of consuming preserved meat varied from year to year. In the Le Strange household at Hunstanton, the consumption of preserved pork was restricted, first appearing in early January 1346 in the account for 30 October 1345 to 28 February 1346; but in the following year it was eaten from October 1347 through to February 1348 and appeared again after Easter.[47] In the household of Hugh Audley the Younger, in 1320, salted pork was used before Lent, but hams not until 17 April, after Easter.[48] Preservation was not always successful. In the household of Robert Waterton of Methley, 8.5% of the hams could not be eaten.[49]

Where was pork preserved? On the Abbot of Westminster's manor of Pyrford, Surrey, in 1285–6, a centre for fattening pigs, the sides of meat were hung not only in the larder, but in the hall as well, the smoke from the open fire doubtless assisting in the process of curing.[50] Sir Hugh Luttrell, in February 1406, paid John Corbet, a smith, for 36 hooks for *bacon* (smoked pork) hanging in the kitchen.[51] An inventory of the goods of Sir Edmund Appleby of Appleby Magna, conveniently taken in mid-November 1374, listed the larder as containing a salting trough, a bin for salt and a table, besides 30 pigs and three oxen.[52] At Horton, Kent, about 1425, the larder was a separate building: as well as the salting trough, it contained a large chest for storing meat and two other large chests.[53] At Hanley Castle, pigs were purchased and killed in bulk in November 1409 for the Duke of York's household. In December, two wagons of preserved pork were transferred from the village to the household, with the meat wrapped in 16d. worth of straw, a very considerable quantity, to protect it.[54]

Pork butchery wasted little. In November 1296, Joan de Valence invested a further 20¼d. on preparing the entrails of her pigs. She bought 104 gallons of ale to put them in, to delay deterioration. The accounts also mention flour (for sausages or pudding), the carriage of water, ½d. for candles and 12 pots bought for 6d. to collect the fat.[55] Many accounts record white fat – or lard – in liquid form, measured by the gallon, when pigs were killed. Bishop Mitford's house-hold bought seven earthenware pots to hold white fat on Wednesday, 24 November 1406, a fish day, probably because pigs were being killed at that time.[56] Lard was subsequently processed and was measured by the pound in a solidified state. The quantities varied according to the opportunities there had been for fattening the animals. In the household of Robert Waterton of Methley, in 1416–17, 12 gallons of white fat were produced by 56 pigs;[57] in the household of the Earl of Oxford, 1431–2, 7 gallons of white fat came also from 56 pigs;[58] but those killed for William Molyns, in 1401–2, had not been sufficiently fat-tened that year to produce lard.[59] The lard was used in cooking, particularly for frying.[60]

The great household was a major consumer of fish. Its supply was less pre-dictable than meat and there was a significant concentration in the demand at Lent. Much of that demand was satisfied by sea fish, some supplied fresh – no part of England was too far from the sea to be supplied with fresh sea fish – but mostly in preserved form. Three principal courses were open for the preserva-tion of fish in a British climate: drying, in company with salting; pickling in brine; and smoking. These solutions aimed at long-term preservation, keeping food edible for months rather than days. For short-term preservation, light salting – 'powdering' – was employed, although some species, eels and oysters, might be kept alive in barrels with changes of water. The main fish preserved for long periods were herring and white-fleshed sea fish, principally of the cod family. The latter were either dried, usually in the open air, and known as stock-fish and by other names – winterfish, markfish, halfwoxfish, cropling, titling – the nuances of which are now largely lost;[61] or salted, pickled in brine, and known generically as salt-fish. Both types were frequently imported from north-ern Germany and Scandinavia.[62]

Domestic in-shore fisheries and deeper sea ventures also made an important contribution. In the Severn estuary, there is archaeological evidence extending into the late medieval period for fishtraps that would have caught thornback ray, gurnard, sea-bream, salmon, grey mullet, plaice and other flat fish, besides occa-sional herring and mackerel.[63] The Bishop of Bath and Wells, in late 1337 and early 1338, when resident in Somerset, drew heavily on fish from Compton Bishop, an episcopal manor close to the estuary. It was perhaps a centre for pro-cessing fish as well as holding them in store (some possibly from the previous winter) until the Bishop wanted them. Available were supplies of deep-water marine fish which had been salted – cod, ling and coalfish, possibly also pollack – or dried, particularly hake; and conger, probably pickled.[64] These fish origin-ated in catches landed locally. Further down the Bristol Channel, Sir Hugh Luttrell of Dunster, whose fish came to him through Minehead, bought fresh cod, paying to have it washed and salted. In the week of 28 February 1406, he purchased for his household a wooden vat for salting fish.[65] At Cockington, in south Devon, in 1439–40, there are records of a seine fishery, with arrangements for both salting and drying fish in summer, as well as for packing mackerel in barrels.[66] These arrangements were fairly typical of the coastal industry. Other fish were not preserved. At Hunstanton in Norfolk in the 1340s, some fish, such as plaice, were caught in great abundance by local fishermen and were eaten fresh throughout the year by the Le Strange household. In this area whiting was also only consumed fresh, caught between late May and early November.[67]

Herring was by far the most important of the other fish that were processed. There was a major industry centred on North Sea ports, especially in East Anglia, at Great Yarmouth and Lowestoft, attracting fishermen from elsewhere, from Rye and Winchelsea, and from northern Europe. Herring was a seasonal catch, found off Lincolnshire, Norfolk and Suffolk coasts in mid to late summer – and it was readily caught elsewhere in the North Sea at this time of year. The herring was sold as a processed product: white herring (salted and pickled) was first available towards the end of season for fresh herring, red herring (smoked) a little later in the year. Sprats were processed in the same way as herring and conveniently had a fishery that succeeded the herring season, although of diminished volume.[68] The produce was then shipped round the coast in its preserved form. Works at Dover Castle were delayed at the start of September 1221 as the boats that were used to carry the building stone had in large part gone to Yarmouth, not necessarily to fish, but to convey the preserved product for resale around the coast.[69] Joan de Valence's household at Goodrich was supplied with preserved herring through the port of Southampton: on 1 February 1297 N. Gascelin accounted for his purchase of 24,000 herring, which had cost him 30s. to transport by cart to Gloucester. There he had to sell 3,600 (for 25s. 6d.) for lack of money to pay for transport. In contrast, another staple – dried, salted cod – was brought to Goodrich from the opposite side of the country. In mid-February, 240, which had come from Joan de Valence's Pembroke estate, were brought by sea to Bristol, whence they were shipped across the Severn to Chepstow, completing their journey to Goodrich on the backs of eight pack-horses.[70] Goodrich was also supplied in early December 1296 with a purchase made by Philip the Clerk, at Chepstow, of dried fish and another 2,400 herring.[71] These three acquisitions would have supplied much of the daily consumption at this time.

Shellfish and crustacea were also consumed, the latter rarely, the former quite frequently, especially in Lent. Oysters were normally available throughout the year, either fresh in their shells, or pickled, without shells, in barrels.[72] Consumption of mussels and whelks was sometimes restricted to Lent; cockles were eaten from the beginning of the year through to about October. Occasionally, close to sandy beaches, razorfish were eaten. Shellfish were usually gathered along the seashore by women. On 20 March 1343, the Le Stranges of Hunstanton bought ¼d. worth of cockles from Maud, daughter of Joan of Burnham.[73] But where the business was substantial, it was male oystermongers who did the trade, the Bernard family supplying in all probability the royal household at Ludgershall with four cartloads from Southampton in February and March 1440; on 17 March 1444, a John Oystermonger left the same town with three cartloads of oysters.[74]

In Joan de Valence's household, fish was usually bought by a senior member of the kitchen staff. When Joan resided at Hertingfordbury, in late June and July 1296, Master Roger the Cook made trips to London at weekly intervals to purchase fish. From Inkberrow, in October the same year, he took the kitchen sumpter-horse to Worcester; in December, from Goodrich, he went to Gloucester.[75] Fresh sea fish was available at inland markets, but specialist markets could have a curious effect. The Duchess of Buckingham, in 1465, while at Writtle, close to small market towns in Essex, well provisioned from the sea, was supplied with fresh fish from Winchelsea; her salt-fish came from London. In London, early the following year, her purchases included eels imported from Flanders.[76] Despite the decline of fairs in later medieval England, Stourbridge remained important for the sale of both dried and salt-fish.[77]

The supply and consumption of freshwater fish were organised on a different basis and related very explicitly to status, to an upper-class diet, and to the monasteries. These fish were considered a delicacy and fetched a comparatively high price. They came from ponds, in the main, which involved large sums both in their construction and their maintenance. The royal household consumed quantities far outstripping all others: under Henry III, it transported to Westminster thousands of fish, the produce of Northamptonshire fishponds at Brigstock, King's Cliffe and Silverstone, using those at Marlborough to supply Windsor, Winchester, Clarendon and Woodstock.[78] At Mimizan, Landes, the works undertaken for Edward I by John Le Convers, making vivaria for pikes in Lent 1287, came to nearly £4.[79] Some vivaria were temporary constructions, as at Marlborough Castle in 1238, where a tank was made from timber by a carpenter and two colleagues over three days, reinforced with large stones, followed by further work filling a related ditch and caulking it with tallow.[80] The fishponds of the Bishops of Winchester were largely constructed between the mid-twelfth century and 1208. They were sited close to the principal episcopal residences and, even today, some, such as Frensham Great Pond, covering about 40 hectares, remain impressive features of the landscape (Plate 45). As well as the main ponds, there were smaller holding ponds, *servatoria*, to keep the fish when the larger pond was drained or scoured, or to hold the catches.[81]

The impact of freshwater fish can be seen in the accounts of Joan de Valence. From 2 February 1297, salmon were taken from the weir on the Wye at Goodrich.[82] That day, the kitchen accounted for 400 herring (120 of which were purchased); cod and ling, preserved in some guise; and freshwater fish. The expense of the last, 18d., as against 2s. 6d. for the cod and ling, should not mislead in respect to the quantities involved. At this price, no more than a handful of freshwater fish could have been purchased. Elsewhere on her estates, Joan de Valence relied on her own fishponds for the provision of freshwater fish. She had a pond in Kent, probably at Sutton Valence; and there was a pond at Inkberrow, which was fished at fortnightly intervals, twice by a fisherman from Bordesley, when she stayed there in September and October 1296.[83] Besides the weir on the Wye near Goodrich, there was some river fishing. On 22 March 1297

45. Frensham Great Pond, Surrey, a fishpond of the Bishop of Winchester. The pond was constructed before 1208 and in 1282–3 a quay was built for a fishing boat.

a net was fetched from Abergavenny and, two days later, 12d. was paid to a fisherman also from Abergavenny for catching fish at Goodrich.[84]

The largest households maintained fishermen of their own, professionals who might, with the assistance of others, carry out the task for them. Eleanor de Montfort's fisherman, Simon, fished at Farnham for 11 days in March to April 1265. He received a stipend,[85] but other households hired workers, along with their equipment.[86] Ponds were fished by seine-net, with between four and six men, in a functional manner. On larger ponds, boats were used, as at Frensham.[87] In contrast to other hunting activities, most fishing was not for sport, although there was some use of rod and line for pleasure.[88] The ponds themselves were status symbols and the fish in them were highly prized. From 1462 onwards, John Howard, later Duke of Norfolk, kept a careful record, partly in his own hand, of the stock of his ponds, including carp, not widely recorded in England before the sixteenth century.[89]

In terms of nutrition, freshwater fish could have contributed to the diet of few. The pond at Dogmersfield, producing in March 1338 five pikes, six pickerels and two bream, was typical.[90] Even then, some species were more significant than others: bream, roach, chub and tench contributed less than pike, eels and lamperns and lampreys. Freshwater fish from streams, aside from salmon and eels, were even rarer. Trout appear in the accounts of Joan de Valence only five times – she was at Hertford or Hertingfordbury on every occasion – and it is unlikely that more than two or three fish were at issue each time.[91] Even in the

Couient ſeſu pere feſoit aporter le peſſon q̃ il auoit peche eu la mer: A la tere ẽ dic. ỿpiſt atrenouc. ⁊ ſeſu pre feſoit metre vngi-ril ſure le ffui.⁊ rouſluc ou pe̅ con.⁊ dic matuſc eurtc eus.

46. The apostles grill fish for Christ, who has appeared to them at Lake Tiberias. According to the French text, St Peter puts the grill on the fire and roasts the fish. The loose fish arrive in wicker baskets. One apostle is blowing on the charcoal. The grill has a ring for hanging it up. The fish are served in bowls, at a table set up on trestles, on which are a round loaf and a short tablecloth. From the Holkham Bible picture book, *c.* 1320–30.

chalklands of Wiltshire, Bishop Mitford's household consumed only a handful of trout in 1406–7.[92] Where fish were not in ponds, fishing was controlled. In 1301–2, at Cheriton and Alresford river-fishing required a payment to, effectively a licence from, the Bishop of Winchester.[93] There were specialist fishmongers who dealt solely in the larger freshwater fish. In 1465–6, Anne Stafford's supplies of pike regularly came from William Waleys; another pikemonger supplied John Howard in 1466.[94] Lampreys were particularly prized: in March 1466, Anne Stafford was sent four which had been acquired by one of her receivers.[95]

Fresh sea fish were often transported by pack-horse, for speed. Like stockfish or salt-fish, they were carried in baskets or wickerwork panniers (Plate 46); fish pickled in brine were transported and stored in barrels of different shapes and sizes.[96] In storage, it was sufficient to wrap or interleave loose fish with straw.[97] Freshwater fish, with the exception of eels which were sometimes salted,[98] were usually eaten within a short time of capture. Where these fish had to be transported – and it was unusual to carry them much of a distance, as the normal practice was to site the ponds close to residences – they could be moved alive, wrapped in wet straw or grass; or they could be baked in pastry (*in pane*) or set in jelly.[99] Where it was essential to move them alive over longer distances, for example for the stocking of ponds, a very expensive operation was undertaken, using barrels lined with canvas and filled with water.[100]

That there is a plethora of information about bread and its baking is not surprising. What is unexpected is the variety in everything connected with the loaf – its size, shape, quality of flour (fineness of milling and subsequent bolting), composition of flour (corn used), shelf-life and age at consumption, and purpose (where and how the loaf was destined to be consumed). Some of this difference was undoubtedly connected with status. Food within the household had to be appropriate to the lord, his guests and his servants. When Master Robert, Edward I's pantler, was suspended from household wages for a month at Ghent in January 1298, his fault was a failure to provide sufficient bread for the knights in the King's hall: he could not obtain money from the royal wardrobe. As a result bread had been bought in the town by the knights' valets and had been served by them in hall to the knights, 'in manifest contempt of the King' – doubtless both in terms of this appalling breach of hospitality and in the quality of the commodity (Plate 47).[101]

47. The Old Testament transposed to a household setting. *Top*: Joseph in prison with Pharaoh's pantler and butler. Bread, after it had been baked, was the responsibility of the pantler. Therefore it was the pantler, rather than Pharaoh's baker, who was imprisoned. *Bottom*: Joseph tells them what will happen as a result of their dreams, that the pantler will be hanged within three days (having dreamed of the crows pecking at three baskets full of bread on his head); and that the butler returns to his office as before. From the Queen Mary Psalter, early fourteenth century.

In the English royal household in the early fourteenth century, there were two principal types of bread, both made solely of wheat. The more numerous was a white loaf, known as a cocket, which was round and intended for the whole community of the household. Its flour was of slightly lesser quality than the other loaf, pain-demaine (*panis dominicus*), which was intended for the king.[102] The finest flour was used to produce pain-demaine: Robert Waterton of Methley, in 1416–17, consumed nearly 104 quarters of wheat in his household, of which 8½ quarters were used for pain-demaine.[103] Flour of this quality was carefully guarded: it was suggested that it should be kept in a sack of good leather, secured with a lock, always to be carried in the cart that followed the lord.[104] Keeping the best flour in leather bags was probably common: the household of Hugh Audley the Younger bought three for this purpose in January 1320.[105]

Wheat was the corn used almost exclusively for bread within the great household in general in the later Middle Ages, but in lesser households, of Sir Hamon Le Strange of Hunstanton for example, about a quarter of the corn baked was wheat mixed with either rye or barley.[106] Different corns were associated with bread for the poor. The household of Dame Katherine de Norwich baked about 35 loaves per bushel of wheat for household use, but for distribution to the poor resorting to her household, a mixture of corn was used, probably of wheat and barley, which produced nearly 50 loaves to the bushel.[107] The bread that Sir John Dinham baked in 1372–3 for the anniversaries of his parents and his wife, probably for distribution to the poor, was made from barley.[108]

Variety in other households is apparent in the size of loaf. A treatise on household organisation of the first half of the fourteenth century advocated at least 20 loaves to the bushel, all to be well cooked (which would reduce their water content and, hence, weight).[109] These, however, would have ranked among the largest household loaves. Those in three episcopal households, all using wheat bread, were smaller, setting aside any differences in the size of bushel or customs relating to its use, for example in the employment of struck or heaped measure.[110] Robert Grosseteste, *c.* 1240–2, proposed to produce 22½ loaves per bushel, white and brown (or black) together;[111] the baker of the Bishop of Bath and Wells, in 1337–8, produced 32 or 33 loaves to the bushel;[112] and in the household of Thomas Arundel, Bishop of Ely, in the 1380s, it was usual to produce between 34 and 37 loaves per bushel.[113] Despite these differences, many households had only one size of loaf, frequently baked at around 25 per bushel of wheat: this was the usual rate in the household of Bishop Mitford in 1406–7.

What contribution did bread make to household diet? At a rate of 25 loaves per bushel, each loaf would have needed 1.38 lb. of the best wheat flour, producing a loaf weighing about 1.1 lb. after baking. At 35 loaves per bushel, 0.98 lb. of flour would have been needed, with the finished loaf weighing 0.79 lb. after baking.[114] A loaf formed a part of each portion (*ferculum*) and from the second half of the fourteenth century it is possible to see a direct equation between numbers of *fercula* and loaves: in Bishop Mitford's household, on 10 December 1406, one loaf was used in each of 41 *fercula*. The ration in this household was probably one loaf per person per day, but even if the ration was two loaves per day, this would still have left the individual, especially in those households baking 30 or more loaves per bushel, below the level of bread consumed, for example, by a monk at Westminster. Not all loaves were allocated to *fercula*: a substantial percentage, in ecclesiastical households and possibly those of women, was used for other purposes, for trenchers, rewards, liveries, all night, and sometimes for alms. In Bishop Mitford's household in 1406–7, 54% of the loaves were used for *fercula*; in the household of Edmund Mortimer, Earl of March, on a diplomatic mission to Scotland in 1378, the proportion was much higher, 71%.[115]

How fresh was the bread? The records of Mitford's household show a regular pattern of baking. When the household removed from Woodford to Potterne, bread was baked almost immediately, on 27 October, again on 30 October, and thereafter every four or five days, first using up the entire stock of the previous baking.[116] In the 1380s, however, Thomas Arundel, as Bishop of Ely, had all his bread baked fresh every day – and the product of the baking was nearly always consumed in its entirety during the day.[117] While Bishop Mitford's household were all eating bread of the same age, sometimes four or five days old, it was the opinion of John Russell, 40 years later, that the lord's bread should be fresh, that all the rest brought to table should be at least a day old, with all household bread three days old, and trencher bread four days.[118]

Loaves for other purposes may have been differently shaped or constituted. Wastel bread, that is made from exceptionally fine flour and baked in a very hot oven, producing a biscuit-like loaf, was used on occasion in the household of Henry, Lord Grey of Codnor, in 1304–5.[119] Ralph of Shrewsbury bought 'French bread' in London in 1338.[120] The loaves – small bread – used for liveries in the household of the Duke of Clarence, in 1468, were half the normal household loaf in weight, with bread for horses and dogs also to be prepared differently.[121] In the household of Edward IV, the loaf for horses, made from bran, was known as a hogman.[122]

Whereas corn was regularly transported and also the best-quality flour, in comparatively small quantities, it was not usual for a household on the move to carry bread. When Joan de Valence moved, an advance party, including a baker, went to the destination a day or so ahead to have bread ready for the main body of the household.[123] Baking was largely carried out within the household, under the direction of specialists. Along with cooks, bakers and pantlers were among the domestic staff who might be described as Master (*magister*). Once the bread was baked, it was handed over to the charge of the pantler and his assistants. In 1295–7, Joan de Valence employed at different times two bakers, John and William, each of whom operated with an assistant; there was at least one valet working in the pantry for some of the time.[124] Edward II, in 1318, had a pantry staff which included a clerk and under-clerk (shared with the buttery), a chief serjeant pantler, a serjeant pantler for the King's food, with a valet under him, a valet for purveying bread for the household, a waferer, a serjeant baker, who had two valets as assistants, one to look after the oven, the other to look after the mill and the preparation of the wheat.[125] Bread was also purchased, particularly when a household was on the move, or residing in a large city. Joan, Duchess of Brittany, bought bread in Boston, when staying there briefly in the October of 1377;[126] and Edward Stafford, in the summer of 1501, bought some of his bread during his stay in London.[127]

Daily consumption of wine was a mark of the highest aristocracy. It was most often purchased in bulk at the point of import. The wine purchased for Joan de Valence in London was moved by the pipe (a wooden vessel like a large barrel), by boat to Kent, by cart to Bampton and Moreton Valence. From Bristol to Goodrich it went by boat and then by land. The verjuice transported to Goodrich from Inkberrow on 25 September 1296 by Richard the Usher and Richard the Saucerer came by pack-horse.[128] Daily consumption at Goodrich between 18 November 1296 and 11 January 1297 was at a rate of ½ sester when there were no guests, rising to 1½ sesters throughout the Christmas period, with 2½ sesters on Christmas Day itself.[129] In February 1407, the household of Bishop Mitford consumed between 2 and 6 gallons of wine daily. In April the same year, he purchased five pipes of red wine and one of white at Southampton for £29, with a further 26s. 4d. in transport costs. His funeral feast required 6 gallons of sweet wine.[130] Other households made purchases on an *ad hoc* basis from taverns, as did Joan Holand, Duchess of Brittany, when travelling to Boston in October 1377; and Edward Stafford, when at Queenhithe, Barnes and Richmond.[131] Besides red, white and sweet wines, hypocras – a richly spiced wine, for service at the end of the meal, with wafers – required the careful selection of spices, the preparation of powders, with different degrees of spicing according to the status of the drinker.[132] Anne Stafford's household bought 2 ells of blanket for straining this drink.[133] Wine was a luxury in the households of gentry and knightly families: the Multons of Frampton, the Le Stranges of Hunstanton, and the Catesbys of Ashby St Ledgers purchased small quantities, the last perhaps in the greatest amounts, with 3s. 4d. worth for the feast of Corpus Christi, probably in 1388, at Coventry.[134] In these quantities, few in the household would have had wine; and fewer still on a regular basis.

The most common drink in the great household throughout the later Middle Ages was ale, brewed from malted grains, typically barley, less usually oats or dredge, a mixture of oats and barley. Brewing either took place within the household, by its own servants or by individuals hired for the purpose (Plate 48); or the finished article was purchased from local producers. The drink was of varying strengths, depending on the quality of the malt and the amount of water used, as well as of different qualities. In the household of Joan de Valence, most ale was purchased and the ale-making occasions were exceptional and insufficient. Just under 1,400 gallons were brewed in the household at Goodrich in March and April 1297; thereafter the bulk was purchased in the surrounding district, particularly at Monmouth.[135] Dame Katherine de Norwich, in 1336–7, largely brewed her own ale, with malt drawn directly from her manors of Blackworth and Mettingham when she resided there. The intervals between

48. The medieval brewhouse at White Castle, Mon.

brewing here stretched as far as 12 or 13 days.[136] Bishop Mitford made purchases from local brewers throughout 1406–7, rather than brew within the household. Typically his supplies came from a small group of individuals, supplying different amounts, qualities and strengths. This household needed to store approximately 300 gallons of ale. Purchases were made at intervals ranging from three days to one week, as the household supply dwindled almost to nothing.[137] In the mid-fifteenth century, John Russell advised that ale should be five days old before it was served.[138]

Ale, in general, had a shelf-life of about one week, but sometimes as much as nearly two; the household consumed its supply almost entirely before restocking, as it was readily available for purchase in almost every location. The daily household ration of ale could be substantial: the practice of issuing a gallon per *ferculum* appears in episcopal households in the late fourteenth and early fifteenth centuries.[139] At the other end of the scale, the Duke of Clarence, in 1468, expected a gallon of ale to be shared between eight at meals, but supplemented as need be; and the household ordinance of Edward IV of 1478 put the ration at four men per gallon of ale per meal.[140]

In the fifteenth century, beer was initially a rarity. With the addition of hops, it had both a different flavour and better keeping qualities than ale. It was a continental innovation and was imported from the Low Countries, north Germany and what is now Poland. The Holland beer, bought at 4s. a barrel for Joan and Margaret, the daughters of the Duchess of Clarence, who resided at Dartford Priory, in 1419–21, was a considerable luxury.[141] The household of Robert Waterton of Methley, in 1416–17, consumed five and a half barrels of beer, at 3s. a barrel; 149½ quarters of malt were needed, however, to provide its ale.[142] It was purchased by the occasional barrel by Anne Stafford in 1465–6; but the part of the household of Edward Stafford, third Duke of Buckingham, residing with him at Queenhithe, Barnes and Richmond had a markedly increased total consumption: no fewer than 15 barrels at 22d. each were bought between 16 and 23 October 1501.[143] To make his own beer, John Howard, Duke of Norfolk, purchased 562 lb. of hops on one occasion in 1481.[144]

Cider was available on a regional basis, especially in the West Country, the Welsh Borders and the south-east. The household of Joan de Valence had cider at Inkberrow in late September and October 1296; at Swindon from May to July 1297; and at Moreton Valence and Goodrich in August and September 1297.[145] At Inkberrow, the amounts ranged between 10 and 20 gallons a day and replaced some of the ale consumption. The household of Hugh Audley the Younger, at Tonbridge in Kent in 1320, had similar quantities of cider from May onwards.[146] The consumption of mead is mentioned more rarely.[147] To drink water alone, rather than at least ale, was a sign of poverty.[148] It might, however, be used in combination with another drink. A silver vessel was used to boil water for Edward I; and his son's wife, Queen Isabella, carried with her on journeys two small barrels, one for water and one for wine, the one to dilute the other.[149]

Milk for drinking is usually associated with the presence of children in the household, from the very young through to early teenage. In the household of Joan de Valence it was bought in Lent 1297 for Edward Burnel; in August to September 1297, at Moreton Valence, for little John Comyn, Joan's grandson, who stayed there in company with his mother.[150] In Joan's household it was also regularly used in cooking, in the making of pottage;[151] it was an essential ingredient in dishes such as furmenty (wheat soaked in milk, with spices) and much else besides.

Dairy produce was not uncommon, particularly in households headed by a woman: Eleanor of Brittany, in 1225–6, consumed milk, cheese and butter most weeks; likewise Joan de Valence in 1296–7.[152] Some cheeses were highly esteemed as gifts: in January 1290, Eleanor of Castile sent cheese to Amesbury for her mother-in-law, Eleanor of Provence;[153] and Queen Isabella sent cheese from Brie to Isabella de Vesci in Yorkshire in January 1312.[154] Hard cheese was commended by John Russell for its digestive qualities.[155] In common with monastic establishments, ecclesiastical households made not inconsiderable use of dairy products. The rich cheese flans eaten at Westminster Abbey in Rogation (the three days before Ascension Day) probably also appeared in 1406–7 in Bishop Mitford's household immediately before Ascension.[156] Cream appeared less often in this household than in that of John Hales, Bishop of Coventry and Lichfield, in 1461, where it was used for dowcet, a sweet custardy dish.[157] Butter was used for frying, supplementing animal fats, particularly lard, and comparatively expensive oils (olive and nut). Eggs were consumed in all households without reserve, except at Lent.[158]

If the demesne economy could supply much of the corn, meat and freshwater fish needed by the household, it was not well placed to supply it with spices. Except for mustard and saffron, spices were imported and were consequently purchased at markets or fairs, or in London, typically by members of the wardrobe staff on their purchasing expeditions. Local purchases were usually of small quantities – and at a greater price. The bulk of Bishop Swinfield's sugar supply (101 lb.) was purchased in London, along with wax and other spices, probably on three separate occasions around Christmas 1289, Epiphany 1290 and Whitsun 1290, at prices between 5½d. and 7d. a pound; a single pound was purchased at Ross-on-Wye on 15 March 1290, for 8d.[159]

There was little difference between households in the range of spices used, but there was a good deal of difference in terms of quantity and frequency of use. Spices were one of the defining characteristics of upper-class diet. The gentry concentrated their use on great feasts and occasions, employing more commonly available flavourings, such as mustard, onions, garlic, salt and vinegar, at other times.[160] When, in the mid-fourteenth century, Henry of Grosmont confessed to gluttony, he had in mind not just rich meats, but ones that were made as delicious as man could, with good spices and the most piquant sauces.[161] While spices had other uses within the household – in washing, beds and clothing[162] – their connection with food was foremost. As well as providing flavouring, they had, by the fourteenth century, an important place in the ceremonial at the end of the meal. At the void, or clearing away of the meal, the final service was typically of spices and wine. They were also taken at the fireside in the chamber, perhaps as we might eat chocolates of an evening.[163] For this service, there was a range of impressive spice plates, frequently emblazoned with the heraldry of the owner, a chivalric episode or other device (Plate 49).[164]

The use of one spice – sugar – changed through the period. The increased availability of sugar had an important effect on the range of medicines in the thirteenth century, in the production of electuaries and cordials, and was an important ingredient in the preparation of confections and preserves. It was used in large quantities in the royal household: in 1287–8, the Great Wardrobe issued 6,900 lb. of sugar, together with 1,434 lb. of rose and violet sugar.[165] Much of the rose and violet sugar was destined for use in electuaries – and had itself been manufactured from ordinary sugar by an apothecary within the household.[166] Much smaller quantities were used in noble households, but increased during the later fourteenth century and into the fifteenth, accompanying a shift in its use from drawing out flavours, as a condiment, to sweetness as an end in itself, especially in conserves.[167] In 1296–7, Joan de Valence acquired only 12 lb. of sugar, 1 lb. of which may have been an electuary.[168] John de Multon of

49. The Bermondsey dish,
c. 1335–45: this silver, parcel-gilt
plate has traces of enamel. It is a
highly decorative piece, intended for
display, or perhaps as a spice dish. The
central medallion depicts a lady placing
a helm on a knight's head.

Frampton purchased small quantities – a little over 4 lb. – largely in preparation
for All Saints and Christmas, in 1343, with a further ½ lb. for the start of Lent in
1348.[169] The accounts of Bishop Mitford in 1406–7, suggest about 50 lb., with
further confections;[170] but this was a fraction of the consumption in the largest
noble households. Humphrey Stafford, in 1452–3, consumed 245 lb.;[171] and
Anne Stafford, at the start of 1466, acquired 84 lb. alone probably in association with an operation to stew warden pears for a compote or conserve.[172]

    In terms of fruit and nuts, while gardens and domestic production were
significant, imports, particularly of almonds, figs, raisins and currants, were
of major use during periods of abstinence. The last four were purchased in
the same way as most of the spices. In 1285, the purchases made by Bogo de
Clare in London, sent to his manor of Thatcham against Lent, included 4,000
onions, half a seam of garlic, three frails of figs, two of raisins and 246 lb. of
almonds, besides 300 stockfish and another 100 dried fish.[173] In the household
of Edward IV, the officers of the confectionary were to get their supplies without
charge according to the fruits to be had in the King's gardens. There were
cherries, pears, apples and nuts for summer; for Lent, wardens and quinces.
There were also presents given to the King. Other fruits and varieties of apple
– blaundrells and pippins – were to be bought.[174] John Russell, outlining the
duties of the butler, counselled the service of plums, damsons, cherries and
grapes before lunch, with pears, nuts, strawberries, whinberries, hard cheese,
blaundrells and compotes and comfits as a fruit course at the end of lunch; then
another fruit course after supper, of roasted apples, pears and white-powder (a
mixture of ground spices).[175] The service of a fruit course probably represents
a continuing tradition: it was the custom in France by the end of the fourteenth

century.[176] Large purchases were made by royal fruiterers. In 1310–11, William of Writtle bought pears, cherries, blaundrells and apples for Queen Isabella.[177] The Duke of York purchased 1,150 wardens, 600 apples and 200 pears between December 1409 and February 1410.[178] In 1501, Edward Stafford, Duke of Buckingham, ate fruit in the afternoon as well as at the end of meals.[179] Citrus fruits were unusual in medieval England. In the fifteenth century they rarely occur in more than the low dozens[180] – and the Spaniard (doubtless in the train of Katherine of Aragon) who brought the Duke of Buckingham a gift of oranges and lemons in August 1501 was well assured of his 20d. reward.[181] Gifts of fruit were prestigious, and likewise the seigneurial gardens that produced them.[182]

There is no reason to think this use of fruit – and the produce of gardens in general – was peculiar to the highest ranks of the nobility: proportionately, it may have been more important among lesser landowners.[183] An agreement from the 1470s, between two members of the lesser gentry, Christine and Robert Battescomb, divided a manor house between them, giving Christine 'a lytell appell hous over þe ovene', the little orchard and six apple trees in the great orchard.[184] Manorial gardens also produced a supply of vegetables, but their impact on diet among the aristocracy would have been limited. Isabel of Lancaster bought leek and onion seeds for her garden at Amesbury in 1333–4; John de Multon bought onions and garlic, besides leek seed, for his garden at Ingleby in 1343–4.[185] The plants were used principally for flavourings, or as ingredients for pottage, with green peas, skirret and worts.[186] The use of herbs from gardens for further flavourings continued the same trend,[187] although there was a prejudice against salad.[188] Vegetables now regarded as commonplace – such as cabbage – were sometimes imported and appear as purchases, perhaps indicative of the underdevelopment of horticulture in Britain as opposed to the Continent.[189] Nuts and berries that could be gathered in hedgerows as well as gardens are harder still to trace. From 4 June to 18 August 1465, the household of Anne Stafford at Writtle purchased 'beries', or soft fruit generally, with strawberries on 14 July.[190] Edward, Duke of York, had strawberries on 17 June 1410.[191]

Vineyards were specialist gardens and redolent of status. Their contribution to the supplies of white wine and verjuice was sometimes of considerable importance, although the quality (if the price is an indication) was inferior to continental products. Bishop Swinfield of Hereford, in 1290, received seven pipes of wine from the Ledbury vintage of the previous year, as well as nearly eight pipes of verjuice. The cost was roughly half that of imported wine.[192] In 1431–2, the vineyard at Wivenhoe, Essex, which belonged to the Earl of Oxford, produced for his household no more than 34 gallons of wine.[193] The royal household had vineyards at Kennington, King's Langley, Rotherhithe and Westminster.[194] But these domestic vineyards supplied only a fraction of the needs of the great household, in terms of white wine, and no red or sweet wines at all. The poorer climate of the fourteenth and fifteenth centuries had a major impact on production.

There were a number of changes in diet in the great household in the later Middle Ages. On one level, there were regional differences in diet – the produce of each *pays* was different. While the purchasing power of the great household could do much to even out these discrepancies, patterns of natural distribution had an impact. Households closer to the sea ate more fresh marine fish and littoral birds, those closer to the wetlands ate more wildfowl, and those with access to large markets, particularly London, had the largest variety. The distribution of some species of sea fish, in particular, could be restricted.

Another source of difference was dietary theory. The belief that cooking contributed to the well-being of the body and soul was drawn ultimately from Greek medicine. Its influence can be seen in the writings of continental cooks, such as Chiquart. Food was derived from three of the four elements – earth, air and water – and was moderated by the fourth, fire, in cooking. In dietaries and guides to health, physicians considered the consequences for diet. The 'Forme of Cury', an English recipe collection prepared at the court of Richard II, paid respect in its proem to the 'assent and avysement of maisters [of] phisik and of philosophie þat dwellid in his court'.[195] In the household of Edward IV, the doctor of physic was 'comynly ... [to] talke with the steward, chambrelayn, assewer, and the master cooke to devyse by counsayle what metes or drinkes is best according with the kinges dyet'.[196] The popularisation of dietary tracts may lie behind some of the changes in English noble diet in the fifteenth century.

What was the substance of these changes (Table 7)? Firstly, the proportion of household expenditure on bread and ale declined between the late thirteenth century and the fifteenth. The proportion of expenditure on the kitchen, however, remained fairly constant at a little less than a quarter. It was about the same in the household of Joan de Valence in 1296–7 as in that of the Earl of Oxford in 1431–2 and the Duke of Buckingham in 1503–4.[197] Within kitchen expenditure, there were changes in the balance of fish and meat. There were three groups of marine fish – herring, salt-fish (principally members of the cod family) and stockfish or dried fish (usually cod) – that households laid in store to sustain fish consumption throughout the year. They form the best indicator of comparative levels of fish consumption, as eating fresh marine fish or freshwater fish may have been restricted on the basis of status. In the second half of the fourteenth century, these staples were used on an almost daily basis on days of abstinence.[198] There was a decline – perhaps by some two-thirds – in both the expenditure on these staple fish and in fish consumption, from the first part of the fifteenth century to the early sixteenth century. At the same time, there was a change in the balance of the three groups, with a decline in proportion of herring by the fifteenth century, in favour of salt-fish, a pattern that continued into the sixteenth century. This decline was then dramatically hastened by the abandonment of abstinence as part of general religious observance, especially from 1538, with Henry VIII's instruction to end fasting in Lent. This change was never reversed by economic legislation in support of the fishing industry.[199]

The decline in fish-eating was matched by increased consumption of meat, particularly fresh meat. At the same time, the great household consumed better-

quality cattle than were available in the market.[200] In the household of the Duke
of Buckingham, in 1503–4, £219 – 44% of kitchen expenditure – went on beef,
mutton, veal and pork; a further £180 or 36% on poultry, pheasants, partridges,
similar fowl and some fresh fish, with £61 or 12% on the staple fish. Among the
heavier meats (beef, mutton, veal and pork), the later Middle Ages also saw a
change in balance, with a marked decline in the use of pork and some increase
in that of mutton (Table 8). There may also have been a regional concentration
of pork, close to large areas of woodland. It is high in proportions in the records
of two households residing close to the Weald: for Hugh Audley the Younger
and his wife, largely at Tonbridge, Kent, in 1320; and for the Bishop of
Winchester, about 70 years later, while his household was at Esher in Surrey. It
is difficult not to conclude that by the sixteenth century there was a definite prejudice against pork, that the meat was not considered wholesome in aristocratic
circles.[201]

Peasant diet, notably that of harvest workers, moved from a largely cereal
base, with dairy products and some pork, in the thirteenth century, to the use of
wheat for bread, a much larger proportion of meat, especially fresh meat, and a
diminishing proportion of fish in the fifteenth century. This was a general cultural pattern, with the peasantry following the lesser gentry, and the lesser gentry
copying what they saw in the households of the nobility.[202]

Evidence for another change at the highest level in the household appears by
the end of the Middle Ages in the records of banquets and feasts. On Monday,
6 September 1501, the Duke of Buckingham entertained the Burgundian
ambassadors at his house at Queenhithe. The account for the meal records five
pheasants, 12 partridges, two dozen chicks, six capons, 12 rabbits, three dozen
small birds (possibly sparrows), furmenty, 2 gallons of milk, 100 eggs, 12 dishes
of butter, 2 gallons of cream and 3 gallons of curd, 20 calves feet and one shoulder of veal for making *le gely*, together with pears, spices and filberts, doubtless
to conclude the meal.[203] What is noteworthy about this list is what it does not
contain – pork, beef or mutton – and this pattern in general was typical of the
accounts of Buckingham's foreign household in London, as opposed to the great
household at Thornbury or Penshurst. For example, in 1501, the household in
London consumed one and a half pigs and two piglets in a period of six months.
In the account of his great household which survives for 1503–4, pork formed
1.8% of all the meat consumed, a small proportion perhaps, but enough to
suggest that while the Duke and his immediate entourage had little taste for pig,
preferring on the whole poultry and fowl, those who ate pork and the other
meats in much greater quantities were the lesser servants of the great household.[204]

The instructions given by the Earl of Northumberland and his council for the
provisioning of his household, in September 1511, indicate a similar pattern.
Projected consumption for 1511–12 included 25 pigs, at a total cost of 50s. as
against £86. 5s. 4d. to be spent on beef and £68. 12s. 2d. on mutton. Capons
were only to be served to the Earl; the chamberlain and steward might have
them too if there were guests; hens and pigeons were only to be served in the

Table 8. Proportions of cattle, sheep and pigs consumed in the great household

Household	Place	Date	Cattle lb.	Pigs lb.	Sheep lb.
Hugh Audley	Kent	1320	(49.5%)	(47.6%)	(2.9%)
Richard Turberville of Sampford Peverell[1]	Devon	1358–9	10,400 (73.9%)	3,037 (21.6%)	629 (4.5%)
Sir John Dinham at Hartland[2]	Devon	1372–3	4,798 (72.5%)	869 (13.1%)	952 (14.4%)
William of Wykeham	Surrey	1393	(47.5%)	(38.7%)	(13.8%)
Robert Waterton of Methley	Yorks	1416–17	9,963 (55.2%)	3,553 (20%)	4,401 (24.8%)
Edward Stafford, Duke of Buckingham	London Newport Thornbury	1503–4	51,989 (65.7%)	1,411 (1.8%)	25,679 (32.5%)

Sources

PRO E101/372/4, E101/505/17, E101/510/17; *HAME* ii, pp. 490–1, 497–8, 508–20; WCM 1; Staffs. RO D641/1/3/8.

Notes

The calculation of meat weights is based on Harvey, *Living*, pp. 228–30. Audley and Wykeham are based on diet accounts, where percentages are easier to establish than total weights.

1. Further meat, not given here, was bought fresh, as part of nearly £37 of foodstuffs. The meat weights here are based on the stock account, the value of which was approximately £23. 10s.
2. A further £9. 6d. was spent on fresh meat, not included here. The meat weights are based on the stock account, the value of which was about £13.

messes of the lord, the chamberlain and steward; plovers were only to be had at Christmas and were reserved for the lord and those sitting at his board-end; cranes, reserved for Christmas and other major feasts, were for the lord's mess alone, likewise heronsews and mallards, woodcocks and 17 other types of bird.[205]

At the enthronement feast of Archbishop Neville of York, *c.* 1466, there is an earlier indication of this movement, with very large quantities of birds falling within the restricted categories, 104 peacocks, 4,000 mallard and teal, 204 cranes, 400 heronsews, and others; 1,000 sheep and 104 oxen were destined to feed more than 400 servants of the noblemen who were present. The enthronement feast of Archbishop Warham, in 1505, which took place in Lent, exhibited a parallel development with fish. The staples were all but absent in the menus for the feast itself, which concentrated on either freshwater fish – lamprey, pike, salmon, carp, tench, sturgeon – or high-status sea fish – conger, halibut, turbot, sole. The general provision for the feast, however, included 14 barrels of white herring and 20 cades of red, part of the supplies for the lesser members of the households present.[206] Further distinctions were made in the way food was prepared, leaving a division that separated game from domesticated animals, the birds from the other meats, and roast from boiled foods.[207]

The food supply to the great household had to meet a range of demands from consumers, predicated on status, on patterns of religious observance, on philosophy and perhaps just plain taste. It had to respond to the logistical questions of sustained availability and to a demand for luxury items, or for items the consumption of which was restricted by social custom or required by social emulation. Much had to be available in a form suitable for long-term preservation – for example, the peak in the medieval demand for fish was at the season of the year least favourable for catching them or for importing them. Conversely fresh foodstuffs were a mark of status and always in demand, however restricted their availability. Some items, such as venison, wine or the use of spices, marked out distinctive elements of an aristocratic diet. The fare destined for the head of the house was also increasingly divided from what might be eaten elsewhere in the household: this was, by the fifteenth century, no longer just a case of choice pieces of meat or fish, but of whole categories of foodstuff. Routines, such as carving, were to focus particularly on these reserved foodstuffs, to the magnificence of the lord. To understand the significance of items in the diet of the great household in a broader canvas than a nutritional analysis might paint, it is therefore necessary to look further than the ingredients, to the cooking and service of the meal itself, to see how these distinctions were followed through.

CHAPTER 7

Cooking and the Meal

To receive, prepare and deliver the substantial quantities of food demanded by the great household was a major exercise of logistics, requiring skilled – and sensitive – personnel. How was the kitchen organised? In 1295–7, the custody of Joan de Valence's kitchen was shared between Master Roger the Cook, Nicholas Gascelin and Ralph the Clerk. None of the three was present in the household continuously. Master Roger took charge of the kitchen whenever he was there, for the major feasts of the year, with the exception of the Purification in 1297. Nicholas Gascelin took over in his absence and sometimes undertook some responsibility for purchasing when he was present. Both received a daily wage of 10d. when they were on business away from the household. Ralph the Clerk, who took charge of the kitchen intermittently, had different responsibilities. His daily wage, on business away from the household, was either 4d. or 6d., and from time to time he accounted for other household departments. He did not have the professional standing of the cook and was probably one of two clerks of the household.[1]

Over the winter of 1296–7, Master Roger handled much of the supply of provisions for the household, a duty elsewhere of caterers or professional purchasing officials.[2] Most purchases made by him were on credit, against tallies. At Goodrich, he owed about 70s., more than half to Thomas Le Saltere, other creditors including a poulterer of Ross and the beadle of Goodrich Castle for one calf. Working with the cooks in Joan's kitchen were two valets, Isaac of the Kitchen and Richard the Saucerer, besides another servant, Robert of the Kitchen. The valets received 2d. a day away from the household and there would have been other less highly ranked servants, grooms, whose names are not recorded. The pantlers were also ranked at this level. There were at least three during the period – John Cely (a valet), John Le Wariner and Roger Bluet – and possibly a fourth, recorded only in Michaelmas 1295, Hugh of the Pantry. The household baker, John, was a valet, assisted by a groom (as noted before, just possibly a woman for part of the period).[3] Like the rest of the household, the kitchen was a male preserve and it was not until the fifteenth century that women generally began to appear.

These male servants were well rewarded: the cooks in the household of Joan de Valence were at the top of the scale of household servants but probably received less than those, such as the household treasurer, at the apex of the financial system. The profession was well remunerated elsewhere. In the household of Edward II the serjeant cooks for the king received 7½d. a day in wages.[4] Stipends, as opposed to daily wages, were also high. Sir John Fastolf, in 1430–1, paid Henry Cook a stipend of 30s.; John Bakere, 21s. 8d.; John Wyles, the butler, 26s. 8d.; and Adam Burgh, the clerk of the household, 20s. The steward of the household, John Rafman, received 66s. 8d.[5] Cooks also had opportunities for casual employment on major occasions that required supernumerary assistance. Robert Waterton of Methley, on the marriage of his daughter to Lord Welles in August 1417, hired a cook of Lord Scrope of Masham, a cook from Wakefield and a cook of the Prior of Nostell.[6] Loyal service was also rewarded at the death of the lord.[7]

Despite their standing, few English cooks of this period – or their cooking – are now well known. The renown of continental chefs, such as Guillaume Tirel, known as Taillevent, cook of Philip VI of France, or Master Chiquart of the court of Savoy, has not been obscured.[8] The association of their names with cook-books, however, indicates as much tradition as personal innovation or a distinctive style.[9] At first sight, there was much in common across Europe in cookery, in the preference for spices, the use of mordant flavourings such as vinegar or verjuice, or the use of oil as a cooking medium. The internationalism is misleading, however: there were distinct culinary traditions in different areas and dishes going by the same name had varying constituents and tastes.[10] While one of the earliest Catalan cook-books, the *Libre de Sent Soví*, dated 1324, claims as its author Peter Philip, cook of the King of England, the recipes it contains are in the Catalan rather than the Anglo-Norman tradition.[11] Cook-books also embody a conservatism that is striking given a mid-fifteenth-century plaint against *nouvelle cuisine*:

> Cookes with þeire newe conceytes, choppynge, stampynge, & gryndynge,
> Many new curies alle day þey ar contryvynge & fyndynge
> þat provokethe þe peple to perelles of passage þrouȝ peyne soore pyndynge,
> & þrouȝ nice excesse of suche receytes [recipes] of þe life to make a endynge.[12]

Medieval cook-books were not instructional manuals, with quantities and cooking times, but more of the nature of *aides-mémoire* to someone who might already know what they were doing, or who wanted a general impression (as might the head of the household) of what to expect. Skills were passed on in a practical way; likewise innovation that survived the test of time.[13]

There were five principal methods of cooking practised in England: frying, roasting, grilling, boiling and baking. Distinctions in method reflected status. Frying employed fat, either lard or butter or an oil, all expensive commodities. In the week of 27 December 1405, Sir Hugh Luttrell of Dunster spent 7d. on fat for frying. Anne Stafford's household at Writtle, on Easter Day 1465, spent

A sequence of four illustrations, on consecutive folios of the Luttrell Psalter, *c.* 1320–45, showing the cooking of food in the kitchen, its preparation for service and its consumption at dinner in hall.

50 (*above*). Two birds, on either side of a piglet, are roasted on a very simple spit, in front of a fire. The spit is turned by one man, while the other puts faggots on the fire.

52. A cook chopping a piglet and poultry for table in a preparation area. At the second of the stave-legged tables, drink is being poured from a flagon into cups. The food is then carried to the table.

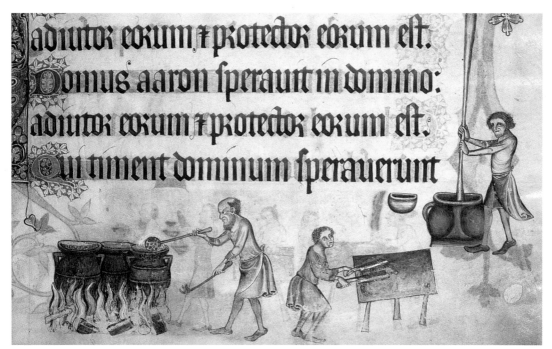

51. Three steaming cauldrons, resting directly on a log fire. The cook has a skimmer and a flesh-hook. Another kitchen servant, with two knives, is chopping green vegetables or herbs, on a rudimentary table with three stave legs. A further servant is using a long pestle.

53. The Luttrell family at table. The trestle table is covered with a plain white cloth. On the table are metal trenchers, knives and spoons; bowls of wood and metal; covered bowls; loaves of bread, some already sliced. Two Dominican friars sit with Sir Geoffrey Luttrell and his wife, his two sons and daughter-in-law. One servant places dishes on the table while the other, the cupbearer or butler (with a towel with embroidered ends and tassels over his shoulder), has just handed over the cup from which Sir Geoffrey drinks, in Eucharistic fashion. It has been suggested that the mournful expressions of the diners have a direct relationship to the Psalm the illumination accompanies, 'Dilexi quoniam', the Psalm of the just man in his affliction, and to the circumstances of Sir Geoffrey's family at this time.

6d. on *flotis*, the skimmings of fat from the top of cauldrons, for frying.[14] While the results were delicious, roasting on a spit in front of a large open wood fire was profligate in its use of both fuel and labour. It was, besides, a technique that must have done much to contribute to the heat of the kitchen (Plate 50). Not everyone was entitled to eat roast meat: in the household of Edward II the defining line came between the esquires of the household on the one hand, and their juniors, the valets and grooms, on the other.[15] Boiled dishes were widely available. In small-scale operations, the food could be cooked in a pot suspended over a fire (Plate 38). Larger quantities required different methods. Cauldrons were placed either directly in the fire (or the fire was lit around them), or in constructions, as at Edward I's Caernarvon, which allowed fires to be lit beneath them (Plate 51).[16] In 1318–19, Thomas of Lancaster acquired two brown robins (large cauldrons) and four copper bowls for the substantial sum of £20.[17] Grilling was employed for cooking fresh fish, typically over a charcoal fire (Plate 46).

By following a single meat, pork, to the table, the variety of dishes can be seen. As fresh meat, it was readily available for roasting or boiling. As a chine, a boiling joint, it was common in winter (the result of butchery to preserve the sides of meat), but less abundant in summer.[18] It was commonly used for mortress, finely ground, sometimes with poultry, with bread, eggs, boiled with spices: on Sunday, 27 January 1320, Hugh Audley the Younger, spent 15d. on half a fresh pig 'pro morterel'.[19] The continuing popularity of this dish is evidenced by its appearance in recipe collections throughout the later Middle Ages.[20] John Russell's *Boke of Nurture* refers to a number of pork dishes. In carving roast meat for the lord, he was to be helped to the shoulder first, then a rib; boar, baked in a pasty, was to be carved and placed on the trencher; bacon was included in pottage of peas; verjuice was used with bacon, ginger sauce with piglet.[21]

The fuel for most cookery was wood or charcoal, although turves were used in some parts, particularly in East Anglia. Cooking on open fires was a difficult process. On the Continent, more use was made of coal, especially from the fifteenth century, which allowed heat to be controlled more effectively. There is little evidence for the use of coal for cooking in the household in Britain before the sixteenth century. Where it appears at an earlier date, it is usually associated with the marshalsea and a forge for ironwork.[22] The main kitchen was a hot, smoky place, and staff dressed accordingly (Plates 50 and 51). In 1526, Henry VIII gave each of his three master cooks 20 marks a year reward 'to the intent they shall provide and sufficiently furnish the said kitchens of such scolyons as shall not goe naked or in garments of such vilenesse as they now doe'.[23] Not all cooking was done on this scale. More delicate work was performed over charcoal, for example, at the confectionary at Hampton Court under Henry VIII. The use of charcoal, in braziers or other vessels, perhaps in ranges, gave more control over cooking and enabled it to take place in buildings other than the principal kitchen.[24]

The design of the main kitchen incorporated what it could to mitigate the inconveniences of its function. It was frequently a detached building, on

54. The kitchen at Stanton Harcourt, Oxfordshire, *c.* 1460–83.

account of the very real risk of fire. In 1284–5, a fire at Bogo de Clare's manor of Melton Mowbray engulfed the kitchen, causing 10d. worth of damage to three lead cisterns and a cauldron which had been hired, besides damage to clothing elsewhere.[25] Early kitchens were of wood, such as the weather-boarded structure at Weoley Castle, roofed with reeds, in use *c.* 1200–60, or made of cob: an example of this type of construction was probably superseded at Wallingford in the 1220s.[26] Many, of timber, and later of stone or brick, were square (Plates 54 and 55). The twelfth-century structure at Clarendon was about 40 feet square; the thirteenth-century kitchen in the Bishop's Palace at Chichester is some 37 feet square; and the fourteenth- or fifteenth-century kitchen at Writtle was about 36 feet square.[27] They were tall structures, frequently with vents in the roof. At Bolton, the kitchen tower commissioned by Richard, Lord Scrope, in 1378 was to be 50 feet high and to measure 10 ells by 8 ells.[28] The hexagonal kitchen tower at Raglan Castle, built in the 1460s, has two large fireplaces, each with an oven. A hatch allowed dishes to be carried away without the servants having to enter the kitchen, past the pantry and probably the buttery, to the hall.

55. Farleigh Hungerford, Somerset. Behind the late fourteenth-century scullery, with its cobbled floor, lies the kitchen. Beyond the well, to the right, was a bakehouse. The castle was held by Richard, Duke of Gloucester (subsequently Richard III), from 1462 to 1483, and by John Howard, Duke of Norfolk, from 1483 to his death in 1485.

In the basement of the kitchen tower there was a storage area, described in the seventeenth century as a wet larder.[29]

At Bishop's Waltham, the kitchen of William of Wykeham's palace was remodelled in 1388–93 and still stands nearly to its full height (Plate 56). An external larder was built nearby at the same time. Besides the well which was integral to the building which the new structure replaced, the kitchen was equipped with a wooden dresser in 1389–90, an internal wooden larder and stone-lined floor in 1391–2, and wooden shutters for its windows in 1392–3. A scullery was partitioned off in 1441.[30] Major furnishings, like dressers, were a common feature of kitchens, butteries and serving areas, providing work-space for the final preparation and ordering of food. Joan de Valence's London house had dressers in both the kitchen and the buttery.[31] In anticipation of Anne Stafford's stay in the Bishop of Worcester's house in the Strand in November 1465, two carpenters made a dressing-board and a ewer-board with trestles. There were preparations for the surveying-place, with a table and lantern, work to an aumbrey (or cupboard) in the kitchen and the larder door.[32] 'Dresser' was used without distinction in the medieval period to apply to anywhere food was prepared, from a board to a piece of furniture in which utensils and dishes, food and drink could be stored. The term was also used for a room where these preparations were made, at Bishop's Waltham in Wykeham's new building, adjacent to the hall, or at Windsor, a room built in 1362–3.[33]

Kitchen equipment was in constant requisition. Joan de Valence's kitchen required an additional skimmer, sieves and two panniers in 1295–7; on Easter Day 1297, to assist with the reprise of the meat diet, three knives and a strainer were required.[34] Cloths were used in the processing of food and drink: for covering dishes, cheese-cloths, cream-cloths, jelly-cloths, ravel (a coarse cloth) for straining and packaging, and linen of many descriptions.[35] Water for washing in basins at table was strained through a towel by the ewerer.[36] In 1393, Wykeham's kitchen department (including the scullery and poultry) had two baskets covered with leather, for the bakehouse; two barrels and a vat for pikes, besides other vats, two costrels for sauce, one vat for the scullery, seven pestles, two vats for wheat- and oat-flour, five knives for the dresser, two knives for herbs (Plate 51), a container for salt, three nets for rabbits, along with nets for fish, 200 wooden plates, three pairs of panniers and two great mortars. In his establishment at Southwark there was a mill for the saucery, five brass covers for pots and six dozen pewter plates. The department was also charged with the care of two boats for the fishponds at Farnham and Bishop's Waltham. The pantry and buttery contained various sacks and there was a great vat for the brewhouse at Bishop's Waltham.[37] Sculleries required a supply of salt for cleaning vessels, as well as large tubs in which to carry out the washing.[38] The royal household had a separate section, under Edward IV, for the storage of vessels: the pitcherhouse and cup-house.[39] In October 1448 Sir John Fastolf's kitchen at Caister, Norfolk, had a series of brass pots and pans, three brass pike-pans, two brass ladles, a cauldron, a gridiron, four racks, two cupboards, three trivets and a frying pan, besides two great spits, two other spits and two little broaches, a brass mortar

56. The kitchen (*right*), dresser and hall at Bishop's Waltham, rebuilt by William of Wykeham, 1388–93.

and pestle, a flesh-hook, two pot-hooks, a pair of tongs, a shovel for the fire, two trays, a strainer and a small container for vinegar. The larder had three large pans, a butcher's axe and two salting tubs, besides the fish stored there. The buttery had knives and containers and in the cellar was kept a large collection of silver dishes and plate, along with napery.[40]

Like kitchens, bakehouses and brewhouses were often separate buildings. Among the later medieval buildings within the inner ward at White Castle, Mon., are the remains of the brewhouse, which include a rectangular roasting kiln, immediately adjacent to a circular structure, which would have supported the main vat for brewing over a fire (Plate 48). At Bishop's Waltham, Wykeham's campaign of building started in 1377–8 with the construction of a new bakehouse and brewhouse, built together on the eastern side of the inner court (Plate 23). There were two ovens, of which one was for baking.[41] At Hanley Castle, in January 1410, the household of the Duke of York – which had evidently outgrown the accommodation available – equipped a brewhouse with large vats, brought from Worcester and Gloucester, stone and tiles for making two ovens, and lead and solder for making a large cistern, at a total cost of 56s. 7½d. The household also hired buildings for storing wheat and malt, for the household butcher and washerwoman, and made stalls for the cattle that were kept for the household.[42]

Just as supplies for the kitchen needed storage, so provision was made for the buttery, cellar and pantry, for keeping ale, wine, bread and other pantry items, such as cheese. In the pantry, bread was kept in bins.[43] Storage was frequently in basement areas where there was little light and which naturally remained cool, if not cold. While wine required storage for a period of time lasting months, ale and bread had a shelf-life that was usually measured in days, not weeks. Comparatively ready access was therefore necessary to supplies and for ease of replenishment – and the areas required by pantry and buttery were also therefore not as extensive. The size of the household dictated which other kitchen offices had a separate existence. A scullery, saucery, spicery, a scalding house (for the preparation of poultry), a poultry, a confectionary, a pastry, a boiling or seething house, larders for meat, fish and the products of hunting: all these can be seen in the largest establishments, as well as offices in the modern sense for the officials in charge and the caterers who made the purchases.[44]

Bakehouse, brewhouse and kitchen all required substantial amounts of water. Evidence for water supply ranges from the abundant, such as the conduit system which fed the royal palace at Westminster,[45] to the enigmatically non-existent, with no trace of wells or piped supplies at Pembroke Castle. At Caernarvon the kitchen was supplied with water from the nearly adjacent Well Tower.[46] At Goodrich, the principal water supply of the castle was its well. In the kitchen there is an area for wet processing, but all water would have been carried to that point. That there is not a separately identified brewhouse or bakehouse in this castle concords with the effort required when brewing took place: it may have been one reason why Joan de Valence's supply of ale was usually purchased. The maintenance of wells is amply documented. John Foucard, a messenger, received 6d. for climbing down the well at the royal palace at Clarendon to retrieve a bucket in 1288–9;[47] and John Catesby paid 6s. 8d. for the making of a new well at Ashby in 1379–80.[48] The stone cistern, with its taps, in the outer court at Henry VII's new palace at Richmond was a source of particular admiration.[49] Elsewhere water was carried. At the Duke of Buckingham's house in Queenhithe, in July and August 1501, Simon Egge, 'waterberer', was paid at the rate of 1d. per five tankards he carried for the use of the kitchen (Plate 38).[50]

The purpose of all these arrangements – the provision of food and drink for the household, in hall or in chamber – did much to dictate the layout of the buildings. At Goodrich, the kitchen was adjacent to the principal hall; and the way to other areas where food might be served was covered by a pentice around the central courtyard. In Wykeham's new-modelled palace at Bishop's Waltham, the food and drink passed directly from the kitchen, up steps, to the dresser, which also had hatches for the buttery and pantry, and thence into the hall (Figure 3).[51] The physical barrier – the bar – between the offices and those collecting the goods served both to control access to the provisioning departments and as an area for assembling the foods. The emphasis now switched from preparation to service, delivering the food and drink in an appropriately ceremonial style, for consumption in hall or chamber.

Bishop Grosseteste, *c.* 1240–2, counselled the Countess of Lincoln to eat in hall in the presence of her household (unless she was ill or overly fatigued), as that would bring her great benefit and honour. At the same time he advised she forbid the eating of meals in secret places or chambers, as it was wasteful and not to her honour or profit. In this monition is the germ of an important shift in habit: the Bishop would not have advised the Countess in this way unless this was already a practice – there was much that induced men to dine in more intimate surroundings.[52] It anticipated the well-known plaint of Piers Plowman (in its final form, probably before 1387) of the flight of the lord and lady from the hall to a comfortable parlour or chamber:

> Elenge is the halle, ech day in the wike,
> Ther the lord ne the lady liketh noght to sitte.
> Now hath ech riche a rule – to eten by hymselve
> In a pryvee parlour for povere mennes sake,
> Or in a chambre with a chymenee, and leve the chief halle
> That was maad for meles, men to eten inne,
> And al to spare to spille [waste] that spende shal another.[53]

In architectural terms, this transition can be traced in domestic buildings from the late thirteenth century through the following century. Typically residential accommodation at one end of the hall was improved. The solar acquired greater status and the chamber beneath it was transformed into a parlour. At the same time the domestic services – pantry, buttery and kitchen – remained at the opposite end of the hall.[54] In domestic accommodation, within castles and more substantial complexes, the opportunities for this transition may have arisen much

57. Bodiam, Sussex: the three arches of doorways from the screens passage, for the kitchen, buttery and pantry. The fireplaces of the kitchen can be seen in the walls on either side beyond the areas for the two other departments. Late fourteenth century.

earlier. By the end of the Middle Ages, it was unusual for a magnate not to eat all except the meals on major feasts in his great chamber.

The servants entered the hall from a group of doorways at one end, perhaps shielded by a screen. In late medieval house design, the pantry and buttery were often located together at one end of the hall, with a doorway each, and a third doorway giving access to the kitchen (Plate 57). Emerging into the hall, in the thirteenth century, they would have faced a U-shaped arrangement of tables (Figure 5). Bishop Grosseteste envisaged a high table, with the lord or lady seated in the middle, and one table down either side. The gentle members of the household (*fraunche maysnee*) and guests were seated all together, not in threes and fours; and the grooms were seated together at the lower end of the room.[55] In the household of Walter de Wenlok, in the 1290s, men of rank (estate) were seated together at table; below them were minstrels and messengers, according to rank; then, the officials of the household offices; and finally, the grooms.[56] Other evidence suggests the grouping of individuals according to rank in the hall. In indentures of retinue of the early fourteenth century, while it was unusual for grooms to eat in the household, when they did eat there, they ate together.[57] In April 1399, when Winchester Cathedral Priory granted a corrody to William Wynford, its master mason (who ranked equal to the prior's esquires), he was permitted to have his meals at the prior's table in the prior's hall unless there were many people of rank present; and his valet was to eat at the table in the same hall where the valets ate.[58]

The furnishings of the hall were usually simple: the aim was to reuse space. A mid-fifteenth-century text, outlining the role of the marshal, enjoined that every morning he was to come into the hall and see that it was clean and in order; stools, trestles and forms used for meals were to be put away at other times; all hangings were to be shaken out or beaten with rods if need be; and there were to be no dogs lying around in the hall from morning to night.[59] The most common form of table was a board, or boards, laid across trestles (Plate 53). It was functional and of comparatively small cost: display was confined to plate and soft furnishings.

Wooden furniture was largely made by carpenters who carried out the wood-work associated with building projects. Some was made by turners and joiners: specialist furniture- or cabinet-makers were very uncommon. In 1438, John Lewys, a carpenter, made new arrangements for setting the trestles under the tables in Cardinal Beaufort's hall at Bishop's Waltham (Plate 56). Unusually, in the same year, a large ash at Beaufort's nearby manor of Marwell was felled for making dormant tables, that is tables which did not come to pieces or fold away, but were rigid. These were also destined for the palace at Bishop's Waltham.[60]

Static furniture of this sort was less usual at this period, an expensive use of space which was normally expected to have many purposes. It was less easily transportable, significant if the household was peripatetic, although it is improbable that much in the way of larger items such as table tops (and some were very large, up to 40 feet long) would have been moved. This type of furni-ture was, however, of some antiquity. In a twelfth-century lease of Ardleigh, a manor of St Paul's, the inventory included a dormant table and a buffet – or dresser – for serving.[61] The choice of furniture used might vary according to the importance of the occasion:

> Then shall þe sewer, yf it be in a grete day and a durmant [table dormant] lye under þe clothe, let þe surnape with þe towell rynne uppon the durmant. In a mene day festyvall þe surnape and towelles rynne uppon þe borde [boards on trestles].[62]

A ruder version of a fixed table might be used in other contexts, such as the stave-legged tables found in kitchens or serving areas (Plates 51, 52).[63]

Seating in hall was usually on forms or benches. Chairs were an exceptional item – although found in chambers as well – associated in part with ceremonial or privilege, but not exclusively so (Plate 58). Unlike their modern counterparts, even chairs of the greatest importance did not necessarily have backs.[64] Carpenters made benches or forms in anticipation of visits or occasions when the press of visitors demanded them: these were not items kept in store for occa-sional use. In 1318–19, in preparation for the visit of Queen Isabella to the household of Thomas of Lancaster in Pontefract, two men spent three days sawing wood for benches and trestles for the hall, which took two carpenters a further three days to assemble.[65] At Bishop's Waltham in 1441, trestles and forms were made for the hall and chambers against the arrival of Cardinal

Saunt Sampson estoyt bien arou: Coment il allat a vne feste en philustien
Si veeyt vne pucele bele qe il amoyt. E a femme la voulst auoyr ~ ~ ~

58. Sampson goes to a feast among the Philistines and sees a woman he wishes to have as his wife. Sampson is seated on a turned chair. The table is dressed typically with a cloth, gathered in folds along the front edge; a flagon; round loaves; meat dressed in bowls; and knives. A man opposite Sampson is cutting or chipping bread. A servant kneels. From the Queen Mary Psalter, early fourteenth century.

Beaufort.[66] Some benches may have doubled as chests (Plate 6). Seating on benches could be cramped:

Yf þou sitt by a ryȝht good man,
þis lesson loke þou þenke apon:
Undur his theȝghe þy kne not pit,
þou ar fulle lewed yf þou dose hit.[67]

One other item of furniture present in the hall requires separate description, the buffet. This was effectively a dresser (and often so called). In origin, its purpose in hall or chamber was the same as that in the kitchen, buttery or else-where, a place for the final preparation and distribution of food. In 1318, in the household of Edward II, it was staffed by a serjeant surveyor, who was to oversee the distribution of the food, once all were seated in hall.[68] As a side-table, or 'cup-board', it was used for the distribution of wine and ale, for the buttery, or to hold the basins and jugs brought from the ewery. The key to much medieval furnishing, however, was the necessity to create display – and it was but a single step from a functional piece of furniture, on which cups, ewers and basins, all of which might be of precious metal, were placed, to a form of tiered buffet, with open shelves, principally for display, on which plate might be exhibited. By the fifteenth century (and probably earlier), the number of shelves was directly related to the status of the lord.[69]

The buffet itself was not an elaborate structure: like the bare wooden boards of the tables, it was always covered with textiles when in use; but its contents could be magnificent. The rich cupboard of John, Duke of Bedford, left behind in England when he went to France for the last time in 1434, numbered 128 pieces, five of gold, 69 of silver gilt, and 54 of silver, worth nearly £850 at the time of his death. This plate was for display. There was further plate for use on the table, some of which was equally impressive, including the object now known as the Royal Gold Cup, acquired from the French royal household some time after 1400 (Plate 59).[70] To the author of *The receyt of the Ladie Kateryne*, recording the proceedings on the arrival of Katherine of Aragon and her marriage to Prince Arthur in 1501, these displays were particularly important. Their effects were intended to be prodigious, in diplomatic terms and as an indication of Henry VII's liberality: he gave away to his Spanish guests the contents of buffets, worth hundreds of pounds. The seven-tiered buffet at the banquet in Westminster Hall ran the length of the Chancery court there.[71]

The tables, side-tables and buffet were covered in cloth of varying sorts and richness: covering anything – cupboards, tables, cups, dishes – was a mark of status. Sir Geoffrey Luttrell of Irnham and his family were served at a table covered with a simple, linen cloth, without decoration (Plate 53). Other tablecloths were more elaborate (Plates 38 and 60), with embroidered and fringed ends (Plate 61); and they were carefully laid, with pleats (Plate 36). In the thirteenth and fourteenth centuries, the finest linen came from Aylesham, Norfolk. Thomas of Lancaster bought Aylesham linen in Pontefract in 1318–19, but other purchases of fine linen were made in Paris on his behalf and imported.[72] High-quality linens were increasingly imported later in the fourteenth century and into the fifteenth, from Burgundy and Flanders, along with cheaper materials, such as crestcloth and plain linens (called canvas or holland), used for tables. From the later part of the fourteenth century, small quantities of figured (decorated) linens were also imported, particularly from the area of Rheims. White, figured linen, diaper or damask, became especially popular towards the end of the fifteenth century.[73] In 1468, it was estimated that the household of the Duke of Clarence would require in linen each year 200 ells of canvas, four pieces of crestcloth, 350 ells of holland (of three different qualities), 40 ells of napery from Devon, 50 ells of Paris napery, 50 ells of diaper and 50 ells of towel, along with four dozen napkins, one dozen of Paris napery.[74] Among the goods held by Sir John Fastolf's butler at Caister in 1448 were four plain board-cloths for his table, two 9 yards long, two 6 yards long; six plain napkins; four plain tablecloths for the hall, each 6 yards long; two pieces of worked cloth, and towels for washing, each 10 yards long. There was also one piece of cloth of Rheims for covering bread:[75] John Russell noted, in his mid-fifteenth-century *Boke of Nurture*, the

39. The Royal Gold Cup, made in
Paris, *c.* 1380, now with a Tudor stem,
was part of the plate of John, Duke of
Bedford.

practice of extravagantly wrapping the lord's bread, after it had been cut, in
2½ yards of towel of Rheims, and opening it before the lord.[76] In London, linen
was available for hire: the Duke of Buckingham hired ewery-cloths for 10 weeks
in 1501, at 2d. a week.[77] The routines for laying the tablecloth and covering side-
tables and dressers became ever more elaborate through the fifteenth century. On
a major feast day, the table was covered with a tablecloth, another cloth known
as a *surnape*, as well as a towel, which was to be laid double if someone was of
sufficient status to have a mess to themselves. The *surnape*, which was probably
decorated in some way, was omitted on other days.[78] Cloth of gold – imperial –
was recommended by John Russell as the final dressing for the cupboard.[79]

   On the table, aside from the cloths, were cups, plates and saucers, serving
dishes or chargers of various sizes and shapes, as well as platters for trenchers,
made of wood, pewter or precious metals. Throughout the period, the high table
at least would have had at its disposal a range of silver or silver gilt dishes.
Prestige had its downside. Hot, silver dishes were difficult to carry and servants
do not seem to have used cloths to assist them (perhaps these were reserved, as
a point of status). One fifteenth-century text recommended the server to hold,
unseen, a piece of bread between his hand and the dish.[80]

The richness of the vessels in the Valence household (Plates 13 and 14) was typical of the quality sought in metalwork. The wills of the nobility and episcopacy enumerate many similar dishes and cups of precious metal. In his will, proved in September 1308, Henry, Lord Grey of Codnor, left to Joan, his wife, a large silver pitcher and a hanap with a foot, with acorns on its cover, together with another hanap, with a foot and enamel decoration, a pitcher for water, six dishes and six silver saucers for messes. He also left to Robert Saufcheverel 12 gilt hanaps, to Margaret de Cromwell a small silver pitcher for wine and a gilt hanap, and to Joan, her sister, a gilt hanap (Plate 62).[81] At the same time, this household used earthenware: around Christmas 1304, more than 100 bowls or cups and more than 200 plates or dishes were bought.[82] Large purchases of earthenware vessels were made around major feasts in other households. In 1265, Eleanor de Montfort made several large purchases a month, with as many as 1,000 dishes purchased on 17 March;[83] in 1320, Hugh Audley the Younger purchased 150 bowls in preparation for Easter;[84] and for the funeral feast of John de Sandale, Bishop of Winchester, in 1319, 1,000 decorated dishes were acquired.[85] Pottery and precious metals functioned side by side, further delineating the social distinctions in the household.

60. The water turned into wine at Mary's intervention at the marriage at Cana. The diners may be seated on a bench (see right-hand edge). Round loaves are being sliced by the left-hand seated figure; the meats in dishes are whole animals, probably roasted, minus heads and feet. The tablecloth, with its quite short overhang, is decorated along the edge. The first cup of wine is served in a mazer or a sort of bowl, not an elaborate cup. Water is brought by the hooded servant (who has probably come from outside) in a wooden bucket, bound with iron hoops. From the Holkham Bible picture book, *c.* 1320–30.

61. The Last Supper: Christ, in the centre of a long table, covered with a cloth that looks like a single runner, with two embroidered bands at the ends. On the table are loaves (some cut or sliced), covered cups, three knives and one spoon, held by the disciple to the left of Christ; and two plates, each with two fish, reflecting the Lenten fare that would have been eaten on Maundy Thursday. Judas kneels in front of the table. From the Luttrell Psalter, *c.* 1320–45.

Other materials, particularly pewter, wood and leather, were used for containers that came to table. Pewter was not used for domestic vessels before the 1290s, but had established its place in this market by the middle of the next century.[86] Sir Hugh Luttrell of Dunster bought pottery, wooden, leather and pewter vessels, including four dozen of the last for 72s. shortly before Christmas 1405.[87] In 1465–6, Anne Stafford bought 10 dozen pewter vessels in anticipation of a visit by the King.[88] Pewter was available in London in 1501 for the Duke of Buckingham to hire.[89] The Earl of Northumberland, in 1511, preferred purchase to hire and reserved the use of pewter for Christmas, Easter, St George's Day, Whitsun and All Saints.[90] Pottery vessels, however, enjoyed something of a renaissance later in the fifteenth century, particularly with the import of higher-quality products from the Low Countries and Germany, of stoneware and (also from Italy) maiolica.[91]

Wooden vessels had a function in most kitchens and found their way to the table in various guises. Mazers – drinking cups made of maplewood, mounted in precious metals – were highly prized. Among the long list of vessels bequeathed by Nicholas Longespee, Bishop of Salisbury, in 1297 to Lambert, his chamberlain, were two mazers with feet and two without (Plate 63).[92] For the funeral of Bishop Mitford in June 1407, 500 cups of ash were bought.[93] One fifteenth-century courtesy book suggested the ewerer use a wooden cup, probably of ash, to assay the water he brought to and strained at table.[94] Along with eight wooden bowls for the kitchen, the household of John de Vere, twelfth Earl of Oxford, purchased 234 cups from turners in Colne and Hatfield Peverel.[95]

These wooden vessels may have been used only by lesser members of the household. The wooden dishes and spoons bought by John Catesby in 1392–3 were possibly for his manorial servants at a harvest meal.[96] Robert Waterton of Methley had wooden bowls and three cheese-vats made from his own timber in 1416–17; 17d. was also spent on repairing leather pots.[97] Bombards, or black jacks – large leather jugs – were used in the great household.[98] Leather had a durability – and the potential for repair – that pottery lacked. In 1511, the Earl of Northumberland proposed leather pots be bought instead of earthenware for serving meals in the household.[99]

During the later Middle Ages, glass tableware in England was largely imported, although some English blue glass is known. Glass vessels may have been more commonly associated with medicine, particularly with the inspection of urine and distillation,[100] but there was some tableware of a high quality. Goblets and enamelled beakers, probably from the Near East, predominate in the thirteenth century; in the fourteenth, there were slender-stemmed drinking-

62. Achan, before Jericho, hides his wealth, frustrating the cause of the Israelites. The valuables going into a lockable chest, on a base of arched woodwork, include a cup with a cover. From the Queen Mary Psalter, early fourteenth century.

glasses.[101] In the kitchen of Henry Le Scrope's London house, forfeited in 1415 were 4s. 4d. worth of 'glassis et verris'.[102] At this valuation, these cannot have been of high quality. Similar, cheap glasses were being imported through Southampton in 1439–40; but the range of imports from the Low Countries through London in 1480–1, with small quantities of crystal drinking-glasses, alongside others brought in by the thousand, suggests a wide spread in the market.[103]

Table vessels came in various forms – chafers, bowls, chargers, shaped dishes for fish, through to platters for trenchers. The use of these last, to hold trenchers – slices of bread – onto which food was served, was common. Flat, metal platters for trenchers, sometimes divided into two, possibly hinged like a book, were found in households certainly by the fourteenth century (Plate 53).[104] Wooden trenchers were used in lesser households.

Objects at table particularly connected with ceremonial and magnificence were distinguished by sumptuous programmes of decoration based on episodes of aristocratic life, religious scenes or heraldry, particularly emphasising family connection. From Grosseteste onwards, there was ceremonial, increasingly elaborate, associated with cups and cupbearers (Plates 59, 64 and 65). The secular ritual associated with them was not far distant from liturgical use (Plate 53).[105] They form part of a group of metalwork which had strong personal or family associations. Humphrey de Bohun, Earl of Hereford (d. 1361), bequeathed to his confessor the hanap from which he was accustomed to drink. Edmund Mortimer, Earl of March (d. 1381), left his son and heir, Roger, a golden hanap and cover called 'Benesonne', as well as a gold-mounted drinking horn (which had belonged to Edward III), to be passed from heir to heir in perpetuity. His bequests also included a cup called 'wassail'.[106] To share these – or any – vessels at table was a mark of trust and distinction.

Equally public in purpose were spice dishes[107] and almsdishes. Alms from the table were a major element in charity associated with the great household. Grosseteste's advice to the Countess of Lincoln was to serve more than ample for the household, so that its alms might be increased.[108] By the second half of the fifteenth century, the passage of the alms took place with much ceremony. In the hall, the almoner was summoned three times by the marshal with the cry 'Almoner take up', collecting the food from the tables, starting with the servants and progressing upwards in rank. The almsdish was made up of such foods as had been served to the lord, 'that is the hole standart of beof on the flesh daies and on the fisshe daies in like maner the lynge and codd and parte of other meates at his discretion', and taken to the gate for distribution.[109]

The special plates or dishes designated for alms were elaborate productions. Richard, tenth Earl of Arundel (d. 1376), bequeathed to his son, Thomas, later Archbishop of Canterbury, a great charger for alms, gilt and engraved, with eight bezants enamelled with various coats of arms and in the middle enamelled with the arms of Warenne.[110] Sir John Fastolf had a substantial silver almsdish, weighing 132 oz.[111] One genre that had particular popularity was a miniature ship, or *nef* (Plate 5). In 1324, Edward II possessed a great *nef* of silver, with a

63. Swan mazer, Corpus
Christi College,
Cambridge, second half
of the fourteenth
century.

64. The King John Cup, *c.* 1340, a covered cup of
silver gilt and enamel, with later alterations and
additions, is the earliest English secular medieval cup to
survive. The elaborate decoration shows scenes of
hunting and hawking. It is probable that very little of
the enamel is now original.

65. Richard Beauchamp, the epitome of courtesy, eating with the King of France and other lords, on Whitsunday. The chamber has a tiled floor. There are two well-dressed servants: a cupbearer, with a covered cup; and a carver. In addition there is a herald or marshal in the French King's coat of arms. From the Beauchamp Pageant, *c*. 1483–7.

gold castle at each end, and four wheels,[112] which may in turn have been the wheeled alms *nef* that belonged to Queen Isabella, repaired in 1311–12.[113] Alms *nefs* were to be found among the goods that Princess Joan proposed to take with her to Spain in 1349 and among the possessions of Humphrey de Bohun, Earl of Hereford (d. 1322), Elizabeth de Burgh and William of Wykeham.[114]

Ornamental salts also graced the table. Edmund Mortimer, Earl of March (d. 1381), had a group of gilt salts, two in the shape of a dog, which he left to his son, Roger, and his daughter, Elizabeth; and one, in the shape of a lion, left to his son, Edmund.[115] Among Sir John Fastolf's goods at Caister in 1448 were four salts – two round gilt salts, adorned with a wreath on top and his motto, and two smaller ones, engraved with a double rose and his arms. After his death, the inventory of his plate included two great salts, both shaped like towers and both of silver gilt, one weighing 86 oz., the other 77 oz.[116]

Alongside the salts and bread, knives and spoons were among the first items set on the table.[117] In terms of cutlery, it was usually only these last two items that were present (Plate 53). These items were shared at table, provided by the lord for his guests. It was, however, usual for most people to carry knives. Table-knives may appear as a distinct form in the early fourteenth century, with longer blades and decorated handles.[118] It was probably table-knives that Queen Eleanor of Castile had re-enamelled in September 1288.[119] Sheaths for knives, probably for use at table, were purchased for Eleanor de Montfort in 1265; and collections of sheaths or scabbards from excavations in London show heraldic decoration from the late thirteenth century onwards.[120] Other types of knives, for carving, cutting and paring bread, would have been seen at table.

Silver spoons are mentioned comparatively frequently and were much less expensive than many items of tableware. Eleanor de Montfort had four repaired in 1265 with eight silver pennies;[121] Nicholas Longespee bequeathed 28 to his chamberlain in 1297;[122] and there were 15, worth 20s., in the pantry and buttery of Sir Edmund Appleby in 1374.[123] They were occasionally paid as a rent, perhaps connected with household service or serjeanty. In 1301–2, Peter of the Hall (de la Sale) of Havant owed the Bishop of Winchester two silver spoons per annum or 2s. 4d.[124] Forks did not appear as table utensils in medieval England, with the rare exception of use with preserves and confections. Piers Gaveston's silver forks were used for eating pears; John II, Duke of Brittany, used his for eating sops; and the silver fork forfeited along with the London goods of Henry Le Scrope of Masham in 1415 was for use with green ginger.[125]

How was the meal served? A fragment of a treatise on household organisation of the first half of the fourteenth century is interested in functional matters, matters of accounting, and avoidance of waste and peculation, to ensure the distribution of food to those to whom it was assigned at the dresser, and to make sure no alms were carried out of the hall without the almoner.[126] Matters of portion control, keeping account of the meals served, remained important.[127] That matters of ceremonial, courtesy and precedence are not mentioned does not mean they were unimportant, but that the emphasis was different later. The fifteenth century recorded the same events with a wholly different character, in a detailed choreography of movement, with social gradation marked at every step.

That many of the practices of the fifteenth century were well rooted in earlier years can be seen from the evidence for washing at meal times. Around 1326–7, Walter de Milemete wrote a treatise on good government for presentation to the new King, Edward III, along with a copy of the pseudo-Aristotelian *De secretis secretorum*.[128] While Milemete's treatise centred on good government and kingship, the advice of Aristotle to King Alexander the Great added much on the overall conduct expected of a wise prince – and the accompanying illustrations are important evidence for the customs of the household (Plate 5).[129] It included advice on eating habits, when to sleep in relation to food, what foodstuffs to consume in particular seasons. The king was shown washing his hands immediately before going to eat, attended by a servant holding a ewer and another holding a basin, while another servant arranged the table (Plate 66).[130] In *Sir Gawain and the Green Knight*, later in the fourteenth century, at Sir Bertilak's castle, Gawain had a table set up in his room and laid. He sat down to eat, having washed his hands – without any apparent ceremony.[131] The *Boke of Curtasye*, of the 1430s or 1440s, however, treats the matter at considerable length, filling most of five pages in the printed edition.[132]

A view of the meal itself – but with no account of the preparations, such as laying the table, or washing – comes from the first half of the thirteenth century, in Robert Grosseteste's 'Rules'. The pantler with the bread and the butler with

66. Walter de Milemete's manuscript of *De secretis secretorum*, presented to the future Edward III, *c.* 1326–7, includes advice on dining. The king stands on the left washing his hands, with an attendant holding a blue basin and another pouring from a blue ewer. Outside the frame, another servant prepares the table.

the cup were to come together side by side in front of the lord at table before grace. Three valets were to be designated by the marshal each day to serve drink at the high table and the two side-tables. No ale container was to be placed on the table but under it. Wine was to be placed on the side-tables only – but at the high table, both wine and ale were to be under the table, except for the lord, whose drink was to be placed in front of him, probably in a costly vessel, well positioned for display. The marshal or steward was to keep order in hall. At each course (*mes*), he was to call the servers to go to the kitchen – there is no mention of an intermediary stage for gathering together the food for distribution, at a dresser or serving area – and he was then to precede the steward to the lord and to stay there until his food was placed in front of him. This done, he withdrew to the middle of the other end of the hall. His task was then to oversee the servers bringing in the food for the two side-tables, taking it to those to whom they were assigned, so that it was distributed without favouritism. The lord was also to watch for this. At lunch, for the free (or gentle) part of the household, two principal courses were to be served and two *entremets*, intervening courses, of a different and probably delicate nature. At supper, there was to be one lighter course and one *entremets*, to be followed by cheese. Strangers, at supper, were to have whatever they needed. The lord was to ask that his dish be refilled and heaped – especially of *entremets* – so that it could be shared both to left and right throughout the high table and elsewhere.[133]

The form of the meal developed in the subsequent centuries. There were attempts to control the amounts of food eaten in households, in total and by rank. The amounts set as acceptable, both at a time of famine in August 1315, and, in 1336, in rather different circumstances, were nearly identical, although in 1315 there were additional injunctions aimed at controlling growing numbers of minstrels and so-called messengers, whose main motive was to acquire food.

Under the statute of 1336, no meal might be served of more than two courses. Each was to have no more than two types of food, be it fish or meat, with soups. If a sauce was needed, it was not to be a costly one, and if fish or meat was to be put in it, then it was to take the place of a *mes*. The only exceptions to this were the great feast days, when three courses might be served.[134] There is good evidence that England in 1336 – or at least the Crown – was quite impoverished. With foreign expeditions in view, royal expenditure on clothing was limited and Crown jewels had to be pledged as security for loans, but the harvest that year had been good, equally that of 1337, and there was no general dearth.[135] Although the statute alleged the less wealthy had been forced to use the rich as a model and had been greatly impoverished as a result, behind it lay both the desire of the rich to maintain their status and shrewd opportunism on the part of Edward III to restrict consumption, leaving funds available for taxation to finance his claim to the French throne.[136] The implication of the legislation was that more than two courses were now usual.

By the fifteenth century, the normal service of a meal, lunch or supper, was three courses (excluding *entremets*), with fruit, followed by spices to conclude. At the marriage feast of Henry IV at Winchester in 1403, there were three courses, probably with fruit as a fourth.[137] Specimen menus in John Russell's *Boke of Nurture* have three courses followed by a course of fruit on both a flesh day and a fish day.[138] Other fifteenth-century menus for banquets frequently gave three courses for the principal parties, although fewer might be offered to those of lesser status. The sumptuary legislation of 1363, for example, restricted grooms to one meal of meat or fish a day, with other foods, cheese, butter, milk, according to their estate. More generally, those who were worth less than 40s. were not to eat and drink excessively, in a manner above their station.[139]

Food was served in messes, the units in which it was convenient to prepare it. Many messes were designed for a number of people, often four, to share, although some smaller dishes were prepared on an individual basis.[140] The messes, or individual dishes, were grouped together to form courses. Courses were arranged in a fashion that combined elements of the sequences in which food is now eaten, one dish at a time (*service à la russe*), and of the bringing together of many dishes to the table, the pattern which prevailed, for example, in France from the seventeenth to the nineteenth centuries (*service à la française*). In general terms, the first course (which was all that many members of the household received) usually contained the boiled and most substantial meats; the second course, the roasts and other foods cooked in the oven, reserving fried foods and other delicacies for the last course (Table 9). Certain things were served either 'out of course' or after dinner, for example spices and hypocras or other wine.[141] The service of fish was broadly similar, starting with sprats, red herring, white ling, salted salmon and other salted fish including all fried, salted fish;

and folowyng þem all rever fyshe aftur as þey bethe of deynte and in gretnesse; and next folowynge all maner of pole fyshe and þen all maner of rostid fyshe,

Table 9. The structure of the menu: the feast to mark the enthronement of John Chandler as Bishop of Salisbury, *c.* 1417

Each course begins with its soups. There is a progression from boiled, to roast, to delicate meats. Subtleties (formerly *entremets*) conclude each course.

First course (including boiled meats)	*Second course (including roasted meats)*	*Third course (including fried meats and delicacies)*
Furmenty with venison	*Vyaund ryal* (sweetened and	*Mammenye ryal* (probably
Vyaund cyprys (wine, with	spiced wine, thickened	minced poultry in almond
sugar and spices, thickened	with rice flour)	milk and/or spiced wine)
with flour, and ground	*Blandyssorye* (a white soup,	*Vyand* (probably a soup)
chicken or pork)	with almond milk and	Bittern
Boiled capons	ground poultry)	Curlew
Swan	Piglets	Pigeon
Pheasant	Kid	Young rabbits
Peacock	Crane	Plovers
Pomys en gele (minced meat-	Roast venison	Quails
balls in jelly)	Heronsews	Larks
Un lechemete (a sliced meat)	Stuffed poussins	*Vyaunt ardant* (with spirits)
Tart royal	Partridge	*Un lechemete*
A subtlety: Agnus dei	*Un leche* (possibly a tart)	*Frytourys lumbard* (fritters or
	Crustade ryal (a sort of	filled pastries)
	quiche, with an egg-based	*Payn puffe* (a filled pastry)
	filling)	Jelly
	A subtlety: a leopard	A subtlety: Aquila

Source

Two fifteenth-century cookery-books ed. T. Austin (EETS, OS, 91; 1888) pp. 60–1.

what so ever þey bee; and þen folowyng all maner of shell fysshe; and folowyng þem all maner of bake metes, be it fishe or doucetes; . . . and laste of all, all maner of leche metes and metes of deynte.[142]

A second development in the regime of food courses was that *entremets*, which were in large part edible delicacies in the time of Grosseteste and later,[143] concluding each course, became more elaborate confections, ceasing to be edible and taking on a political or allegorical character, subsequently even including live performers. Each course of Henry IV's 1403 marriage feast concluded with a subtlety, as *entremets* had become known. By 1501, at the marriage of Prince Arthur to Katherine of Aragon, subtleties had developed into separate dramatic productions.[144] At the same time, the preparation of food emphasised the differentiation between groups within the household. Gold foil was used to decorate food, at least for the most distinguished in the household, for example during the New Year festivities in the household of Anne Stafford in London in 1466.[145] The development of carving was aimed particularly at meats reserved for the lord's table, for the service of game and ornamental birds, such as peacocks or swans, or at fish of similar quality.[146]

The food and the diners did not arrive all at once. A treatise of the second half of the fifteenth century, describing the order of service for an earl's household, with the earl eating in his great chamber and two sittings for others of the household in hall, shows that there was a good deal of preparation of the rooms before the meal. This included laying the table and taking assays, as well as bringing the food for the meal in readiness. It was only at this time that the gentleman usher, with the gentlemen waiters, went to the earl to let him know that the food was ready to serve. At this point the most senior household staff, the steward and the controller, were in the great chamber in readiness. The lord then washed and grace was said by the almoner. Next, the lord sat in his chair at table; and those who were to sit at the reward at his table were seated there on stools and place settings brought for them. At a second table – the knights' board – were then seated gentlewomen of presence and gentlemen ushers, that is those of the degree who served the earl's table. This table was served by yeomen of the chamber who, in turn, were seated at another table, outside the great chamber (and probably in the hall), along with chamberers and ladies' gentlewomen, served by grooms of the chamber. At this stage the second course of the meal was brought through the hall, with due reverence, on its way to the great chamber. The conclusion of each course (the void, or taking away of the course) and the meal, and the dismantling of the tables, took place in reverse order to its setting down. The earl was the last to rise, having received courtesies from all. The almoner said a concluding grace and the earl washed. At this point musicians arrived and the room was given over to dancing. A similar progression took place in the hall, although it was the intention that the meal in hall, or at least the first sitting, should be completed within the time taken for the meal in the great chamber. The head officers of the household took the principal places in the first meal in hall. The second sitting was reserved for those who served at the first session.[147]

Bread, ale and wine were distributed on the tables. It was the duty of the almoner to see that all were amply served, so that there would be a good measure for alms. In 1445, in the household of Henry VI, every mess in hall was to have a loaf, every two messes a gallon of ale at lunch and every three messes a gallon of ale at supper. At both meals, every three messes of gentlemen were to have half a pitcher of wine and every five messes of yeomen, half a pitcher; grooms and chamberlains were to have none.[148] The allowances were presented more generously in 1478, in a way which demonstrates how many individuals partook of a mess. Every two persons in hall were to have a loaf, every four men a gallon of ale, every three men a mess from the kitchen. On feast days and whenever else it was thought appropriate, every two messes of gentlemen (six people) were to have half a pitcher of wine and every three messes of yeomen (nine people) half a pitcher of wine. Rewards of bread, wine and ale were additional.[149] In the establishment of the Duke of Clarence, in 1468, there was a loaf between two people, eight were to share a gallon of ale, with additions ('sufficyauntlye rewarded') as need be; and four people were to share a mess from the kitchen.[150]

Figure 5. Table layouts

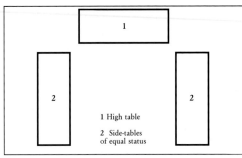

(i) *c.* 1240–2, in hall. *Source*: WH, pp. 402–7.

1 High table

2 Side-tables of equal status

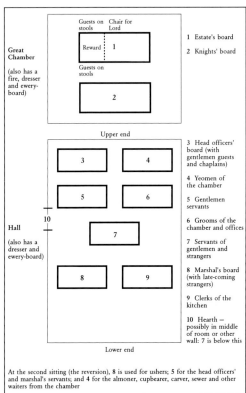

Great Chamber

(also has a fire, dresser and ewery-board)

Guests on stools   Chair for Lord

Reward : 1

Guests on stools

2

1 Estate's board

2 Knights' board

Upper end

3

4

5

6

10

7

Hall

(also has a dresser and ewery-board)

8

9

Lower end

3 Head officers' board (with gentlemen guests and chaplains)

4 Yeomen of the chamber

5 Gentlemen servants

6 Grooms of the chamber and offices

7 Servants of gentlemen and strangers

8 Marshal's board (with late-coming strangers)

9 Clerks of the kitchen

10 Hearth – possibly in middle of room or other wall: 7 is below this

At the second sitting (the reversion), 8 is used for ushers; 5 for the head officers' and marshal's servants; and 4 for the almoner, cupbearer, carver, sewer and other waiters from the chamber

(ii) Late fifteenth century. *Source*: BL MS Harley 6815, ff. 29r-33r.

Lord

③ ③   1   ③ ③
                   ②   ②

Upper end or reward

1 Trencher, napkin, spoon, knife, under a cloth

2 Salt

3 Trencher

Other tables laid for two messes each, with four loaves at each end of the table

(iii) Mid-fifteenth century: the lord's table. *Source*: MM, pp. 130–1.

67. The Black Book of the household of Edward IV, transcribed by Sir Simonds D'Ewes, with one of two drawings he asserted he copied from the fifteenth-century original, showing the space between the King and other members of his household. On the table dormant are trenchers and covered cups. The King has a chair of state; his almoner, a bishop, is seated to his right.

In order to prepare bread for service, it was pared of its hard crusts (which had helped to preserve it), leaving the crumb. John Russell expected the pantry to be equipped with three knives, one to chop or slice the loaves, the second to pare them, the third 'sharpe and kene to smothe þe trenchurs and square'.[151] Only the bread for the lord and his table was pared in the household of the Duke of Clarence, *c.* 1468; that for others was chipped, which may indicate that not so much was cut off.[152] Just as his trencher, napkin, spoon and knife were concealed by cloth, the lord's bread was wrapped and placed on the table to be opened in front of him.[153] Bread was brought from the pantry in a port-pain, or cloth, and set on the other tables. Russell's tables probably had eight diners each, with four loaves to be set at each end of the table.[154] The service of the meal continued with drink and food. In the most elaborate cases, there was a division of labour: it was brought from the kitchen or the cellar by one group of servants, but set on the table by another, in the late fifteenth century by gentlemen waiters.[155] All messes of the course were placed on the table together, then taken one by one by the servers and offered to those eating. The soups in each course were eaten while other food was being carved.[156] Service was traditionally made on bent knee (Plate 4).

The descriptions of the service of meals provide some evidence for further changes in etiquette and formality, setting out who might sit by whom. Bishop Grosseteste's dining arrangements were comparatively simple. At the top table,

68. The disciples prepare to eat: a picnic, with a tablecloth spread on the ground, fish in bowls, knives and round loaves. Jesus declines, as he has eaten a meat that is unknown to them. From the Holkham Bible picture book, *c.* 1320–30.

he was able to distribute food from his *entremets* to both left and right: these fellow diners were close to him. With the withdrawal of the lord from hall, to more intimate surroundings in the great chamber, space assumed a greater significance. Not only was access to the great chamber a test of status, but to endow individuals with more space in a restricted area emphasised their distinction. At the same time, books of courtesy identified more closely the groups that sat at increasing numbers of tables, especially in the hall (Figure 5).

When Leo of Rozmital visited the court of Edward IV in 1465, he dined in hall in the absence of the King. The guests ate together with the greatest nobles, apart in hall, and Leo sat at the King's table. The King was represented by one of his greatest earls and Leo sat 'at the same table only two paces from him. No one else sat at that table.' The service, in terms of carvers, dressers and side-tables, was said to have been the same as if the King had been present. Rozmital's account of the feast to celebrate the churching of Queen Elizabeth Woodville records her sitting alone at table, on a costly gold chair. Her mother and her sister-in-law had to stand some distance away, sitting down only after the first dish was set before her. All the servants knelt as long as she was eating: the meal is said to have lasted three hours, not untypical in the usual order of meals at this time.[157]

The Luttrell Psalter's sequence of illustrations of *c.* 1320–45 underscores the differences of fifteenth-century service and dining. The preparation of meat for the table was done by the cook, with a cleaver: this was not carving by a gentle servant. Likewise, wine was poured into bowls at a side-table in the same area, not at a cupboard covered with a fine cloth for all to see (Plate 52). The diners at high table are seated close together, side by side (Plate 53). In the 1480s, Richard Beauchamp, Earl of Warwick, was depicted eating on Whitsunday with the King of France, a mirror of courtesy, where Beauchamp 'so manerly behaved hymself in langage and norture that the Kyng and his lordes with all other people gave hym greet lawde'. This was a meal in a chamber, with a cupbearer and carver at the table, as well as a herald and possibly another servant at the board-end (Plate 65). An illustration of King Edward IV at table (Plate 67) shows a fixed table, the King under a canopy of estate, with little on the table, except trencher platters and possibly salts or cups. Besides the King, three individuals and a bishop are seated – the bishop to the King's right, at the upper end of the board, much as outlined by the 1493 ordinances, and with a great deal of honorific space between them and the King.[158] The use of the lord's right-hand side for the seating of clerics may have had a longer (and perhaps biblical) tradition (Plate 53).

The formalities of these meals might, however, be diminished in certain circumstances. The hall or great chamber was not the venue for all meals. Picnics, or fêtes champêtres, were popular. In August 1465, the household of Anne Stafford paid for the carriage of food for lunch from Writtle to the lodge in Horsefrithpark (Plate 68).[159] This, in part, must have been a regular use of many of the hunting lodges of medieval England.[160] Equally, however, it was the nature of the occasion that determined the formality: a meal for the lord, even in a tent, might be served with all the pomp expected in the great chamber.[161]

Despite the opportunity for open-air diversion at some meals, by the fifteenth century the formality of the meal and its service provides further evidence for the scale of the commitment made to social competition by the great household. The elaborate ritual and the specialised servants that accompanied it had developed from more general practice. The length of time taken at meals, in their preparation and service, from the foodstuffs reserved for the lord to the political messages of *entremets*, from the quality of the table linen to the splendour of the plate on the buffets, all represented a significant investment, an elaboration of the purpose of the household beyond the honour and profit of the lord, to a statement of his magnificence. The quality of the establishment, however, might also be judged by much that was less overt. It is therefore important to consider some of the intangible aspects of life in the great household.

CHAPTER 8
The Senses, Religion and Intellectual Life

Smell, sound, sight, touch and taste may seem difficult to gauge at historical distance, but there is a good deal of evidence to show how responses of pleasure or repugnance to their manifestations – cleanliness, dirt, noise – were viewed in the great household and how its routines were organised to effect certain standards in daily life. Medieval ideas of what was clean, what was dirty or unfit for consumption, what was beautiful or displeasing, are some way removed from our own. Our drive for cleanliness is associated with hygiene. Upon the fastidious of medieval England, honour and status made the same demands. To cover food or drink was a mark of the recipient's status, likewise to wrap it. The effect was to promote hygiene – but that was incidental. Wrapping the lord's bread, advised John Russell's *Boke of Nurture* in the mid-fifteenth century, was a mark of honour; his injunctions to have the pots for ale and wine exceptionally clean and to look out for flies were concerns not just with cleanliness, but with appropriate standards for the lord's house.[1] There was a litany of personal behaviour best eschewed: not to scratch as if after a flea, or to pick one's head as if 'for a flesche mought [louse]', 'put not youre handes in youre hosen youre codware for to clawe', not to cough or spit, not to put fingers in the cup. The servant was to

> Be glad of chere, curteise of kne & soft of speche,
> Fayre handes, clene nayles, honest arrayed, y the teche.

This was a matter of courtesy, encompassed in general directions for behaviour: a dirty servant was no more credit to his lord than an ill-dressed or ill-mannered one.[2]

There is a psychology to cleanliness, that what looks clean is clean, that what smells good is good. A strong but pleasant smell might be used to overcome less pleasant ones, without removing their source. It is all a matter of perception: we purchase scented disinfectants, although their efficacy may be no different from those that do not smell as agreeable. Herbs and spices were used by the medieval household to generate these smells, to ensure that napery, for example, was not only fair and clean but also sweet, that is having a pleasing smell.[3] Curiously, however, in the context of food smell and taste were not frequently discussed. Spices in cooking must have had a considerable impact, but it was only in the case of foodstuffs that were difficult to prepare, such as crustacea, that explicit mention was made of smell. Crab, which had to be reheated after carving, was spiced beforehand: '. . . Cast þer-on powdur, the bettur it wille smelle.'[4]

Henry of Grosmont recorded how he delighted in smelling flowers, fruits and women, even scarlet cloth, but recoiled from the offensive odour of the sick and the poor.[5] Personal cleanliness was a mark of gentility. Its associated smells disguised human and other odours.[6] To this end, the ritual of the upper-class day placed considerable emphasis on washing – before and after meals, on rising, on going to bed (Plate 66). The chamberlain was always to be ready with water and towel for his lord, after sleep or visiting the lavatory.[7] Even if vessels used for washing were shared in the hall, those used by the lord and his family were personal. Richard, Earl of Arundel (d. 1397), bequeathed to his wife, Philippa, vessels for her ewery including a pair of ewers and a pair of basins which she was accustomed to use for washing before lunch and supper.[8] Separate, equally personal, arrangements were made for washing hair. Henry III had a wardrobe at Westminster in which his head was washed.[9] Humphrey de Bohun, Earl of Hereford (d. 1361), left to his sister, the Countess of Devon, the brass basin in which he used to wash his head and which had belonged to their mother.[10] Preparations for washing hair included spices. In September 1501, the chamber-servant of Edward, third Duke of Buckingham, purchased cinnamon, licorice and cumin for washing his master's head.[11] Strong-smelling spices, including ambergris and nutmeg, were worn on the person in scent- or must-balls.[12] Spices, probably in bags, were kept with clothing, linen and in bedding;[13] in bathing, they were used as a herbal infusion and in conjunction with the sheets that might be hung around the bath.[14]

Bathing took place frequently. A payment made to the servant who arranged the bath, as a special fee, almost certainly represented a series of baths, not one occasion. Thus Eleanor de Montfort, in 1265, paid Roger of the Chamber on two occasions probably for a series of baths at Odiham.[15] Joan de Valence's bath was repaired in October 1295, but there is no mention of payments to servants for its use.[16] The bath was a wooden vessel, like a vat, bound with hoops (Plate 69), although some examples may have been sheathed with copper. In the *Boke of Nurture*, the chamberlain was to ensure that there were half a dozen sponges in the bath, including a large sponge on which the lord was to sit. He was then to wash his lord using a sponge and basin full of herbs 'hote & fresche', rinsing him with warm rose-water.[17]

Royal bathing arrangements at Westminster in the reigns of Henry III and Edward I included water supplies from a cistern to the chambers of both the king and queen – there were separate bathrooms for each – and, in 1351–2, separate taps for hot and cold water.[18] Elsewhere hot water was carried to the bath. Other refinements of royal bathing included a canopy for the bath, partitioning off the bathing area, as well as mats for stone and tiled floors.[19] Henry of Grosmont wrote of the benefits of sweating – presumably in some form of

69. The Virgin attending a holy woman standing in a bath, possibly intended to be the Virgin bathing in preparation for her death bed. The bath is constructed of staves and bound with iron hoops. From the Luttrell Psalter, *c.* 1320–45.

steam room – after a bath. The bath-water itself, if possible, was to be running and tepid, like the water that ran from Christ's side.[20] In this vein, in the reign of Henry VIII, the royal bath made a transition to something more akin to a Turkish bath.[21]

Soap was frequently used for personal washing,[22] purchased by the loaf or cake.[23] Other items associated with personal hygiene included toothpicks and implements, possibly straws, with silk loops attached, for cleaning ears.[24] It was the duty of body-servants to help the lord or lady get clean, dress and prepare themselves. Hair was combed with ivory combs (Plate 43).[25] Barbers were bought in, or retained, for shaving the lord.[26]

For clothing and linen to be clean and smell pleasant, there had to be satisfactory laundry arrangements. Joan de Valence made an allowance of 12d. three times a year to her washerwoman for ashes and the hire of pots.[27] Her functions, like those of many others of her sort, were largely confined to napery and linen.[28] In 1465–6, when in residence at Writtle, Anne Stafford paid Joan Sigore, her washerwoman there, at the rate of 4d. a week, and 2d. a week when she was away; but the expenses of her laundry in London were greater, and there Rose Vernon received 1s. a week for washing her napery.[29] The laundry required fuel for hot water, as well as wood-ash itself.[30] In the household of Edward IV, the ewery, napery and laundry were to ensure the linen was clean, that there were clean basins and pure water (assayed as often as the king was served); and the linen was not to be handled by strangers. Washing used white, grey and black soap, drawn from the Great Spicery, as well as ashes from the chambers and kitchens of the court.[31]

It was quite impractical, however, to wash many medieval garments. Usually only linen and unlined garments, such as shirts, were washed.[32] How often was linen clothing washed? John Russell's chamberlain in the mid-fifteenth century was expected to produce clean linen underclothes when the lord dressed (and probably on each occasion): 'Se that youre soverayne have clene shurt & breche.'[33] In practice, linen may not have been changed that frequently. Anthony Woodville and Edmund Berners, the two henchmen who attended the Duke of Buckingham in London during the summer of 1501, together had 11 shirts washed between 3 July and 21 August, a period of eight weeks, with a further six in the next three weeks, that is a shirt a week each at the very most. The details of the Duke's washing suggest more frequent changes of linen, with 16 shirts, six head-kerchiefs and five pairs of linen sheets washed for the seven-week period ending on 11 September.[34]

It was difficult to clean woollens and silks, as well as composite garments, with linings, decoration and furs. Light sponging would remove some stains and a heated iron spoon was used to remove wax, possibly in conjunction with an absorbent cloth.[35] John Russell recommended that woollen garments in the wardrobe be brushed and shaken at least once a week to avoid damage by moths, and that other garments and furs be checked.[36] Other protection for goods in the wardrobe was given by nets.[37] In storage in the royal wardrobe garments were hung on cords.[38] In smaller households, garments might be stored in rooms used for other purposes: Henry de Vere of Great Addington (d. 1493) had his clothes kept in the parlour chamber.[39] The use of fumigants or strong-smelling 'swete flowres, herbis, rotez' countered insect infestation and made garments smell pleasant.[40] Furs could be detached from garments, partly for cleaning purposes and partly for reuse or replacement. Richard Derrant, a skinner, spent nearly a week at Penshurst in October 1501, furring two gowns for the Duchess of Buckingham, in preparation for their use over winter.[41]

As part of the preparations for the arrival of the household, it was usual to have buildings cleaned. Joan de Valence's return to Goodrich in September 1297 was marked by the cleaning of the castle and the purchase of rushes, the work of an advance party.[42] Despite a general move towards the commutation of labour services, in 1301–2 the customary works expected at Farnham were designed to facilitate arrangements for residence by the Bishop of Winchester and the King. Those continuing in force included the carriage of firewood to the castle and the duty of six of the lesser cottars to clean the castle buildings in anticipation of the Bishop's visits.[43] In the 1370s and 1380s, manorial works on the Bishop of Ely's manor of Wisbech were used in a similar fashion, to clean and prepare rooms in the castle in readiness for visits by the Bishop and his sister.[44] Aside from renewing the floor coverings, other routines included dusting with canvas cloths,[45] sweeping,[46] and, by the mid-fourteenth century, washing the building down with hot water to kill fleas – which must have been more effective on tiled and stone-flagged floors.[47]

Some of this work must also have taken place when a household resided at a single spot for a long period of time: the references to the renewal of rushes and other floor coverings suggest as much.[48] Bedstraw also had to be changed. In the household of Edward, Duke of York, at Hanley Castle, straw was bought for bedding in December 1409 and March 1410, which may indicate a three-monthly cycle of replacement.[49] This was an improved regime over, for example, Westminster Abbey, where, even though it might have happened more frequently, the thirteenth-century custom was that the straw should be changed at least once a year.[50]

Prolonged residence necessitated effective arrangements for the removal of household waste and rubbish from the kitchen and other departments, as well as the unpleasant task of cleaning latrines that emptied into cesspits rather than discharging into flowing water: few outside the monasteries were flushed in this way.[51] Garderobes were attached, increasingly, to the principal chambers of the residence. At Goodrich, not only did they appear here, but there was also a common battery of three, in the east range of the castle (Plate 70). Batteries of latrines were not unusual: Beaufort's works at Bishop's Waltham in 1441 included a common latrine with six seats.[52] In the sixteenth century, some latrines were partitioned off, with thin, matchboard divisions, as at the Tower of London, *c.* 1525.[53]

In 1354, Henry of Grosmont, writing of the joys of the heart of the Virgin, compared them to the cistern which received the water from the gutters around the roof and clarifed it, so the water became good and wholesome. His own heart was like an underground cesspit, collecting all the waste from the household by the gutters that came from the kitchen, the common chambers and garderobes; but just as the cesspit was below ground and its true awfulness could not be seen or sensed – that is, this was an effective way of preventing the smell extending through the household – his heart was covered by flesh.[54] Other devices to protect the household from the unpleasant smell of garderobes included the use of double doors and right-angled turns within the thickness of a wall to give access to the privy.[55] The lord's chamberlain was responsible for the maintenance of the sanitary arrangements in the chamber, looking after the chamberpot and the garderobe:

Se þe privehouse for esement be fayre, soote [sweet], & clene,
& þat þe bordes þer uppon kevered withe clothe fayre & grene,
& þe hoole hymself, looke þer no borde be sene,
þeron a feire quoschyn [cushion] þe ordoure no man to tene
Looke þer be blanket cotyn or lynyn to wipe þe neþur ende.[56]

If cleanliness was one mark of gentility, the visual magnificence of the great household was equally important as an indicator of its status. While the wardrobe (*garderoba*) in another guise, as a repository for clothing, would have supplied the blanket, cotton or linen for the privy, it was also the source of some of the most important visual messages in the household. Colour and signs had enormous importance in the Middle Ages as means of identification and understanding in a largely illiterate world. Their use in cloth and clothing deserves

70. The battery of three latrines in the east range of Goodrich Castle, Herefordshire.

particular examination, for clothing had an important part to play, not only for warmth and protection, but in transforming the household into a community identifiable on sight, for marking out groups within it on the basis of their social standing, and for providing the props for spectacle and pageantry.

It was no accident that King Arthur's court was at Camelot – camelot or camlet was, in origin, a silk, probably from the Middle East, of great value and magnificence, a quality well known to a medieval audience. Clothing could be a very exceptional item, consuming 10% or more of the expenditure of the great household.[57] Contemporaries were alive to the distinctions implicit in the high cost of some fabrics, with furs forming a greater expense but a more durable product. The most sumptuous materials were imported silks, such as velvets; but not all silks were so restricted in their use – samite, cendal and cindon, while luxurious, were more widely purchased. By the end of the thirteenth century, technological changes had the effect of increasing the amount of lesser-quality silks available. About this time, native woollen cloth began to include a higher-quality product. In all cloths there were distinctions in colour, with silk taking a range of dyes producing strong and striking hues; in texture, with weaving patterns producing different finishes; and there were differences in quality.

What were the typical garments? Clothes were thought of as 'suits' or *robe*. In the mid-fourteenth century each one might be composed of between four and six separate garments. Underclothes of linen were worn by both men and women, men's clothing consisting of an undershirt and braes or under-breeches (Plate 10), women's, solely of a long, linen undertunic or chemise. The principal garment worn over this by both sexes was a tunic or *cote* and, on top of that, an over-tunic or supertunic and perhaps a cloak and a hood. Hose of fine woollen cloth was worn on the legs, besides footwear. Garments were added or subtracted according to the season, with thicker cloths and furs in winter.[58] John Russell's chamberlain, helping his lord to get dressed, had for him a shirt and breeches, a petticoat (that is, an undercoat, a tunic), a doublet (a lined supertunic), a long coat or gown, hose, socks, shoes or slippers. The lord also wore a stomacher under his doublet. The chamberlain was there to lace or buckle his shoes, to pull up and tie his hose, to lace his doublet and to hand him his kerchief to go about his neck. His gown was then given to him, together with his belt, hood or hat. In the evening, the reverse procedure was followed, with the lord putting on a gown to keep him warm, a kerchief and a cap.[59] It was unusual to wear clothes in bed, although attire was available for those rising during the night.[60] Illuminations often depict individuals unclothed in bed (Plates 27 and 33), although sometimes they appear in their daytime garments.[61]

In the thirteenth century it was unusual outside the households of the royal family for new suits to be prepared for the lord and lady more than three times a year. The clothing was invariably purchased as cloth, then made up by the lord's own, or contracted, tailor. Its arrival was targeted on the most important feasts, frequently with two winter liveries, at All Saints and Christmas, with the winter clothing making full use of the addition of furs, and summer clothing prepared for Whitsun. The process was designed to produce new clothing, in pristine condition, for maximum effect at a limited number of great occasions in the year, when the household would have been at its busiest. The practice of shearing the cloth again (*retonsio*), particularly closely, would have had the effect of making it shiny, but for a short period only; likewise the quality of the colour may not have endured long. Thus Eleanor de Montfort, in early May 1265, purchased cloth for her Pentecost clothing. Along with the 9 ells of Parisian ray (a striped or banded cloth) for her own suit of summer clothes and the 6½ ells bought for her daughter, she acquired for herself and her daughter a single scarlet red cloth, doubtless of silk, from Lucas de Lucca, an Italian merchant in London, for the enormous sum of £8. 6s. 8d.[62] In 1295–7, Joan de Valence's purchases of clothing fell into two groups: small items, such as hose, shoes and boots, which were bought quite often, on an *ad hoc* basis, together with running repairs; and the major purchases of livery, which focused on winter clothing, prepared for All Saints and for Christmas, with summer clothing at Pentecost. Purchases for Joan's daughter-in-law, Beatrice de Nesle, included various small items, hose, shoes, buttons for her tunic and the costs of sewing linen garments,[63] as well as having clothes made for her, along with Joan, for All Saints 1296.[64]

The way servants were clothed varied in thirteenth-century households. In some a distribution of cloth or made-up clothing was offered; in others, there was a cash distribution instead, or a mixture of the two, as in the household of Bogo de Clare in 1286. Here 20 esquires were given livery at a cost of £31. 4s. 10d. in preparation for Whitsun, while other servants were given a cash sum. There was no single uniform for the household: the quality and quantity of cloth distributed varied from rank to rank, from distribution to distribution; but within rank there was frequently a unity of colour. Bogo de Clare's esquires were bought three cloths of scarlet ray and three of yellow cloth, together with furs and hoods of budge (lambskin). Bogo himself had bluet (blue cloth) and perse (dark-blue cloth), Master Gilbert of St Leophard also had perse, and both had fur and hoods of budge. The two knights had blue cloth of the same quality as Bogo, along with furs and hoods.[65]

Household livery may not have been worn all the time, or indeed for much of it, but it was the intention that it should be worn on great occasions and when the lord wished to make an effect.[66] At a later date, a man of substance might possess liveries from more than one lord. John Howard, later Duke of Norfolk, had made up for him a gown of the Duke of Clarence's livery in 1465 and, the following year, received cloth for a gown of the Earl of Warwick's livery.[67] Lower down the social scale, purchases were much less elaborate in terms of clothing, but still concentrated temporally. The immediate family of John Catesby had new clothing at Christmas 1392 and, in 1393, for the Purification, around Easter, for Corpus Christi, possibly something for the summer and in mid-October. While it is difficult to separate the costs of clothing from the accounts of the family as wool and cloth producers, at least £13. 12s. 4d. was spent on clothing and shoes for John, his wife, his two sons and his daughters, from receipts of about £109.[68]

Visual impact might also be achieved by variety of clothing. Among the knightly class the scope for this was limited. The contents of the wardrobe of Osbert de Spaldington, a knight of the royal household, at the end of the thirteenth century, contained only three complete suits of clothing, and parts of a few others.[69] The clothes of Henry de Vere, inventoried in 1493, ran to five gowns (two with furs of marten), a doublet of satin and a silk jacket.[70] In contrast, in the late thirteenth century it is probable that the King's clothes in the royal wardrobe numbered more than 100 garments.[71] The goods of Thomas, Duke of Gloucester, at his castle of Pleshey in 1397, included 45 gowns and other garments of good or high quality, besides pieces of material.[72] The wardrobe of Sir John Fastolf, at Caister in 1448, had 28 complete gowns, jackets and doublets, besides parts of others, and he had further clothing in London.[73]

More frequent acquisitions of clothing were common by the end of the fourteenth century. At the same time, the character of livery changed, with the addition of heraldic devices, colours or badges. In 1393–4, Roger Mortimer, Earl of March, had a gown made against the feast of St George and another for a tournament at Christmas, as well as livery for himself and his household at Christmas; but he also had clothes for other occasions, among them a magnificent dancing doublet and hanselin (jacket). This required 9 ells of white satin, extensive embroidery and silver gilt oranges, whelks and mussels fastened to the clothing, at a cost of at least £25. This was display that could only be seen in its detail at close quarters, by the restricted company that might approach close.[74] Cloth was selected carefully: the receiver general of the Earl of Devon and two colleagues made two journeys in 1392–3 to pick out his livery, £89 worth of cloth.[75] The quality of the tailoring was also worthy of remark. It was probably the protest of a Lollard that prelates had 'so greet multitude of meyne [household] of kny3tes, squyers, 3emen and gromes, myche more nyseli disgisid than any seculer lordis meyne'.[76]

While colour and rich clothing emphasised the position of the lord and the magnificence of his entourage, it was not English custom to change colour of clothing (aside from ecclesiastical vestments) to reflect seasons of the year, a pattern present in some continental establishments.[77] It was, however, the intention of sumptuary legislation, from the 1330s through to the early sixteenth century, to reinforce the distinctions of status embodied in clothing. In 1337, those who could spend less than £100 a year were forbidden the use of fur on clothing.[78] In the household, the difference between ranks would have been plain. The statute of 1363 defined the costs of materials and the accessories each rank might wear. Grooms, their wives and children were forbidden to use fabric that cost more than 2 marks a cloth, whether they bought it or it was bought for them; nor were they to use gold, silver, embroidery, enamels or silks; and their wives and daughters were not to use veils that cost more than 12d. At the upper end of the scale, knights and their families, with rents from 400 marks to £1,000 a year, might use ermine, lettice (a light grey fur) and cloth with jewels, except on headwear.[79]

The renewed interest of legislation in 1463, 1483 and 1509–10 matched the nice distinctions of precedence and courtesy developed contemporaneously to order other aspects of household behaviour. Additionally, the dignity of household service allowed senior domestic servants, particularly in the royal household, to wear clothing appropriate to a higher rank than they would otherwise have been entitled – increasing the magnificence of the establishment. In 1463, exceptions were made for royal household servants, the steward, chamberlain, treasurer and controller, and the carvers and knights for the King's body (and their wives), to allow them to wear sable and ermine. Exaggerations of fashion also went with status: no valet or person below this degree was to wear bolsters or stuffing for his purpoint (doublet), except the lining belonging to it; shoes with pikes more than two inches long were restricted to peers; and the use of embroidered materials was also closely controlled.[80] The legislation of 1483 reserved cloth of gold of silk or purple silk to the King, the Queen, the King's mother and the immediate royal family. No one below the rank of duke was to wear cloth of gold of tissue; and no one but a peer was to use cloth of gold or to wear any woollen cloth made outside England, Ireland, Wales and Calais, or any fur or sable.[81] The legislation of 1509–10 applied also to cloths used for horses.[82]

These distinctions can be seen in practice in the household of Isabella, Lady Morley. In 1463–4, she bought woollen cloth for the liveries of her servants. Cloths for her own personal use were bought separately: some may have been used for the two, possibly three, gentlewomen who attended her. Eleven bellies of miniver (dressed squirrel fur) were bought for her clothing. She also had Flemish linen and holland for her own use. Two other women residing with her, Anne and Emma Arundell, were clearly of rank, as the cloak that was made for

Anne was furred with 69 skins of grey pured (trimmed squirrel fur). In contrast, 6 ells of pightling, a coarse and cheap textile, were purchased for tunics for the poor.[83] The distinctions of rank were clear to onlookers: high quality and costly materials, with linings, embroidery and jewels, worn with costly accessories, together with the use of furs.[84]

While much could be done to establish the magnificence of a lord through a day-long round of ceremony, the display embodied in clothing, particularly in its decoration and quality, and in the further adornments of jewellery and personal ornament, made a substantial contribution. In cash value, personal ornament and jewellery could easily exceed that of the plate and cloth on display. The most important piece of Sir John Fastolf's jewellery was a rich collar with a diamond, known as 'the white rose', given to him by Richard, Duke of York, and reputedly worth 4,000 marks (Plate 71). He also had, from the same source, an ouch (a buckle or brooch) worth 500 marks. The value of these pieces is so great they can only be compared to Fastolf's investment in real estate. Caister, his castle in Norfolk, had cost Fastolf some £6,000 to build; his estates in East Anglia and Southwark he had purchased between 1415 and 1445 for a little

71. The Middleham jewel, second half of the fifteenth century, an engraved gold case, with the Nativity on one side and the Crucifixion, with a sapphire, on the other. High-quality jewels like this were worn attached to a necklace or collar.

under £14,000.[85] These jewels were perhaps exceptional outside the royal household, but they are indicative of the investment that might be made in items of personal ornament. At the same time distinctions of allegiance were made patent in the wearing of livery badges and collars, equally sometimes jewelled,[86] and in the wearing of colours (Plates 2 and 6).

* * *

If clothing and jewellery were visible proof of the magnificence of the household, its splendour might also be audible. Noise could both enhance and diminish status. On the one hand, music and drama were essential parts of entertainment and ceremonial; on the other, the clamour of meals in hall could degenerate to the uproar of a modern school lunch. The management of grooms at meal times was particularly aimed at controlling noise and riotous behaviour.[87] Personal noises were best not heard at meal times. Children were not to speak unless spoken to; they were to sit when told and were not to make gestures.[88] The meal could also be disturbed by 'noises off'. In the household of Edward IV the serjeants and masters of the household offices were to restrain the conversation of their juniors, let alone anything more enthusiastic, especially while the King dined.[89]

There is some fifteenth-century evidence that formal meals at court were held in silence.[90] The household of Cicely, Duchess of York, in the 1470s, followed the monastic pattern of readings during meals, her household ordinances suggesting that she might listen to the works of Hilton and Bonaventura.[91] Other fifteenth-century households permitted quiet conversation in hall, but no more than would allow the commands of the head officers to be heard by other staff. In the presence of the lord, conversation was to be restricted to the motions of quiet hospitality, so that he might speak as he wished with his guests and household.[92] Two centuries earlier, Bishop Grosseteste advised that there be no noise in hall and that those serving food do so silently, but probably in the expectation that there would be some conversation at least among the diners.[93] Music accompanying great feasts thus made a considerable contrast.[94] Outside the hall but within the household confines, there were the sounds of semi-industrial activities, a horse-mill for corn at Caister, a forge at Maxstoke and Writtle in 1452–3,[95] besides woodyards.[96] There was the noise of the animals and birds kept within the household; and there was the toll of bells announcing the hour and services in chapel.

* * *

The influence of another intangible, religion, was all pervasive in the medieval household, in its beliefs, its sounds, its smells and its personnel. Much of this has been discussed above as the motivation for many customs, the ritual year and the celebrations and commemorations of life. Here it is important to emphasise the role of the household as a religious community.

Clerical personnel were ever present in the household, to conduct services, to act as confessors, almoners and advisers, besides performing the more secular tasks of writing letters, administrative records and accounts (Plates 28 and 53). In larger households the clerks formed a substantial element. The servants of

Joan de Valence in 1295–7 included at least nine clerks or chaplains and one friar. Not all were employed primarily for their ecclesiastical talents. One chaplain was treasurer, resident not in the household but in London. Two others, Thomas the Chaplain and Ralph the Clerk, were probably household clerks or stewards, although the purchases of wax by the former may indicate a stronger connection with the chapel. John the Chaplain appears only in the context of his accounting responsibility and Philip the Clerk is noted once, buying dried fish and herring at Chepstow. Aside from these, the principal chaplain was probably Clement. He was present in the household for the main feasts, attended Joan and her husband at Bradsole Abbey in January 1296 and went to the Archbishop of Canterbury to have the seal of his late master broken in June 1296. John the Clerk drew half the footwear allowance of a valet on two occasions and departed to study at Oxford in January 1297. A full allowance for footwear was made to an unnamed clerk of the chapel throughout 1295–7. Milo the Clerk was probably foremost a messenger and negotiator. Brother Guydo is mentioned once, going to London on 30 April 1296; and the evidence of diet suggests the presence of other friars in Joan's household.[97]

During the fourteenth century, under the influence of the friars, particularly as confessors in many households, there was a growing emphasis on the personal in religion, on new liturgical feasts (first celebrated in private chapels), on the saints and religious objects, particularly reliquaries and images. The chapels of the lay upper classes became more individual in their conduct and more elaborate in their ceremonial. Private oratories became common in gentry households by the fifteenth century.[98] The household chapel of Henry VI, *c.* 1448–9, had 49 members: a dean, 30 cantors, half of whom were in priest's orders, 10 choirboys, a choirmaster and a master of grammar, a priest to read the daily Mass of the Virgin and another, the reader of the gospel at High Mass, besides a yeoman, a serjeant and two servants. Their functions, in contrast to continental royal chapels and those of lesser households in England, were almost exclusively liturgical or ceremonial.[99] Musical skills, both those of composer and performer, were highly prized. The composer, Lionel Power, had a place as master of the children of the chapel of Thomas, Duke of Clarence, in 1418–21; another composer, Thomas Farthyng, was the choirmaster of Lady Margaret Beaufort.[100] Robert Bygbroke, the organist and choirmaster of St Swithun's Cathedral Priory in Winchester, was poached in the 1430s by Cardinal Beaufort for his own chapel, much to the outrage of the Prior, who asked Beaufort to consider whether it was more fitting that Bygbroke should take his place among the nightingales of the Cardinal's wonderful chapel or among the rustics of the Cathedral Priory, who now murdered the psalms and lacked the sound of the organ.[101] The fifth Earl of Northumberland had nine gentlemen of his chapel – a master of the children, two tenors, four countertenors, one to read (or sing) the epistle and two for the organ – besides six children.[102]

The household had a number of physical settings for worship. At Goodrich, there was both a large chapel, adjacent to the gatehouse, and a small one, above the vestibule between the lord's accommodation and the hall. A fine chapel was an integral part of Warkworth as rebuilt by the Percies in the late fourteenth century.[103] Wykeham's works at Bishop's Waltham, in 1395, encompassed the oratory within his own accommodation; the works of his successor, Henry Beaufort, included the building of a new chapel, between 1416 and 1427, with minor alterations through the 1430s and early 1440s. In 1438, glazing was replaced in the chapel and in one window of the Bishop's oratory; the glass in the oratory was cleaned in 1441.[104] At Caister in 1448, the chapel was well equipped with service books – two antiphonaries, a legendary, two missals (one noted), a psalter, with silver clasps and the arms of Fastolf and his wife, and a martyrology. Its inventory included vestments and altar cloths, two crucifixes (one enamelled with the Virgin and St John and fleurs-de-lis, possibly a prize from France), a silver and gilt chalice, paxbread, and silver or silver gilt candle-sticks, cruets and sacring bell, as well as carpets and a French chair.[105] Portability was a prerequisite for chapel equipment, as it was for most household goods. In 1286–7 Robert Alward, clerk of the King's chapel, was paid for transporting the royal chapel to various places in France and preparing altars at the main feasts as well as an Easter sepulchre.[106]

Many among the aristocracy were strongly attracted to the religious life, to living in close association with a religious community. On one level, individuals resided within religious establishments. A succession of high-born women, including Mary, sister of Edward II, and Isabel of Lancaster, spent time at Amesbury, a house of the Order of Fontevrault, and were professed as nuns.[107] Others endowed religious communities.[108] Clerical staff, a daily round of liturgy and the maintenance of groups of poor within the household also created the possibility of turning household life itself into something akin to that of a religious foundation.

Most of the books in the household were closely associated with the religious arrangements of the chapel or personal devotion. Religious books fall into four principal groups: psalters; missals; primers, breviaries or books of hours; and other devotional works. Psalters, containing the text of the Psalms, well known from the elaborate productions of the thirteenth and fourteenth centuries (Plates 50–53), later declined in popularity. They were overtaken by primers or books of hours, in origin an elaboration of the psalter. To it was added the text of offices, such as the short office of the Virgin, and prayers – and eventually the psalter was omitted. These were among the earliest books effectively to be mass produced. This change mirrored the transition to a more personal religious devotion.[109]

The status of the psalter can be seen in a comparatively late reference, of 1475, to a volume which was subject to an arbitration agreement between William Stonor and his mother Jane. Jane Stonor was to have the volume during her life-time, but she was then to leave it to the chapel at Stonor for ever.[110] Missals were primarily for priests or chaplains celebrating the religious offices, rather than for personal devotion. Other service books appeared in the chapels of the great. Margaret, Duchess of Clarence, placed orders for two graduals for the chapel of her husband in 1418–21, at a cost of £7. 13s. 4d., besides the preparation and illumination of a great antiphonary for more than a further £5.[111] Psalters and missals were most commonly owned by men, whereas women more frequently owned primers or books of hours and often bequeathed them to other women.[112] In 1265, Eleanor de Montfort purchased 240 pieces of vellum for a breviary for her daughter Eleanor, which was written at Oxford under the supervision of a friar, G. Boyun.[113] On 18 August 1296, Joan de Valence, residing at Bampton, spent 9d. on having books for her chapel repaired at Oxford.[114] In 1388, Joan Catesby, the young daughter of John Catesby, was bought books containing the service of Matins (of the Virgin) for 2s. 6d.[115] Lay women, rather than men, owned devotional literature.[116]

Service books and religious works also had a prominent place in the collections of the royal household. In May 1288, Eleanor of Castile had lives of St Thomas and St Edward illuminated and covered. Other work was carried out later in the same year and in 1289–90, when she bought a psalter and seven primers.[117] Under Edward II, the collection of books in the Tower of London, possibly an early royal library, was the responsibility of John de Flete, the keeper of the Privy Wardrobe, 1324–41. He accounted for at least 67 liturgical books, but here there were other texts, including no fewer than 59 romances, either whole books or fragments.[118] Romances and histories, from the *Romance of the Rose* to *Bevis of Hamtun*, works of law and biblical and patristic texts featured in the library of Thomas of Woodstock at Pleshey in 1397, which numbered 84 volumes, besides nearly 40 books for the chapel.[119]

Other manuscripts themselves suggest association with particular households. Recent work on the localisation of BL MS Harley 2253, one of the most important collections of Middle English lyric verse, probably dating from the late 1330s, points to a strong connection with Ludlow and possibly with the Talbot family of Richard's Castle. The binding of the volume with pastedowns taken from an account of the household of Roger Mortimer, first Earl of March, may link the book's scribe, at an earlier stage in his career, with that establishment.[120] The ideals of chivalry and courtly love pervaded aristocratic and knightly society. The maid of Ribblesdale, the subject of admiration in the Harley lyrics, had red lips 'romances for to read'.[121] John de Multon of Frampton (d. 1368) concluded a letter, otherwise in French, to his wife possibly with a line of poetry: 'Have here my lovee and keppe it welle' – and two lyric poems found endorsed on a copy of a deed in his family archive show an interest in the poetry of courtly love, familiar from some of the contents of MS Harley 2253.[122]

Other interests were professional. At his death in 1303, Richard Gravesend, Bishop of London, had biblical, patristic and legal texts, a Bible in 13 volumes worth £10, with at least another 87 volumes, including a five-volume *Corpus juris civilis*, worth £20, the whole amounting to more than £116.[123] The household of Sir John Fastolf was keenly interested in literature. In 1448, his books at Caister included a French Bible, chronicles of France and England, works of Livy, Caesar and Lucretius, a book of geomancy and four books of astronomy, the *Romance of the Rose*, a Vegetius, a Justinian, a rhyming Brut, tales of King Arthur and an etiquette book, as well as works ascribed to Aristotle and St

Bernard.[124] Shortly after his return from France, around 1439, at Fastolf's request, his stepson Stephen Scrope (*c.* 1396–1472), who had a room at Caister, made an accomplished translation for him of Christine de Pisan's *Epistle of Othea*.[125] Another member of the household, Fastolf's secretary, William Worcester, was an author and antiquary, and also reworked one of Scrope's translations. Around 1438, he prepared astronomical tables on his master's behalf; and he may also have written a memoir of Fastolf, the *Acta domini Johannis Fastolf*, which no longer survives. A further four members of the household were authors.[126]

Large collections of books were, however, very unusual. Humphrey, Duke of Gloucester, who may have possessed about 1,000, and his brother John, Duke of Bedford, who acquired nearly 850 from the French royal library, were wholly exceptional: the collections attributed to them are much larger than that of their brother, Henry V. In many aristocratic households, books cannot have numbered more than a few dozen.[127] Original works by the aristocracy and knightly class are fewer in number. Foremost among them might be counted Henry of Grosmont, author of the *Livre de seyntz medicines*. Sir Thomas Gray, whose *Scalacronica* was compiled during his captivity in Edinburgh Castle in the 1350s, digested and abbreviated much material from the collections of chronicles he read there. Translators of note included Edward, Duke of York, who made his own additions to his translation of Gaston de Foix's work on hunting, and John Tiptoft, Earl of Worcester.[128] The upper classes were primarily consumers rather than authors, patrons whose tastes for de luxe manuscripts have left a lasting monument to medieval culture. The household also provided an important market for the earliest printers: books of courtesy, carving and household texts were a genre that sold.[129]

If they were not authors, the literacy and numeracy of the nobility and aristocracy should not be underestimated. It encompassed the ability to work with administrative and financial documents. The formal auditing of accounts might take place in the presence of the lord: in the fifteenth century, in the greatest households, they might be signed by him; in lesser households, he might write them himself.[130] Correspondences such as the Paston letters show that the gentry of the fifteenth century not only wrote for themselves but employed an array of clerks to do so on their behalf. Women at this level may have been less literate, in the sense that they may have been less able to write. At the same time, however, they had sufficient letters to enable them to read and to participate more widely in intellectual activity.[131]

The great household was a site of sensory and imaginative importance. Its inhabitants were alive to the distinctions of quality that might be perceived by smell, sight and sound, to links between cleanliness and gentility, between the wearing of furs or embroidery and a person's status, to the dignity implicit in the control of noise. At the same time, clerics within the household were a manifestation of common devotional expectations. Literacy linked the household to chivalric society and its ideals. Both consciously and subconsciously, the household and its members played a distinctive role in the culture of the later Middle Ages.

CHAPTER 9
Travel, Horses and Other Animals

For much of the medieval period, the great household was itinerant. One department, the marshalsea, was particularly charged with its transport, its horses and the associated tack and equipment, carts and coaches. At its head was a marshal or master of the horse. In the household of George, Duke of Clarence, in 1468, under the master of the horse there was a yeoman of the horse (to look after the daily needs of the horses and supervise the grooms), a clerk of the stable (to record the comings and goings of horses and grooms) and a clerk of the avenary (for the provision of oats).[1]

Almost everything in the great household was designed to be packed and moved. The goods taken by the household of Princess Joan, in 1348, for her prospective marriage to Pedro of Castile, were intended for travel, right down to two folding chairs, one to use while washing, the other while dressing.[2] In the largest households, those of the Crown, the departments had their own carts. Accounts contain many references to packing cases, to *males* (travelling bags, hence mailbag, now a bag for letters), coffers, hanapers, standards and chests. Special containers were made for some objects. The vessels Edward I gave the Prince of Salerno in 1287–8 were carried in two leather containers padded with 25 lb. of cotton.[3] Thomas of Lancaster had two containers of leather, bound with iron, made at Pontefract in 1318–19 for the carriage of silver dishes.[4]

There were three principal vehicles used by the great household, the cart (*carecta*), the wagon (*chariota*, sometimes *chara*) and the coach (*currus*).[5] In addition, the term *quadriga* is sometimes encountered: this refers to a vehicle customarily pulled by four animals, rather than a type of vehicle itself.[6] The cart was a two-wheeled vehicle, pulled by horses. It was available with a body in different lengths, short and long, both of which were used by households, drawn by as many horses as necessary (Plate 72).

Wagons, four-wheeled vehicles, were not commonly used in agriculture in England until the seventeenth century. By that time a number of technological improvements, beyond the moving fore-carriage (which appeared in the fourteenth century), had been made. They were used, however, by the medieval great household. Two of these vehicles were refitted to take the household equipment of the Earl of March from Hertfordshire to Scotland in 1378.[7]

Wagons were generally pulled by horses, harnessed in pairs.[8] They were cumbersome and often experienced difficulties, but these problems were exacerbated by their use for the heaviest loads, such as wine and other major provisions. Bishop Mitford's wagon was regularly pulled by seven horses and, on one occasion, when carrying salmon and iron from Bristol to Potterne, required in addition the hire of two yokes of oxen.[9] The households of both the Earl of Oxford, in 1431–2, and Sir William Mountford of Kingshurst, in 1433–4, sent their wagons to Stourbridge Fair for the bulk purchases.[10]

The coach was also a four-wheeled vehicle, in construction very much like a wagon. It was frequently decorated and well furnished, and it was often the conveyance used by the ladies of the household. Three cloths of gold were allocated in 1311 for cushions in the coach for the ladies of Queen Isabella.[11] In her will of 1355, Elizabeth de Burgh left her daughter, Elizabeth Bardolf, her coach with all the horse-covers, tapets, cushions and other things belonging to it.[12] The covering of the coach of the Duchess of Clarence, that went to Normandy with her in November 1419, was of velvet cloth of gold.[13] Coaches were often drawn by as many as five horses (Plate 73).

As well as vehicles, households made considerable use of sumpters, or pack-horses. A pack-horse was roughly half as effective at hauling as a cart: the loads carried were lighter but were moved with greater speed. They were used in particular for the carriage of less heavy items or precious goods and, at this date, little in the way of equipment was employed, beyond a sumpter-saddle and fastening.[14] When the household of the Bishop of Salisbury was at Potterne in 1406–7, the caterer took one of the sumpters with him when he went to market at Warminster or Salisbury; a sumpter also went to Southampton, for fish, and to Ramsbury, for swans for Christmas. The horse was equipped with a barehide, girths (and presumably a sumpter-saddle), but no other harness is mentioned.[15] Sumpters were often used for the carriage of fresh fish, as the quickest method of transport. The merchant's horse that was given bread each Saturday at Acton

72. The two-wheeled cart was the most common vehicle in agriculture and saw service provisioning the household, alongside the household wagon. This cart, from the Luttrell Psalter, *c.* 1320–45, is pulled by three horses, with one carter, assisted by two men pushing and one steadying the sheaves with a pitchfork. The wheels have corrugated iron tyres. Cart-horses were not as large as those that pulled the household coach.

73. A coach carrying four ladies of an aristocratic or royal household. The four-wheeled vehicle, with iron tyres on the wheels, has fixed axles: the front axle carriage does not swivel. It is pulled by five dexters harnessed in file, with one principal driver and a postilion. One of the ladies has a pet squirrel; another is being handed a small dog. The cloth inside the coach is decorated and the canopy on the outside is luxurious, probably of cloth of gold, stretched over hoops (or bails). The wooden body is painted, possibly carved, with a chest suspended under it. Three horsemen follow. From the Luttrell Psalter, *c.* 1320–45.

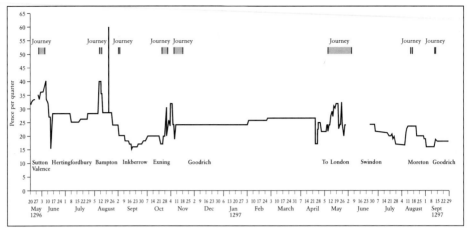

Figure 6. The costs of travel: Joan de Valence and the price of oats, 1296–7. *Source*: PRO
E101/505/25–7.

Hall, Suffolk, at the household of Dame Alice de Bryene, in 1412–13, almost
certainly brought the week's fresh fish on its back.[16] 'Rider' and 'dosser', words
used for the loads carried on a pack-horse's back, came also to mean measures
of fresh marine fish.[17]

In the household of Joan de Valence, there was a group of sumpter-horses,
belonging to different departments or having particular functions. The kitchen
sumpter required a saddle, halter and saddle-cloth during 1296–7; a new horse
for the kitchen was bought on 9 May 1297 for 6s. 8d.[18] There was a sumpter for
carrying Joan de Valence's bed[19] and probably one for the use of Joan's
chamber.[20]

Joan's household had two principal vehicles, a coach and a long cart. Both
were usually pulled by four horses, although sometimes five were used.[21] If the
horses were harnessed in file (Plate 73), the fifth gave extra traction; if they were
harnessed in pairs, the fifth might have been a shaft-horse, or wheeler, for extra
manoeuvrability.[22] Between December 1295 and September 1296, more than
17s. was spent on repairs to the coach, harness and grease.[23] A new coach was
acquired, at unknown cost, around 21 October 1296, in London: over 23s. was
spent collecting it. On its first major journey, from Inkberrow to Exning and
back to Goodrich Castle, it needed a further 2s. 0½d. on repairs and grease; 8d.
was then spent on getting a man from Gloucester to repair the wheels. Another
13s. worth of repairs were necessary between Christmas 1296 and February
1297. While at Goodrich, there was little need for the transport (and little space
for stabling horses at a busy season): the coach-horses were sent to Moreton
Valence on 13 December 1296 and remained there until 17 February 1297.[24]

The long cart was also in constant need of attention, with repairs to harness,
grease, nails and clouts always in requisition. A new long cart was bought on 9
July 1296 for 17s. 8d.[25] The real expense of the vehicles was, however, in the
costs of the horses and men that went with them, that is in the running costs,

not the capital costs. For example, in August 1296, the long cart, with five horses, two carters, Roger the Tailor and four other men assisting, went from Bampton in Oxfordshire to Goodrich Castle and back. The total expense for the four days was 10s. 10d.[26]

Unless a household moved constantly, it was not worth maintaining horses and equipment that were largely supernumerary. The consequence was that it was unusual for Joan to move residence without requiring assistance, either with hired carts and those borrowed from family manors, or with additional horses and equipment loaned by local magnates or monasteries. It must have been an impressive convoy that arrived at Goodrich Castle on 18 November 1296. Besides the coach and the long cart, there were three hired carts, one horse carrying silver, and another two carts belonging to the Abbots of Gloucester and Nutley. The previous day an additional horse had been hired to carry the vessels belonging to the buttery. The cart from the Valence manor of Chearsley had been damaged on the way, as had the cart of the Abbot of Nutley. The Inkberrow cart was paid off that day and returned to its manor from Gloucester with two carters.[27]

The loan of monastic carts was far from unusual. For the journey back towards Moreton Valence from Swindon and Cirencester in August the follow-ing year, both the Abbot of Abingdon and the Abbot of Cirencester loaned carts or men. For the move from Moreton to Goodrich around 12 September 1297, the Abbot of Gloucester loaned a groom and two horses and the Prior of Lanthony loaned two runceys and a groom.[28]

There was one other factor which served to enhance travel costs – the motor-way service station effect. The supply of oats and fodder was more expensive for the household on the move than for one based at a single location. For this reason horses often travelled with their own oats. The expenses of the sumpter that went to London from Joan de Valence's household around 24 July 1296, to get wax, amounted to 2d. 'and not more because it had oats with it'.[29] Joan de Valence was supplied with oats at a steady price while resident in one location, but as soon as the household moved, the costs increased (Figure 6). Her accounts also suggest that in 1296–7 oats were generally cheaper (probably because more plentiful) in the western Midlands and central England, and more expensive in the London area.

Why did travellers pay a raised price for oats? Although oats were fairly widely cultivated on demesnes in England, they were not usually grown for sale, but for consumption by the household. The amount available in the market was probably small – or made up of the surpluses of many small-scale producers – and more difficult to buy. The demands of the travelling household were sudden and substantial. It was perhaps for this reason that Bishop Grosseteste advised the Countess of Lincoln, *c.* 1240–2, not to have any of her oats sold or threshed before Christmas, but to keep them back until sowing time when she might get a better price for them.[30] If the movement of the Valence household, with five carts and sometimes as many as seven, was sufficient to create this effect – and this was a comparatively modest train – the impact of a household removal on the scale of the fifth Earl of Northumberland (who expected to use 17 carts, besides the household wagon) must have been enormous.[31]

A removal on the scale of Northumberland's household, however, would have been unusual in the early sixteenth century. The more the household had established residences, with some staff based permanently at them, the less materials and personnel needed to move between them. When, in 1501, the Duke of Buckingham moved to and from his London house at Queenhithe, he did so in the company of few individuals. On 21 August, he set out from London for Penshurst for three days, in the company of six yeomen (*valecti*), whose hackneys were hired for the occasion. Likewise, in London, if goods were lacking in the Duke's wardrobe, others, such as pewter vessels and cloths, could be hired. More occasional use was made of carting to transfer items between establishments. In January 1502, the Duke's cart brought two hogsheads of wine, spices, 200 oranges and 50 quinces (which all came together in a sugar case), along with, for the Duke's own use, a pair of shoes, a pair of slippers and a pair of saddle bags. There was also a great chest with harness, a barrel with harness and embroiderers' frames.[32]

In the household of Joan de Valence, servants were attached to each vehicle. The two main conveyances came under the marshalsea. The coach was in the charge of Hamo, who was senior enough sometimes to be responsible for the accounts of the whole marshalsea. He had an assistant, a valet, Hec, as well as a second man, Davy, who also ranked as a valet but only received half the allowance, possibly because he was only present part of the time. The long cart was in the charge of Adam the Carter, also a valet, and there was between Michaelmas 1296 and Easter 1297 a second carter, again ranked as a valet but with half the allowance. This pattern of transport seems to have been typical. The household of Eleanor de Montfort in 1265 had a coach and two long carts of its own, one of which, described as the 'small long cart', needed at least five horses. Additional carts were hired, and the driver of the Countess of Gloucester's coach was on hand to take Eleanor from Chippenham to Odiham.[33] Driving a four-wheeled vehicle of this size required skill and experience few would have had. In November 1289, Eleanor of Castile gave a clasp worth 14s. to the driver of her mother-in-law's coach, who had stood in to take her six-horsed coach from Amesbury to Clarendon when her driver, Michael, was ill.[34]

Households were unusual in terms of transport in medieval England as their journeys were overwhelmingly by land. Water transport was cheaper for carriage, on rivers by a factor of four and by sea by a factor of eight. Water had the advantage where there were bulky goods to be shipped or where there was a network of connecting waterways, as in parts of eastern England, making it relatively straightforward to reach a range of destinations.[35] The household of Joan de Valence used ferries to cross the Wye and the Severn, but it was probably only in London that she made, briefly, any more substantial use of water transport. In 1409, when the household of the Duke of York moved from Cardiff to Hanley Castle, part of the household went by land, but the wardrobe was shipped up the Severn all the way to Hanley.[36]

A few households maintained their own water transport. Thomas Arundel, as Bishop of Ely, used his barge on the waterways of the Fens, eating on board *en route* to Downham on at least one occasion. In London in November 1383 while Parliament was held, he hired a barge, but he may also have kept one there at other times.[37] The Earl of Oxford had a barge and his own waterman in 1431–2;[38] in 1501, the Duke of Buckingham made extensive use of the Thames for travel around London and its environs, particularly to Barnes and Richmond.[39] The barge of Henry Le Scrope of Masham (d. 1415) had an awning of black and red wadmal (a coarse, woollen cloth); that of Henry V had coverings of cloth of gold and of red cloth, embroidered with royal mottoes.[40] A journey by sea required different vessels, often hired, and stringent preparations. The deck of the boat which took Eleanor of Castile and her household from Bordeaux to Oléron in July 1287 was strewn with rushes.[41] When Margaret, Duchess of Clarence, crossed from Southampton to Normandy in November 1419, new standards (packing-cases) were made for carrying saddles, other standards were covered in barehide, old leather was newly curried and sacks were lined with fresh canvas.[42]

How far did a household travel? In 1265, there are records of seven journeys undertaken by Eleanor de Montfort. The shortest distance covered in a day was 14 miles, the longest was 38 miles, the average being 26 miles.[43] Between 21 May 1296 and 12 September 1297, Joan de Valence spent 47 days travelling, in total 735 miles or about 16 miles per day. Aside from two journeys from Hertingfordbury to Tring on 8 August 1296 when the household covered 28 miles, and from Buckingham to Arlesey (32 miles) on 28 October 1296, and one short journey from Gloucester to Churcham (5 miles), the distance fell each day in the range 10 to 23 miles.[44]

The routes of the medieval road network are known from a handful of medieval maps, principally the Gough Map and the maps of Matthew Paris, and there was besides the residue of the Roman road system still in use. A good deal less is known about cross-country routes, although some information has been compiled from royal itineraries.[45] Joan de Valence's journeys demonstrate she could make reasonable progress across a range of cross-country routes, but at a rate somewhat diminished from households traversing the major routes (Map 2). On 24 October 1296, she moved 17 miles from her manor of Inkberrow to Pillerton in Warwickshire. The next day she managed 11 miles, to Banbury, but required the household to mount the huge escarpment at Tysoe. The following day, moving on to Buckingham, the household managed about 15 miles, or close to its average. Edward I, on the other hand, managed a daily average of 20 miles. In fifteenth-century Flanders, France and Burgundy, Isabella of Portugal often travelled between 30 and 40 kilometres a day, but exceeded 60 on some occasions.[46]

Maps were not what most people used to find their way: reliance on guides was commonplace. When Joan de Valence moved from Inkberrow to Exning, on 26 October 1296, a guide between Banbury and Buckingham was paid 1d. to escort her coach.[47] In October 1409, the Duke of York needed a guide between Monmouth and Ross-on-Wye and between Ross and Ledbury.[48] The Earl of March paid a guide 20d. for assistance from Hertford to Barnet while he was probably part of a larger group accompanying the body of Richard II from King's Langley to Westminster in December 1413.[49] There was foresight in the actions of William de Felton and others of Edward I's carters who went ahead to look at the French roads the King and Queen had to pass over.[50]

In assessing rates of travel, there is seldom information about when in the day the household started out (although references to breakfast taken on the way suggest it was early) or when it arrived. Moving from Cardiff to Hanley Castle in 1409, the part of the household of the Duke of York that travelled by road reached Newport in time for supper, that is by mid-afternoon, on Friday, 25 October, a distance of 12 miles.[51] The following day, it travelled from Newport to Monmouth, about 20 miles, where it arrived for lunch and spent the rest of the day and the night. On the Sunday, the household moved 27 miles, to Ross-on-Wye for lunch and to Ledbury for supper and the night, covering the final 9 miles to Hanley the day following.[52] In the accounts of Joan de Valence, there is one instance of travel taking place in the afternoon of the day only, on 17 May 1297, when she had lunch in London, but slept at Merton.[53] On 1 June 1265, Eleanor de Montfort's journey from Odiham to Portchester (33 miles) started after lunch and went on into the evening.[54] If it was unusual to start a journey in the afternoon, it was even more out of the ordinary – and dangerous – to travel by night. Guides were essential. On 10 December 1296, William de Munchensy and a guide went from Joan de Valence's household at Goodrich to Moreton Valence, carrying £10 to be paid to the King's sub-escheator there; on 2 January 1297, Walter the Usher went by night to Berkeley from Goodrich with two guides in search of Sir Roger de Inkpen.[55]

There were other perils for travellers. Few disasters, however, can have matched the loss of King John's baggage train in the Wellstream in 1216. An accident to a wardrobe cart in October 1289 at Burgh in Norfolk cost Eleanor of Castile more than 30s. in repairs to clothing. Likewise Joan de Valence had to lay out 5s. 10d. for the repair of furs, damaged by water, presumably in crossing the Thames, leaving Chearsley in August 1296.[56]

Different parts of the household travelled at different speeds. When the Bishop of Bath and Wells left London in March 1338 for Dogmersfield, his carts moved half a day behind him. While the Bishop reached Egham where he slept on 4 March, the carts stayed overnight at Brentford, along with two household officials and three grooms.[57] It was common practice to divide up the household, with an advance party to make preparations for the lord's arrival and to take lodgings. The riding houschold of the Earl of Northumberland, *c.* 1511, was divided into four groups, three to precede the Earl (Table 10). Just as portions of the household preceded the main body, contingents were left elsewhere to look after property and horses, or were lodged elsewhere because there was insufficient room. Joan de Valence sent Ralph the Clerk to Kent in September 1296 to pay the household remaining there, probably at Sutton Valence.[58] There is evidence that, despite the absence of the lord and reducing to a minimum the

Table 10. The household on the move: the riding or foreign household of the Earl of
Northumberland, *c.* 1511

1. *Preceding party of five, to take up the lodgings*
    To act as harbingers for servants: 1 yeomen usher of the chamber; 1 clerk of the kitchen;
        1 yeoman usher of the hall
    To keep the lord's chamber: 1 groom of the chamber
    Also 1 yeoman or groom cook

2. *Preceding party, with the clothsack (the lord's baggage)*
    1 yeoman or groom porter for keeping the gates; 1 groom sumpterman with the clothsack
    for the bed; 1 groom sumpterman for the clothsack with the coffers; gentlemen servants to
    wait on the clothsacks

3. *Party preceding the lord*
    1 yeoman of the cellar with the cup; marshals of the hall; 1 officer of arms; all other
    gentlemen; 1 gentleman usher of the chamber; 1 sewer for the lord; 1 carver for the lord; 1
    cupbearer for the lord; 1 chaplain for the lord

4. *Party attending and following the lord*
    Yeoman of the robes; yeoman of the horse; yeoman of the chamber; yeoman of the pantry;
    yeoman of the buttery; yeomen waiters; groom of the chamber; groom of the ewery; clerk
    of the signet; clerk of the foreign expenses; groom of the wardrobe; groom of the stirrup;
    all other yeomen to ride behind the lord

Source
NHB, pp. 150-2.

staff of a residence, the country round about might continue to see it as a focus
for hospitality – something lords tried to avoid.[59] Margaret Paston, in 1465,
thought nothing good came of this practice at Caister:

> Item, as for youre houshold at Castere, savyng youre betere avyse me thynkyth
> that v or vi of youre folkys such as ye wyll assyngne were [to . . .] kype the place,
> and thay for to go to bord wyth the prustes [priests] and ye not to kype no
> houshold there yet, and that ye shall fynd more profettabyll than for to doo as
> we do nogh; for there expens, as I understond, have not be moch the lesse
> byfore Wytsontyde than it shold be thogh I had be at hom, bycause of
> resortyng of pepell thedere. And yf the houshold were broke thay myȝt have a
> gode excuse in that, who som ever com.[60]

Accommodation was necessary on longer journeys, especially those away
from demesne manors. Securing the use of inns or temporary lodgings was the
task of the harbingers. The larger the household, the more problematic the task.
The accommodation arrangements envisaged for the household of Edward II
distributed the staff throughout the verge.[61] It was customary for harbingers to
mark all the doors and entrances of a building with a sign to indicate that it was
to be used as lodging for the household.[62] But more modest parties, such as that
accompanying Sir John Dinham in 1393–4 (which numbered four esquires,
three valets, three pages and 12 horses at its largest), could find lodgings

together in inns.[63] Temporary accommodation in tents appears to have been restricted to the royal household or to military expeditions on campaign.[64] Not everything could be housed indoors: the royal household used its porters to keep watch at night over carts temporarily at rest on their journeys.[65]

* * *

Household life was carried on in close proximity to animals, which, aside from providing a source of food, were enormously important to the medieval house-hold.[66] Horses (and, to a much more limited extent, oxen) were essential to transport arrangements. Dogs and hawks were the necessities of huntsmen. Pets or tame animals kept within the household included cats, caged birds, squirrels, monkeys and more dogs (Plate 73). These animals were the companions of many and we know the names of some of them. Horses were frequently called after their place of origin or colour. In the stable of Hugh Audley the Younger, in 1320, were two dexters named Ferant de Roma and Grisel Le Kyng.[67] In January 1287 the fewterer (or keeper of the hounds) of the Bishop of Durham brought Edward I a gift from his master, a bercelet called Chasteleyn.[68]

The household stable had a range of horses for different functions. Horses were markedly smaller than their modern counterparts: most, even cart-horses, would have been under 14.2 hands. The medieval dexter, the 'great horse', is not likely to have exceeded 15 hands. 'Great' probably referred to its strength and manoeuvrability, possibly to nobility of form, rather than its height.[69] Except at the upper end of the market, the principal expense of a horse was its running costs, not its purchase price – much like the second-hand car today.[70] The most expensive, the dexter or war-horse, the price of which could reach £80 or more,[71] was also used for show (as well as strength) as a coach-horse. Coursers were used for hunting. Palfreys were good riding-horses: runceys, hobbies, nags and hackneys were of lesser grade. Amblers and trotters were famed for the easier ride they gave, as a result of moving both right legs together, then both left. The stable also had cart-horses and pack-horses.[72]

Both Joan de Valence and her daughter-in-law, Beatrice de Nesle, had palfreys and palfreymen. There were great horses in the stable at Hertford, some prob-ably belonging to her husband William de Valence, when Joan stayed there in October 1295, besides the cart- and pack-horses of the establishment.[73] In February 1320, the Countess of Gloucester's coach was pulled by five dexters (Plate 73) and she had a palfrey to ride. Her husband (Hugh Audley the Younger) had three dexters and a palfrey. There were five sumpters and eight cart-horses, besides the horses of other retainers and servants attending the household, making a total of 39 horses and one hackney.[74] At Thornbury, on 5 January 1508, the stable of the Duke of Buckingham contained 49 of the Duke's horses, including 15 coursers, eight hobbies, eight palfreys, four sumpters, two mail- or bag-horses, seven cart- or coach-horses (*equi quadrige*) and three horses belonging to yeomen in the stables (the valets of the horses, the avenar and the farrier). In addition, there were 62 horses of other servants of the Duke.[75]

Prima facie, Buckingham kept proportionately more horses for riding than traction, the reverse of Audley's stable composition. It is difficult, however, to compare stables. For practical purposes – to keep within reasonable bounds the fodder, oats or grazing that had to be assembled – it was usual to disperse horses when a household lodged at a single place for any period of time. In 1337, the Bishop of Bath and Wells kept some of his stable at Evercreech, where he resided, with another part at Wookey in the company of some of his household on detached duty;[76] Bishop Mitford of Salisbury, shortly after he arrived at Potterne in 1406, kept part of his household at Ramsbury to look after horses there;[77] and Anne Stafford, while residing at Writtle in April 1465, kept some of her stable at Ongar.[78]

Horses in this quantity required a substantial amount of stabling, associated yards, and storage for fodder and corn, usually oats. The remains of the four-teenth-century stable in the outer ward at Goodrich cover 81.25 m²; at Hadleigh in Essex, the stable covered about 60 m² and at Farleigh Hungerford, built at the end of the 1420s, it was about 80 m² (Plate 74).[79] These are low figures and there must, at Goodrich, have been additional accommodation of which no trace now survives. Even allowing as little as 3 m² stallage per horse, 80 m² would not have been sufficient to house the average of 31 horses Joan de Valence had with her household at Goodrich in 1296–7. Other evidence – reliance on the well for water and the movement of the coach-horses to Moreton Valence at Christmas 1296 – may reflect the difficulty of keeping a large number of horses at this site. Joan's stable was modest in number compared with the average of more than 400 horses at Pontefract in 1318–19 with Thomas of Lancaster (Table 1). At Bishop's Waltham in 1388–9, there were at least three separate stables or major divisions of the stable building, one for William of Wykeham's palfreys, another for the cart-horses, with a third for the horses of esquires.[80] In 1441–2, works on the west side of the stable in the outer court included new racks and mangers, with 90 holes dug for the footings of the mangers, as well as partitions and divi-sions within the building, separating the accommodation of individual or groups of horses.[81]

The main expense of horses was their provisioning. What were horses fed? In the household of Joan de Valence, as in most great households, the horses were mainly given oats and hay. There was a period, however, in June to early July when horses were fed freshly mown green fodder, as opposed to hay.[82] Beans and bran were added to the feed in the household of Hugh Audley the Younger in March 1320.[83] There were also assorted horse-breads: in the household of Ralph of Shrewsbury the horses were watered before they were fed on these, around lunchtime.[84] Away from the stable, food could be given in nose-bags: 32 linen sacks were purchased to this end in October 1289 for the horses of Eleanor of Castile.[85] Joan de Valence's horses each consumed, on average, a little under half a bushel of oats per day, a considerable helping of a high protein diet that reflected the hard work and sustained performance expected of these important animals.[86] Hackneys received a lesser quantity: in Ralph of Shrewsbury's house-hold, their livery of hay was half that of the other horses. Where the horses had been worked hard during the day or travelled a long distance, they were given extra rations.[87] In this household, as well as that of Bishop Mitford in 1406–7,

74. Farleigh Hungerford,
Somerset: the fifteenth-century
stables, with the central drain
running through the cobbled floor.

if the hackneys also received a reduced portion of oats, the horses would each have had a little under half a bushel of oats per day.[88] Rations suggested by a fifteenth-century courtesy book were somewhat less: the lord's horses were to have two armfuls of hay and a peck of provender a day.[89]

    In terms of harness and fittings, the minimal necessities were matched by elaborate cloths and metalwork appropriate to the magnificence of the household. Metal fittings, enamelled with heraldic devices, decorated harness (Plate 15). Bishop Bek of Durham is recorded as using the most expensive cloth for the housings for his palfreys, although contemporaries, such as Bishop Swinfield of Hereford, were content with materials such as coarse basset or russet.[90] Horse-housings made for the Duke and Duchess of Clarence, in 1418–21, were embroidered with greyhounds and hinds.[91] Saddles and other accoutrements of chivalry could be elaborately decorated.[92] Most stable accounts record the shoeing of horses, the removal and provision of shoes for both front and rear feet. In the household of the Bishop of Bath and Wells, in 1337–8, it was the practice, doubtless common elsewhere, to rework old shoes whenever possible, to produce stronger iron.[93]

Veterinary care was closely associated with farriery. The range of treatments for horses was limited, frequently confined to the purchase of fat or grease (tallow, often applied to the legs and feet). On 25 October 1296, a more elaborate preparation, including spices, grease and bran, was made for one of Joan de Valence's limber horses.[94] Honey and butter were bought for the palfrey of Aymer de Valence and special purchases of horse-bread were made for a sick coach-horse.[95] The primary expense was often the maintenance of the horse away from the household. On 6 November 1296, the costs of one of Joan's coach-horses which had remained sick in London for 13 days, together with a reward for the farrier who had cured it and the wages of one groom looking after it, came to 4s. 5½d.[96] Besides honey and grease, other items called for in curing horses included wort (unfermented ale), lard, garlic, olive oil, plasters and pills.[97]

*   *   *

Veterinary medicine was not confined to horses. Efforts to assist gerfalcons in the royal household in 1285–6 extended to enlisting the efforts of Master Peter the Surgeon, using the herb *saundragon* (or 'dragon's blood'), and making an image of a sick falcon in wax which was offered at the shrine of St Thomas at Canterbury.[98] Sick dogs likewise attracted both veterinary attention and the additional benefits that came from religion.[99]

The presence of dogs in almost all great households was a source of some ambiguity. Favoured as pets and adjuncts to hunting, they could also be a nuisance. Household ordinances enjoined keeping dogs out of the bakehouse and watching the alms to prevent canine depredation. Henry VIII expected courtiers and servants to keep their dogs in kennels out of court, except by the King or Queen's special command and with the exception of 'some few small spaniells for ladyes or others', so that 'the house may be sweete, wholesome, cleane and well furnished, as to a prince's honour and estate doth apperteine'.[100] Like cats, they were not to be stroked at meals and they were to be excluded from chambers.[101]

Hunting dogs were highly prized and some households maintained packs (mutes). Joan de Valence's pack spent most of its time away from the household, at work, hunting. Its visits were occasional, joining up with the household at Hertford in October 1295, when litter was supplied for the dogs' bedding, and at Brabourne, in Kent, in May 1296.[102] Similarly, in 1265, Eleanor de Montfort's household lodged both her own dogs and packs belonging to visitors, one pack probably containing 34 animals, with other visiting dogs and the Countess's greyhounds making a total of 52 on 16 May.[103] Under Henry VI, the royal hunts were only to be in court during their seasons.[104]

Food was sent from the household of Ralph of Shrewsbury, Bishop of Bath and Wells, in 1337, to the Bishop's huntsmen, with his dogs, nearby at Cheddar.[105] In 1406–7, Bishop Mitford required at least two loaves per day for dogs in his household and sometimes considerably more; his hunting dogs, however, were kept elsewhere in the charge of his huntsman and fewterer.[106]

Dogs within the household were fed on scraps and indulgence as well as bread. In some cases, this may have been ordinary household bread, but in others a black bread was specially baked, largely from bran. Hunting dogs were probably fed almost entirely on cereals, with some game meat out of season. Cereals were given in the form of a fairly coarse bread, possibly similar to biscuit; they were also fed a corn mash, sometimes made of oats or barley, or mixed with peas, or a preparation made with oats, rye and bran.[107] Out hunting, they were normally rewarded at the kill with the entrails of the beast, sometimes cooked over embers and mixed with bread.[108]

What dogs were kept? Many dogs were distinguishable by function or by breed, although the characteristics of breeds have developed since the Middle Ages. The *Master of Game* included separate sections on greyhounds, alauntes, spaniels, mastiffs and hounds, different animals being used for different quarry; the principal beasts of the chase were deer and hares, after wild boar had largely disappeared.[109]

Greyhounds were popular hunting dogs, kept by aristocracy, gentry and clergy alike. Bishop Bitton of Exeter (d. 1307) had among his goods two greyhound collars, made of silk and silver thread, as well as harness for a further six collars.[110] Anne, the wife of John de Multon of Frampton, kept greyhounds in 1343–4;[111] and the treasurer of the second Earl of Salisbury bought eight collars for them at 4d. each in 1367–8.[112] Isabel of Lancaster, a nun at Amesbury and a daughter of Henry of Lancaster, kept four greyhounds at the start of 1333–4, the number falling to two later in the year, at which point she borrowed two more for hunting.[113] In the 1460s, John Howard, later Duke of Norfolk, who took his hunting very seriously, kept a careful note of dogs he had or was promised.[114] Foxes were considered vermin and, *inter alia*, a threat to rabbit warrens. In 1285–6, Edward I's servant, William Le Foxhunte, and two assistants, had 30 dogs, probably hounds, to help them, but sometimes archers were used.[115] Setters were employed, in conjunction with falcons, and probably with nets, for catching partridges.[116] Greyhounds were used in otter-hunting,[117] spaniels (a breed which originated in Spain, looking more like sheep than their modern counterparts) for rooting out game and retrieving.[118]

Careful thought was given to the kennels for hunting dogs. The *Master of Game* recommended a structure with a gutter running through the ground floor, with a loft above for warmth in winter and to keep the kennel cool in summer. A chimney gave further warmth in winter and there was also to be a fenced run.[119]

Hawking was extremely popular as a pastime. Birds were maintained in many households, with regular supplies of meat and fish.[120] The largest and most noble species were reserved for those of the highest rank. Edward, Duke of York, translator of the *Master of Game*, had a goshawk in 1410.[121] Joan de Valence kept sparrowhawks, at one stage keeping eight nests or chicks at ½d. each per day. She had her own falconer. Her son, Aymer, with his wife, had up to four falcons in Joan's household and later one gerfalcon.[122] While, in 1406–7,

Bishop Mitford's falconer looked after his young birds at Upavon, Wilsford, Patney and Marden, on the northern edge of Salisbury Plain,[123] birds were not usually reared or obtained locally. A late fourteenth-century Abbot of Shrewsbury was doing nothing out of the ordinary when he sent one of his servants to Ireland to purchase goshawks and tercels.[124]

There was special accommodation for hawks and falcons. Towards the end of 1287, a wooden chamber was made for the falcons of John of Brabant, probably at Windsor, with a thatched roof and walls of daub. In 1288–9, the clerk of the mute (responsible for arrangements for Edward I's hunting animals and birds) had a construction made for bathing gerfalcons. As well as supplying vinegar, soap and dandelion for their needs, three cranes were kept as lures.[125] The birds might also be kept for some of the time inside the house. Edward III, around 1353, had a partition made in his chamber at his manor at Rotherhithe as a perch for his falcons.[126]

Besides the professional huntsmen and falconers, who went hunting? Purchases made by Roger Mortimer, fourth Earl of March, in 1393–4, indicate the composition of one hunting party. Dressed in green hunting gowns (at a cost of more than £4. 10s.), besides Roger and Thomas Mortimer, was a group of courtiers, with one exception all knights of Richard II's chamber: George Felbridge, Simon Felbridge, William Le Scrope (the King's under-chamberlain), Stephen Le Scrope, John Littlebury, Philip La Vache and William Arundel. Roger Mortimer's hunting knife was newly gilded and sharpened, along with the other furbishments of his belt. There were two bells for his great belt. A new bow, eight bolts, two dozen bowstrings, an archer's glove and a cloth cover for the bows were acquired.[127] It was expeditions like this that used hunting lodges such as Wardour Castle.[128]

Cats were present for their hunting propensities as much as for society. They had considerable freedom to wander: Eleanor de Montfort's chamberlain acquired one for her in 1265, along with milk for the dogs that probably also shared her chamber, much against the advice of later courtesy books.[129] Ferrets were also employed for hunting. The work of the ferret was well rewarded with eggs in the household of Dame Katherine de Norwich in 1336–7.[130] They needed control, however, and their owners had to be restrained from rabbiting in jealously guarded warrens, unless specifically invited.[131]

More exotic animals provided greater symbols of status. Caged birds – parrots and finches – were kept in chambers.[132] Bears were kept by a number of households, including those of the Countess of Warwick in 1420–1 (a living embodiment of the Beauchamp heraldic device) and of the Duke of Buckingham, in 1507–8.[133] The royal menagerie in the Tower of London represented the most majestic accompaniment of wild animals the household might have. In the Tower, it was relatively safe and the animals were regularly supplied with meat. In 1288–9, the menagerie included at least two lions and a cub, a leopard and a bear.[134] When the king moved parts with him, or accepted gifts away from home, less regal consequences ensued. On Oléron in 1287, one of Edward I's lions killed the horse of a local man.[135]

The fine horses that pulled the lady's coach, the lord's war-horses, the hunting dogs and hawks, the costly pets, the exotic species, all reflected the quality of the household and the gradations of status. While households moved less in the later Middle Ages, there were few establishments that did not maintain a range of transport, from pack-horse to highly decorated coach. The investment associated with them was both a practical necessity and an important measure of the household's standing. To hunt with the finest hounds, to ride the best horses, might define a man as a leader of his class. In all these activities, however, the scale of the investment could vary widely. Even those of more modest means could readily feel they were participating fully in this pattern of living.

CHAPTER 10
Conclusion

Looking at a household of the end of the fifteenth century, a thirteenth-century servant would have been struck by the range of changes. The economy and geography of the household had altered. It was no longer supplied by food rents from its properties but by a more fluid system, part derived from the market, part from estates. Domestic service, maintained by serjeanty tenure, had largely disappeared in favour of servants who received board and other emoluments. The household was no longer continually itinerant, but based at a few residences, with increasing importance accorded to a London house, essential for any courtier.

The differences were also qualitative and social. The household was smaller (albeit increasing in size at the close of the fifteenth century) and there were fewer servants, but a higher proportion of gentle rank. Within buildings, there was growth in luxury, in intimacy of the domestic setting, and in numbers of chambers, with individual rooms or suites for members of the household, lord and servants. This was still public living, with no loss of formality: privacy, in the modern sense, was a development of the seventeenth century onwards. Smaller units brought to the lord an immediacy of control. Fifteenth-century courtesy books elaborated social convention to enforce hierarchy in closer confines. Who could do what in an intimate surrounding needed to be controlled, who sat where, who might approach whom, when and for what purpose. John Russell's *Boke of Nurture* has a long list covering questions of precedence, questions which did not feature in the description of the duties of the marshal of a century previously.[1] Precedence emphasised social distance in a more compact environment – precedence rather than rank, the former relative, the latter absolute – as well as the more obvious elements of display in costume and ornament. Paradoxically, social distance increased with intimacy of surroundings. Sequences of smaller rooms replaced a single large chamber, in which the lord of the thirteenth century had been much more accessible.

When and why did these changes occur? The latter part of the fourteenth century probably saw the greatest alteration. From this time the proportion of gentle servants in the household grew. It is also probable that the highest levels of expenditure per person within the household occurred between 1380 and

1410, especially in episcopal households (from which most of the evidence comes) (Table 2). At other times the largest households aimed to impress by presence of numbers. It may be significant that these changes coincide with the reign of Richard II. His vision of kingship relied on majesty surrounded by elaborate ritual, perhaps inspired by familiar continental examples, his father's court in Aquitaine and that of Charles V of France. Its exaggerated form included periods of crown-wearing during which Richard's courtiers were expected to kneel if his gaze fell upon them.[2] Royal magnificence and ritual were emulated in lesser households.

The highlighting of magnificence has helped to characterise the great household as both greatly profligate and living beyond its means.[3] In any assessment, it must be recognised that the maintenance of the household itself was the first and most substantial call on the lord's resources. It gave the lord honour, profit, standing and a way of life, political credit and influence. Next in order of magnitude, depending on the household, came purchases of cloth for livery or building expenses, for new projects or continuous expenditure on the upkeep of properties. Looking at his treasure, the other options open to a lord were to purchase land, to loan the funds, to store it as treasure or to turn it into plate (a form readily convertible into specie), to invest in charitable works or to invest for the future of his soul and that of his friends and relations. The balance varied from household to household.

To assist the lord in his choice, concepts of financial management were developed and applied to the household. Some establishments, such as that of Dame Katherine de Norwich, like some monasteries, probably had a close idea of what the household costs were per person and what was necessary to balance the books.[4] Advising the Countess of Lincoln, *c.* 1240–2, Robert Grosseteste demonstrated how it was possible both to establish what estates contained and what they produced, in order to regulate domestic expenses. The income from surplus corn, rents and other profits was to be employed for the kitchen expenses, wine and wardrobe and chamber of the household; once that was done, a reserve was to be built up, equivalent to a year's supply of corn.[5] Thomas de Bitton, Bishop of Exeter (d. 1307), held at his death cash that would have been sufficient for the annual expense of his household; and it is probable that the £96 held by Henry de Vere of Great Addington at his death in 1493 would have covered much of his expense for a year.[6] Bishop Fox's new college of Corpus Christi in Oxford had its statutes revised *c.* 1528, forbidding the college to spend the rent receipts from the current year. For its living expenses, it had to draw on the revenue of the previous year.[7] Less than 20 years later, Andrew Boorde proposed the lord should divide his income into three parts, one to cover his food and drink; the second, for clothing for himself and his household, together with servants' wages; and the third part, as a contingency

75. Tattershall Castle, Lincolnshire, built by Ralph, Lord Cromwell, between 1434 and 1446, with his profits as Treasurer.

against sickness, repairs and other urgent necessities. Nor did Boorde think it wise to set up a household unless there was the equivalent of two or three years' rent in the coffers.[8] Prudence dictated the provision of an appropriate reserve: maintaining a household was expensive and the costs not confidently predicted.

Beyond such a reserve, some households had large assets in movable wealth and other readily convertible assets. Those of Richard, Earl of Arundel (d. 1376), were worth £72,245 on his death. More than £60,000 was to be found in his coffers, with nearly half deposited in the High Tower of Arundel Castle. About £4,500 was loaned out.[9] The total represented about three times the annual expenditure on the household of Edward III in the 1360s, or four times the annual expenditure in the 1370s.[10] John of Gaunt left £2,000 in cash to his wife.[11] Sir John Fastolf's cash, plate and jewels were far from exhausted at his death in 1459, having a combined value of at least £8,000.[12] These substantial funds were all potentially available to the household.

In addition, by the fifteenth century, lords had increasing flexibility to convert fixed assets, or future interests, into credit, systems that required considerable confidence and security. Private administration evolved mechanisms and sophisticated financial instruments, much in the mode of the royal household, with the development of debentures, as well as the postponement of payment on other bases. William Wistowe, the treasurer of the great household of Humphrey Stafford, first Duke of Buckingham, rendering his account for 1452–3, although disbursing £2,123, noted debts of nearly £730, some dating back to 1439–40.[13] There was no suggestion, however, that Buckingham found it difficult to obtain cash or goods. The contrast with the finances of the household of Joan de Valence is instructive. The amounts of cash available to her household were restricted, perhaps a consequence of the death of her husband. Her credit was also severely circumscribed and she had to go to great lengths to transport and borrow specie. Loans were sought from Aymer de Valence (the comparatively small sum of £10) and from Agnes de Valence, both around 28 May 1297;[14] missions went to various estates after money, to Collingbourne and Newton Valence in July 1296, to Pembroke in November the same year;[15] and delays were incurred in paying debts other than those for which the household officials had accepted responsibility, for example paying the Kent debts around 20 December 1296, when the last day spent by the household there was 9 June 1296.[16] This household was also indebted to its own officials. Adam Rimbaud, the marshal, for the stay at Inkberrow from 3 September 1296 to 24 October 1296, had laid out a total of £4. 0s. 2½d., of which he had been paid 55s. 2d., with the balance left owing to him at the time of departure.[17] The £100 taken to London around 26 June 1296 to retrieve silver vessels that were in the hands of the Lombards, however, shows what store might be set at the same time on magnificence.[18]

Of the other possibilities for expenditure, major building projects could easily consume 20% of annual income. Expenditure on maintenance might run at 2% or 3%: the works carried out, largely on a single chimney, by the Multons of Frampton in 1343–4 amounted to just over £2 out of £61 total expenditure.[19] Building work in the thirteenth and early fourteenth centuries was probably generally financed from revenue, from the substantial resources of the thirteenth-century Crown and aristocracy.[20] In his work on Winchester Castle from 1234 to 1272, Henry III spent about £8,500; Edward III's works at Windsor in 1363–5 alone reached a similar amount.[21] The new royal castles in Wales between 1277 and 1304 cost a little under £80,000 in all, with the most expensive, Conway, at a little under £14,000.[22] Thomas of Lancaster spent nearly £1,900 on building in 1313–14.[23] In modernising the palace at Bishop's Waltham, William of Wykeham spent at least £1,509 between 1369 and 1404. Cardinal Beaufort spent a further £1,032 there in a single campaign of 1438–43.[24]

By the latter part of the fourteenth century and in the fifteenth, the resources of the aristocracy were considerably less than they had been. The scale of some building projects was such that they could only be financed by windfalls, rather than by the sustained income of estates. The profits of the French wars in the early fifteenth century funded one spurt of residence building. Sir John Fastolf, whose estates in England and France combined produced a total income of £1,463 in 1445, spent more than £6,000 on his castle at Caister (Plate 24). While this was spread over 30 years, £1,425 was spent on the project in 1432–5; the building works on Fastolf Place in Southwark, acquired for £139, cost him another £1,100; and Fastolf also paid some £616 for works on the south choir aisle at St Benet at Hulme, an investment with an eye on his spiritual future.[25] It was also exactly at this time that some of Fastolf's major land purchases were made in East Anglia, between 1430 and 1436 amounting to about £5,750.[26] Herstmonceux Castle in Sussex (Plate 25), financed in a similar way, is reputed to have been built for Sir Roger Fienes, *c.* 1441, for about £3,800.[27] The building works of Ralph, Lord Cromwell, from the late 1430s until his death in 1456, were supported by the profits of his office as Treasurer of England. In the early 1440s he was spending £700 per annum on his building work at Tattershall (Plate 75) and Wingfield, and charges for works at his new acquisition, Collyweston, and Lambley may have brought this closer to £1,000, the total level of his income in the 1430s and nearly two-fifths that at the time of his death.[28] The cost of any castle, residence or major alteration ran into thousands of pounds. The incomplete Kirby Muxloe (Plate 76), on which rebuilding was carried out in earnest from 1480 until Lord Hastings' execution in 1483, cost, even in its partial state, £994.[29]

While these sums were large by any reckoning, the concentration on fewer residences enabled greater sums to be made available for single projects. They should also be compared with the other peaks of expenditure. The household's costs at major feasts, the focus, perhaps, of no more than a single day, might consume up to about a sixth of annual expense and, in absolute terms, in the greatest households, an enormous sum (Table 11). The cost of ceremony – and social competition – was one that had increased greatly by and during the fifteenth century. In the later Middle Ages the possibilities for the use of credit to liberate this display were extended. Here was perilous temptation. In 1480,

76. Kirby Muxloe Castle, Leicestershire, left incomplete at the execution of William, Lord Hastings, in 1483.

William Harleston wrote to his nephew, Sir William Stonor, whose wife had recently died, advising him to break up his household, so as not to incur too much expense:

> And of certen thynges I wold desire you and pray you in the name of God, that ye wolle not over wissh yow, ner owyr purches yow, ner owyr bild you; for these iii thynges wolle plucke a yongman ryth lowe. Ner medyll not with no gret materis in the lawe. For I truste to God to see you the worshipfullest of the Stoners that ever I sawe or shall se be my days.[30]

This study should not conclude without a prospective look at the great changes that came to the household with the end of the Middle Ages. A most striking transition in the sixteenth century was the growing female presence in the household, both in terms of servants and service, and female control of domestic arrangements. The speed of change varied from establishment to establishment. That Robert Dudley, Earl of Leicester, had a household that was

Table 11. Costs of feasts

Anniversary feasts	
Joan de Valence, 15 May 1297 (death of husband)	£11 (out of £414 p.a.)
Katherine de Norwich, 20 January 1337 (death of first husband)	£11 (out of £66 p.a.)
Marriage feasts	
Henry IV and Joan of Navarre, February 1403	£523
Funeral feasts	
Richard Mitford, Bishop of Salisbury, 1407	£137+
Thomas of Lancaster, Duke of Clarence, 1421	£135+
Entertaining the king	
Thomas Arundel, entertaining Richard II, 6 July 1383	£162
William of Wykeham, entertaining Richard II, 1393	£26
Episcopal enthronement	
William Warham as Archbishop of Canterbury, 1505	£513+

Sources

PRO E101/505/26, m. 24r; *HAME* i, p. 178; M. Biddle, *Wolvesey: the Old Bishop's Palace, Winchester, Hampshire* (1986) p. 19; *HAME* i, pp. 403, 407–9, 412, 429–30; ii, pp. 679–82; CUL EDR D5/7a, mm. 1, 2r; WCM 1; *JLBC* vi, p. 31.

largely male is testimony to the strength of tradition.[31] That Lady Grisell Baillie of Mellerstain, Hannah Glasse in her *Servant's directory, or housekeeper's companion* of 1760, and Susanna Whatman, in her own notes, had taken firm control of the domestic establishment is evidence of how far this movement was to travel by the end of the eighteenth century.[32] Accompanying the women in the household were children, bringing it closer to our contemporary perception of household membership.

The effects of the Reformation reached far inside the household. While piety had its place – few households were without an act of collective worship at some stage in the day – the domestic establishment was rarely the mirror of a monastic community with its routine of chapel and oratory services, and elaborate dietary observances. It was now the possessor of a calendar quickly relieved of its patterns of liturgical celebration and commemoration. The dietary regime changed dramatically from the 1530s, with a rapid decline in the amounts of fish eaten and the practice of fish days and seasons of fasting falling into desuetude. At the same time, domestic charity and alms-giving were largely replaced by Poor Laws, administered as a secular function of the state.

The size and shape of domestic accommodation changed, becoming increasingly filled with furniture. It was no longer the soft furnishings that dominated: craftsmanship – cabinet-making, sculpture and carving – turned what had been functional woodwork into art, part of a scheme of decoration, enriching the opulence of the household. Architectural changes gave more comfort, more seclusion and, eventually, privacy to the members of the household, more splendour and a unity to the construction. The elaboration of areas for guests, sequences of rooms for lord and visitors, became possible as the labour force supporting the household changed in character, with many servants living out rather than in, releasing space within the buildings. In domestic planning, it was, on the whole, no longer physical barriers (or only slight ones) which kept the lord apart, but social divisions, an etiquette enforced by servants in waiting. At the same time, gentle service became ever more refined. The arrival of humanism and the new learning placed a premium on the educated servant, who had a wider range of accomplishments, performing as servant, companion and courtier.

The sixteenth-century English monarchy and its court dominated aristocratic society in more marked fashion than at any time in the Middle Ages. The position of the great ecclesiastical magnates was on the wane. While monastic prelates disappeared entirely, even the position of the households of others, such as Wolsey, was untenable in the long term. The Reformation represented the greatest redistribution of property in English history since the Norman Conquest and, in the transfer of huge amounts of accumulated wealth, the position of the household changed. By the end of the sixteenth century, the opportunity to make investments other than in social competition had greatly expanded – and with that, the predominant position of the household was never to be regained.[33]

The stage had also changed. Although we may now see England as a land of country houses and castles, the present pattern is more like that of medieval England than of the intervening centuries. The politics of display, in household and residences, concentrated wealth where it could be seen to greatest effect, in London, especially by the early nineteenth century. These metropolitan buildings are now largely demolished. Only one or two, such as Apsley House, now survive with any vestige of their former splendour. Their contents now adorn their country cousins, endowing them with riches they never possessed in their working lives.[34]

We have today unparalleled opportunities to view household antiquities at first hand. In so doing, we should not mistake the commonplaces of 1300 for those of 1500 or those of 1900. Equally, the false emotion of nostalgia and the accidents and inventions of heritage must not be confused with the realities of medieval society. There is much still to learn, but in exploring the remains of the great household, whatever one may think of its purpose and the fashion of household living, one cannot fail to be impressed at the scale of the endeavour.

Abbreviations

The place of publication is London unless otherwise stated.

AgHR	*Agricultural History Review*
Amyot, 'Transcript'	T. Amyot, 'Transcript of two rolls, containing an inventory of the effects formerly belonging to Sir John Fastolfe' *Archaeologia* 21 (1827) pp. 232–80
Annales ESC	*Annales: Économies, Sociétés, Civilisations*
AntJ	*Antiquaries' Journal*
ANTS	Anglo-Norman Text Society
ArchJ	*Archaeological Journal*
Aston, *Arundel*	M. Aston, *Thomas Arundel: a study of church life in the reign of Richard II* (Oxford, 1967)
BB	*The household of Edward IV: the Black Book and the ordinance of 1478* ed. A. R. Myers (Manchester, 1959)
BI	*The Bedford inventories: the worldly goods of John, Duke of Bedford, Regent of France (1389–1435)* ed. J. Stratford (Reports of the research committee of the Society of Antiquaries of London, 49; 1993)
BJRL	*Bulletin of the John Rylands Library*
BL	British Library
Bodl.	Bodleian Library, Oxford
Boorde, *Dyetary*	Andrew Boorde, *The fyrst boke of the introduction of knowledge . . . A dyetary of helth . . .* ed. F. J. Furnivall (EETS, Extra Series, 10; 1870)
Bryene	*The household book of Dame Alice de Bryene, of Acton Hall, Suffolk, Sept. 1412 – Sept. 1413 with appendices* ed. M. K. Dale and V. B. Redstone (Ipswich, 1931)
CClR	*Calendar of Close Rolls*
Challenger, 'Marlborough'	S. B. Challenger, 'Accounts for works in the royal mills and castle at Marlborough, 1237–8 and 1238–9' in *Collectanea* ed. N. J. Williams (Wiltshire Archaeological and Natural History Society, Records Branch, 12; 1956) pp. 1–49
CI	*Curye on Inglysch: English culinary manuscripts of the fourteenth century (including the Forme of Cury)* ed. C. B. Hieatt and S. Butler (EETS, Supplementary Series, 8; 1985)
CIPM	*Calendar of Inquisitions Post Mortem*

CP	*Complete peerage of England, Scotland, Ireland, Great Britain, and United Kingdom . . .* ed. G. E. Cokayne, revised by Vicary Gibbs *et al.* (13 vols, 1910–59)
Crawford, 'Private life'	A. Crawford, 'The private life of John Howard: a study of a Yorkist lord, his family and household' in *Richard III: loyalty, lordship and law* ed. P. W. Hammond (1986) pp. 6–24
CUL	Cambridge University Library
Dillon and Hope, 'Inventory'	Viscount Dillon and W. H. St John Hope, 'Inventory of the goods and chattels belonging to Thomas, Duke of Gloucester, and seized in his castle at Pleshy, co. Essex, 21 Richard II (1397); with their values, as shown in the escheator's accounts' *ArchJ* 54 (1897) pp. 275–308
DMT	*Du manuscrit à la table: essais sur la cuisine au Moyen Âge et répertoire des manuscrits médiévaux contenant des recettes culinaires* ed. C. Lambert (Montreal, 1992)
Duffy, *Altars*	E. Duffy, *The stripping of the altars: traditional religion in England c. 1400–c. 1580* (1992)
Dyer, *Everyday life*	C. Dyer, *Everyday life in medieval England* (1994)
Dyer, *Standards*	C. Dyer, *Standards of living in the later Middle Ages: social change in England c. 1200–1520* (Cambridge, 1989)
Eames, *Furniture*	P. Eames, *Furniture in England, France and the Netherlands from the twelfth to the fifteenth century* (1977)
EC	*The court and household of Eleanor of Castile in 1290: an edition of British Library, Additional Manuscript 35294* ed. J. C. Parsons (Toronto, 1977)
EconHR	*Economic History Review*
EETS	Early English Text Society
EFC, 1986	*England in the fifteenth century: proceedings of the 1986 Harlaxton symposium* ed. D. Williams (Woodbridge, 1987)
EFC, 1992	*England in the fifteenth century: proceedings of the 1992 Harlaxton symposium* ed. N. Rogers (Stamford, 1994)
EHR	*English Historical Review*
EMI	*English medieval industries: craftsmen, techniques, products* ed. J. Blair and N. Ramsay (1991)
Executors	*Account of the executors of Richard Bishop of London 1303, and of the executors of Thomas Bishop of Exeter 1310* ed. W. H. Hale and H. T. Ellacombe (Camden Society, 2nd series, 10; 1874)
Expeditions	*Expeditions to Prussia and the Holy Land made by Henry Earl of Derby (afterwards Henry IV) in the years 1390–1 and 1392–3* ed. L. T. Smith (Camden Society, 2nd series, 52; 1894)
FCCB	*A fifteenth-century courtesy book* ed. R. W. Chambers (EETS, OS, 148; 1914)
Gawain	*Sir Gawain and the Green Knight* ed. and trans. W. R. J. Barron (Manchester, 1974)
Giuseppi, 'Bogo'	M. S. Giuseppi, 'The wardrobe and household accounts of Bogo de Clare, A. D. 1284–6' *Archaeologia* 70 (1918–20) pp. 1–56

Given-Wilson, *English nobility*	C. Given-Wilson, *The English nobility in the late Middle Ages: the fourteenth-century political community* (1987)
Given-Wilson, *Royal household*	C. Given-Wilson, *The royal household and the King's affinity: service, politics and finance in England 1360–1413* (1986)
GMH	A. Emery, *Greater medieval houses of England and Wales 1300–1500* (3 vols, Cambridge, in progress, 1996–)
Griffiths, 'King's court'	R. A. Griffiths, 'The King's court during the Wars of the Roses: continuities in an age of discontinuities' in *Princes, patronage and the nobility: the court at the beginning of the modern age c. 1450–1650* ed. R. G. Asch and A. M. Birke (1991) pp. 41–67
HAME	*Household accounts from medieval England* ed. C. M. Woolgar (British Academy, Records of Social and Economic History, new series, 17–18; 1992–3)
Hare, 'Bishop's Waltham'	J. N. Hare, 'Bishop's Waltham palace, Hampshire: William of Wykeham, Henry Beaufort and the transformation of a medieval episcopal palace' *ArchJ* 145 (1988) pp. 222–54
Harris, 'Buckingham'	M. Harris and J. Thurgood, 'The account of the great household of Humphrey, first Duke of Buckingham, for the year 1452–3' in *Camden Miscellany XXVIII* (Camden, 4th series, 29; 1984) pp. 1–57
Harvey, 'Consumer'	B. F. Harvey, 'The aristocratic consumer in England in the long thirteenth century' in *Thirteenth-Century England VI* ed. M. Prestwich, R. H. Britnell and R. Frame (Woodbridge, 1997) pp. 17–37
Harvey, *Living*	B. F. Harvey, *Living and dying in England 1100–1540: the monastic experience* (Oxford, 1993)
HBJDN	*Household books of John, Duke of Norfolk, and Thomas, Earl of Surrey, temp. 1481–90, from the original manuscripts in the library of the Society of Antiquaries, London* ed. J. P. Collier (1844)
HBJH	*The household books of John Howard, Duke of Norfolk, 1462–1471, 1481–1483* introduced by A. Crawford (Far Thrupp, 1992)
HBQI	*The household book of Queen Isabella of England for the fifth regnal year of Edward II 8th July 1311 to 7th July 1312* ed. F. D. Blackley and G. Hermansen (University of Alberta Classical and Historical Studies, 1; 1971)
HKW	*The history of the King's works* ed. H. M. Colvin *et al.* (6 vols, 1963–82)
HMC	Royal Commission on Historical Manuscripts
HO	*A collection of ordinances and regulations for the government of the royal household made in divers reigns, from King Edward III to King William and Queen Mary. Also receipts in ancient cookery* ed. Anon. (1790)
HRO	Hampshire Record Office
'Isabel of Lancaster'	R. B. Pugh, 'Fragment of an account of Isabel of Lancaster, nun of Amesbury, 1333–4' in *Festschrift zur Feier des zweihundertjährigen Bestandes des Haus-, Hof- und Staatsarchivs* ed. L. Santifaller (2 vols, Vienna, 1949–51) i, pp. 487–98

JBAA	*Journal of the British Archaeological Association*
JHG	*Journal of Historical Geography*
JLBC	*Johannis Lelandi antiquarii de rebus Britannicis collectanea* ed. T. Hearne (2nd edition, new printing, 6 vols, 1774)
JMH	*Journal of Medieval History*
Jones and Walker, 'Indentures'	M. Jones and S. Walker, 'Private indentures for life service in peace and war 1278–1476' in *Camden Miscellany XXXII* (Camden, 5th series, 3; 1994) pp. 1–190
JWCI	*Journal of the Warburg and Courtauld Institutes*
Kingsford, 'Forfeitures'	C. L. Kingsford, 'Two forfeitures in the year of Agincourt' *Archaeologia* 70 (1918–20) pp. 71–100
Ladie Kateryne	*The receyt of the Ladie Kateryne* ed. G. Kipling (EETS, OS, 296; 1990)
Le Strange, 'Household accounts'	H. Le Strange, 'A roll of household accounts of Sir Hamon Le Strange of Hunstanton, Norfolk, 1347–8' *Archaeologia* 69 (1917–18) pp. 111–20
LPL	Lambeth Palace Library
MA	*Medieval Archaeology*
Maddicott, *Thomas of Lancaster*	J. R. Maddicott, *Thomas of Lancaster 1307–1322: a study in the reign of Edward II* (Oxford, 1970)
McFarlane, *England*	K. B. McFarlane, *England in the fifteenth century: collected essays* (1981)
McFarlane, *Nobility*	K. B. McFarlane, *The nobility of later medieval England* (Oxford, 1973)
MCO	Magdalen College, Oxford
MHE	*Manners and household expenses of England in the thirteenth and fifteenth centuries* ed. B. Botfield (1841)
MM	*Manners and meals in olden time* ed. F. J. Furnivall (EETS, OS, 32; 1868)
MOM	*Mémoires d'Olivier de la Marche* ed. H. Beaune and J. d'Arbaumont (4 vols, Paris, 1883–8)
NHB	*The regulations and establishment of the household of Henry Algernon Percy, the fifth Earl of Northumberland, at his castles of Wressle and Leckonfield, in Yorkshire. Begun Anno Domini MDXII* ed. T. Percy (new edition, 1905)
Nicolas, 'Observations'	N. H. Nicolas, 'Observations on the institution of the most noble Order of the Garter' *Archaeologia* 31 (1846) pp. 1–163
NMS	*Nottingham Medieval Studies*
OED	*Oxford English Dictionary*
OS	Original Series
Phillips, *Aymer*	J. R. S. Phillips, *Aymer de Valence Earl of Pembroke 1307–1324: baronial politics in the reign of Edward II* (Oxford, 1972)
PL	*Paston letters and papers of the fifteenth century* ed. N. Davis (2 vols, Oxford, 1971–6)
PP	*Past and Present*
PRO	Public Record Office
'Ralph of Shrewsbury'	J. A. Robinson, 'Household roll of Bishop Ralph of Shrewsbury (1337–8)' in *Collectanea I* ed. T. F. Palmer (Somerset Record Society, 39; 1924) pp. 72–174

Rawcliffe, *Staffords*	C. Rawcliffe, *The Staffords, Earls of Stafford and Dukes of Buckingham 1394–1521* (Cambridge, 1978)
RO	Record Office
Rulers	*Rulers and ruled in late medieval England: essays presented to Gerald Harriss* ed. R. E. Archer and S. Walker (1995)
RW	*A collection of all the wills now known to be extant of the Kings and Queens of England . . .* ed. J. Nicholls (1780)
RWH, 1285–6	*Records of the Wardrobe and Household 1285–1286* ed. B. F. Byerly and C. R. Byerly (1977)
RWH, 1286–9	*Records of the Wardrobe and Household 1286–1289* ed. B. F. Byerly and C. R. Byerly (1986)
Salzman, *Building*	L. F. Salzman, *Building in England down to 1540: a documentary history* (Oxford, 1952)
Seyntz medicines	*Le livre de seyntz medicines: the unpublished devotional treatise of Henry of Lancaster* ed. E. J. Arnould (ANTS, 2; 1940)
SL	*Kingsford's Stonor letters and papers 1290–1483* ed. C. Carpenter (Cambridge, 1996)
SR	*Statutes of the Realm* ed. A. Luders, T. E. Tomlins, J. Raithby *et al.* (11 vols, 1810–28)
Staniland, 'Clothing'	K. Staniland, 'Clothing and textiles at the court of Edward III 1342–1352' in *Collectanea Londiniensia: studies in London archaeology and history presented to Ralph Merrifield* ed. J. Bird, H. Chapman and J. Clark (London and Middlesex Archaeological Society, special paper 2; 1978) pp. 223–34
Steane, *Archaeology*	J. Steane, *The archaeology of the medieval English monarchy* (1993)
Swinfield	*A roll of the household expenses of Richard de Swinfield, Bishop of Hereford, during part of the years 1289 and 1290* ed. J. Webb (Camden Society, 1st series, 59, 62; 1854–5)
Thurley, *Royal palaces*	S. Thurley, *The royal palaces of Tudor England: architecture and court life 1460–1547* (1993)
Tout, *Chapters*	T. F. Tout, *Chapters in the administrative history of medieval England: the wardrobe, the chamber and the small seals* (6 vols, Manchester, 1920–33)
Tout, *Edward II*	T. F. Tout (revised by H. Johnstone), *The place of the reign of Edward II in history* (2nd edition, Manchester, 1936)
TRHS	*Transactions of the Royal Historical Society*
Turner, 'Humphrey de Bohun'	T. H. Turner, 'The will of Humphrey de Bohun, Earl of Hereford and Essex, with extracts from the inventory of his effects' *ArchJ* 2 (1846) pp. 339–49
UL	University Library
VCH	*Victoria History of the Counties of England*
WAM	Westminster Abbey Muniments
WCM	Winchester College Muniments
WH	*Walter of Henley and other treatises on estate management and accounting* ed. D. Oschinsky (Oxford, 1971)

Woolgar, 'Diet'   C. M. Woolgar, 'Diet and consumption in gentry and
                                   noble households: a case study from around the Wash' in
                                   Rulers, pp. 17–31
WPR 1301–2   *The Pipe Roll of the Bishopric of Winchester 1301–2* ed.
                                   M. Page (Hampshire Record Series, 14; 1996)
WW   *Documents illustrating the rule of Walter de Wenlok,*
                                   Abbot of Westminster, 1283–1307 ed. B. F. Harvey
                                   (Camden, 4th series, 2; 1965)

Notes

CHAPTER 1
Household Antiquities

1. N. Elias, *The court society* trans. E. Jephcott (Oxford, 1983); D. Starkey, 'The age of the household: politics, society and the arts *c.* 1350–*c.* 1550' in *The later Middle Ages* ed. S. Medcalf (1981) pp. 225–90.
2. *MOM* iv, pp. 1–94.
3. *Executors*, p. 100.
4. BL MS Lansdowne 1, ff. 84–5; BL MS Harley 642; D. A. L. Morgan, 'The house of policy: the political role of the late Plantagenet household, 1422–1485' in *The English court: from the Wars of the Roses to the Civil War* ed. D. Starkey (1987) pp. 25–70.
5. J. Bryant, *Turner: painting the nation* (1996).
6. A notable exception is M. Girouard, *Life in the English country house* (1978). See also J. Newman, 'The Elizabethan and Jacobean great house: a review of recent research' *ArchJ* 145 (1988) pp. 365–73; M. Johnson, *Housing culture: traditional architecture in an English landscape* (1993); H. M. Baillie, 'Etiquette and the planning of the state apartments in Baroque palaces' *Archaeologia* 101 (1967) pp. 166–99; S. J. Klingensmith, *The utility of splendor: ceremony, social life, and architecture at the court of Bavaria, 1600–1800* (Chicago, 1993).
7. C. Coulson, 'Cultural realities and re-appraisals in English castle-study' *JMH* 22 (1996) pp. 171–208.
8. Harvey, 'Consumer', pp. 19–20.
9. Given-Wilson, *English nobility*, pp. 29–56; McFarlane, *Nobility*, pp. 142–76; R. E. Archer, 'How ladies who live on their manors ought to manage their households and estates: women as landholders and administrators in the later Middle Ages' in *Woman is a worthy wight: women in English society c. 1200–1500* ed. P. J. P. Goldberg (Far Thrupp, 1992) pp. 162–4.
10. Maddicott, *Thomas of Lancaster*, p. 27.
11. McFarlane, *Nobility*, pp. 134–5, 177–86, pointing at the same time to the diminishing fortunes in private hands in the fourteenth century.
12. S. Walker, *The Lancastrian affinity 1361–1399* (Oxford, 1990) pp. 18–19.
13. Griffiths, 'King's court', pp. 41–67.
14. Le Strange, 'Household accounts', pp. 111–20; Norfolk RO, Le Strange of Hunstanton accounts, NH8, m. 2d.
15. *CP* x, pp. 377–82; H. Ridgeway, 'William de Valence and his *familiares*, 1247–72' *Historical Research* 65 (1992) pp. 239–57.
16. *CClR 1296–1302*, pp. 2–3; *CP* x, p. 382; *CIPM* iii, pp. 220–3; v, pp. 21–2.
17. PRO E101/505/26, mm. 2r, 24r.
18. Phillips, *Aymer*, pp. 240–52, for the value of the lands of the earldom of Pembroke. I estimate Joan's share to be worth £1,000. PRO E101/505/26–7.
19. Phillips, *Aymer*, pp. 2, 5–6, 8–9; B. F. Harvey, *Westminster Abbey and its estates in the Middle Ages* (Oxford, 1977) p. 375.
20. PRO E101/505/25–7.
21. Rawcliffe, *Staffords*, pp. 132–3.
22. Rawcliffe, *Staffords*, pp. 66–8, 86–7.
23. W. O. Massingberd, 'Notes on the pedigree of Multon of Frampton, co. Lincoln'

The Ancestor 2 (1902) pp. 205–7; for other details, *HAME* i, pp. 227–8.

24. J. Birrell, 'The *status maneriorum* of John Catesby 1385 and 1386' in *Miscellany I* ed. R. Bearman (Dugdale Society, 31; 1977) pp. 15–28; N. W. Alcock, 'The Catesbys in Coventry: a medieval estate and its archives' *Midland History* 15 (1990) pp. 1–36.

25. PRO E101/510/21, E101/511/15, E101/512/5.

26. K. B. McFarlane, 'The investment of Sir John Fastolf's profits of war' in McFarlane, *England*, p. 186.

27. A. Smith, ' "The greatest man of that age": the acquisition of Sir John Fastolf's East Anglian estates' in *Rulers*, pp. 137–53.

28. H. D. Barnes and W. D. Simpson, 'The building accounts of Caister Castle A. D. 1432–1435' *Norfolk Archaeology* 30 (1947–52) p. 179; M. Carlin, *Medieval Southwark* (1996) p. 52.

29. McFarlane, 'Profits of war', p. 190; MCO Fastolf papers 8, 43; Estate paper 176/9.

30. WCM 1; *HAME* i, pp. 261–430; C. Dyer, 'The consumer and the market in the later Middle Ages' in Dyer, *Everyday life*, pp. 257–81.

31. Aston, *Arundel*; for his London house, C. M. Barron, 'Centres of conspicuous consumption: the aristocratic town house in London 1200–1550' *London Journal* 20 (1995) pp. 1–16.

CHAPTER 2
Size, Membership and Hospitality

1. *MOM* iv, pp. 1–2.
2. *EC*, pp. 153–60.
3. *Dialogus de scaccario* ed. C. Johnson, revised by F. E. L. Carter and D. E. Greenway (Oxford, 1983) pp. 128–35; C. M. Woolgar, 'The development of accounts for private households in England to *c.* 1500 A. D.' (University of Durham Ph. D. thesis, 1986) pp. 18–23.
4. Tout, *Chapters* ii, pp. 49–51.
5. Jones and Walker, 'Indentures', pp. 1–190; see the comments on the annuitants of Humphrey Stafford, first Duke of Buckingham, pp. 12–13.
6. PRO DL 25/2026; also DL25/929; MCO Deeds, Multon Hall 122.

7. J. M. W. Bean, *From lord to patron: lordship in late medieval England* (Manchester, 1989) pp. 143–5.
8. *WH*, pp. 402–3.
9. N. Saul, 'The Commons and the abolition of badges' *Parliamentary History* 9 (1990) pp. 302–15; Given-Wilson, *Royal household*, pp. 234–45.
10. P. D. A. Harvey, *A medieval Oxfordshire village: Cuxham 1240 to 1400* (Oxford, 1965) p. 135.
11. Tout, *Chapters* ii, pp. 158–63.
12. Tout, *Edward II*, pp. 241–84.
13. Given-Wilson, *Royal household*, pp. 259, 278–9.
14. McFarlane, *Nobility*, pp. 109–10.
15. PRO E101/92/23.
16. *HAME* i, pp. 28–30.
17. Below, pp. 124–5, for a discussion of bread, standard measures and patterns of consumption.
18. PRO E101/510/17, E101/372/4, E101/505/17.
19. CUL EDR D5/5.
20. *MHE*, p. 20; H. Johnstone, 'Poor relief in the royal households of thirteenth-century England' *Speculum* 4 (1929) pp. 149–67; PRO E101/505/25–7.
21. LPL ED 1973; BL MS Harley 6815, f. 35.
22. Maddicott, *Thomas of Lancaster*, p. 27; Jones and Walker, 'Indentures', p. 32; Given-Wilson, *English nobility*, pp. 69–83. I am grateful to Simon Payling for discussing this point.
23. East Sussex RO MS GLY 3469 (20); S. Walker, *The Lancastrian affinity 1361–1399* (Oxford, 1990) p. 19.
24. Walker, *Lancastrian affinity*, pp. 18–19.
25. WAM 9223; LPL ED 1973.
26. *HBJH*, pp. xiv–xvii, xli–xlii.
27. *NHB*, pp. 150–2, 291–6.
28. *HAME* i, pp. 264–430.
29. PRO C47/3/33, part printed in J. C. Davis, *The baronial opposition to Edward II* (Cambridge, 1918) p. 569.
30. *WH*, pp. 400–5, 414.
31. Below, p. 136.
32. PRO E101/505/26, dorse.
33. *WW*, pp. 246–8.
34. P. R. Coss, 'Knights, esquires and the origins of social gradation in England' *TRHS* 6th series, 5 (1995) pp. 155–78.
35. N. Saul, *Knights and esquires: the Gloucestershire gentry in the fourteenth*

century (Oxford, 1981) pp. 16–29; D. A. L. Morgan, 'The individual style of the English gentleman' in *Gentry and lesser nobility in late medieval Europe* ed. M. Jones (Gloucester, 1986) pp. 24–6; *Rotuli Parliamentorum* (6 vols, n.p., n.d.) iii, p. 58.

36. *HAME* i, pp. 264–404.

37. Somerset RO DD/L P37/10 B, m. 3r; P37/10 C, m. 2r.

38. *HBJH*, pp. xl–xlii.

39. CUL EDR D5/2; PRO E101/400/28.

40. LPL ED 1973.

41. M. Hicks, *Bastard feudalism* (Harlow, 1995) pp. 139–64.

42. Dyer, *Standards*, p. 83.

43. P. R. Coss, *The knight in medieval England 1000–1400* (Far Thrupp, 1993) pp. 100–34.

44. *SL*, p. 298.

45. F. Heal, *Hospitality in early modern England* (Oxford, 1990) pp. 23–90.

46. *HAME* i, pp. 111, 114.

47. PRO E101/505/26, mm. 14r–15r, 25r.

48. PRO E101/505/17, m. 8r.

49. Harvey, 'Consumer', pp. 23–5.

50. *RWH, 1285–6*, pp. xxvii–xxviii.

51. CUL EDR D5/7a, mm. 1d, 2r.

52. WCM 1; Given-Wilson, *Royal household*, pp. 36; 295, n. 24.

53. HRO 11M59/B1/152, Wolvesey account.

54. Aston, *Arundel*, pp. 411–14.

55. CUL EDR D5/2–4.

56. PRO E101/400/28; CUL EDR D5/5–6.

57. J. Gage, 'Extracts from the household book of Edward Stafford, Duke of Buckingham' *Archaeologia* 25 (1834) pp. 320–7.

58. *EC*, pp. 98–9; PRO E101/505/25–7.

59. Staffs. RO D1721/1/5.

60. *WH*, pp. 400–7.

61. *Gawain*, pp. 70–5.

62. *The book of Margery Kempe* ed. S. B. Meech and H. E. Allen (EETS, OS, 212; 1940) pp. 36, 274–5; Aston, *Arundel*, pp. 165–6.

63. BL MS Harley 6815, ff. 35v–36r.

64. *HAME* i, p. 316.

65. Dyer, *Standards*, pp. 151–76; C. Dyer, 'English diet in the later Middle Ages' in *Social relations and ideas: essays in honour of R. H. Hilton* ed. T. H. Aston, P. R. Coss, C. Dyer and J. Thirsk (Cambridge, 1983) pp. 198–9.

66. MCO Fastolf paper 8, mm. 2r, 5r; *HAME* i, p. 62.

67. *HAME* ii, p. 576.

68. *SL*, p. 198.

69. *HAME* ii, p. 598.

70. *OED; Expeditions*, pp. 259–62, 335.

71. *RW*, p. 129.

72. *WH*, p. 409.

73. *BB*, p. 128.

74. For example, BL MS Harley 6815, ff. 36v–37r.

75. *JLBC* vi, pp. 9–10, 13.

76. G. Mathew, *The court of Richard II* (1968) pp. 107–8; J. C. Holt, *Robin Hood* (2nd edition, 1989) pp. 102–5.

77. A. Wathey, *Music in the royal and noble households in late medieval England: studies of sources and patronage* (1989) p. 5.

78. C. Bullock-Davies, *Menestrellorum multitudo: minstrels at a royal feast* (Cardiff, 1978) pp. 154, 171; PRO DL28/1/13, mm. 4r, 4d.; compare *RWH, 1285–6*, p. 167, £12 for robes of six minstrels.

79. PRO E101/505/27, m. 1r.

80. G. R. Rastall, 'The minstrel court in medieval England' *Proceedings of the Leeds Philosophical and Literary Society (Literary and Historical Section)* 18 (1982) pp. 96–105.

81. *WW*, p. 243.

82. *HAME* ii, p. 587; PRO E101/505/17, m. 3r.

83. Below, pp. 94–5.

84. *BB*, pp. 131–2.

85. Bullock-Davies, *Menestrellorum multitudo*, pp. 50–3.

86. *RWH, 1286–9*, p. 268.

87. *JLBC* vi, pp. 36–7.

88. Bullock-Davies, *Menestrellorum multitudo*; C. Bullock-Davies, *Register of royal and baronial domestic minstrels 1272–1327* (Woodbridge, 1986).

89. *RWH, 1286–9*, pp. 85, 94, 98.

90. Bullock-Davies, *Menestrellorum multitudo*, pp. 55, 138.

91. *EC*, p. 104.

92. *HBQI*, p. 102.

93. *HAME* ii, pp. 653, 667, 669.

CHAPTER 3
The Servants

1. *The political songs of England from the reign of John to that of Edward II* ed. T. Wright (Camden Society, 1st series, 6; 1839) pp. 237–40.

2. W. E. Wightman, *The Lacy family in England and Normandy 1066–1194* (Oxford, 1966) pp. 98, 105, 114; J. M. W. Bean, *From lord to patron: lordship in late medieval England* (Manchester, 1989) p. 152, n. 86; E. G. Kimball, *Serjeanty tenure in medieval England* (Yale, 1936) pp. 18–68.
3. *MHE*, pp. 56–7.
4. *WH*, p. 402.
5. PRO E101/505/25–7.
6. Turner, 'Humphrey de Bohun', p. 347.
7. BL MS Harley 4971, f. 7r.
8. *WW*, p. 245.
9. PRO E101/370/2, dorse.
10. *WH*, pp. 400–1.
11. C. Dyer and S. A. C. Penn, 'Wages and earnings in late medieval England: evidence from the enforcement of the labour laws' in Dyer, *Everyday life*, pp. 167–89.
12. *HAME* i, p. 169.
13. *HAME* i, pp. 261–430, especially pp. 268–9, 405, 421.
14. *HAME* i, p. 424.
15. *HAME* i, p. 420; below, p. 91.
16. Tout, *Edward II*, pp. 244–81.
17. *HO*, p. 94.
18. For example, *MM*, p. 320.
19. Below, pp. 172–5.
20. *Swinfield* i, pp. 111–14, 183–4.
21. *BB*, p. 64.
22. *BB*, p. 84.
23. *HO*, pp. *32, 95–6.
24. Somerset RO DD/L P37/12, m. 1r.
25. E. G. Millar, *The Luttrell Psalter* (1932) pp. 4, 52–4.
26. *Executors*, pp. 58, 109.
27. PRO E101/505/25, mm. 18r, 20r.
28. *RWH, 1285–6*, p. 10.
29. PRO E101/505/26, mm. 13r, 21r, 31d.
30. P. W. Fleming, 'Household servants of the Yorkist and early Tudor gentry' in *Early Tudor England* ed. D. Williams (Woodbridge, 1989) pp. 19–36.
31. Fleming, 'Household servants', p. 25.
32. PRO E101/505/26, m. 3r. C. H. Hartshorne, 'Illustrations of domestic manners during the reign of Edward I' *JBAA* 18 (1862) p. 147, has a limited discussion of Joan's servants, based on the listings of the valets receiving an allowance for footwear. He misread some names: Lucia, 'mistress of the Countess's wardrobe', was John of the Wardrobe; Jaket, the maid of Beatrice de

Nesle, was also a man.
33. PRO E101/505/26, m. 2r; E101/505/25, mm. 2r–3r, for the female assistant – *garcionis sue*.
34. PRO E101/505/27, dorse.
35. *HAME* ii, pp. 651–5.
36. *HO*, pp. 100–1.
37. Giuseppi, 'Bogo', p. 26.
38. *WW*, pp. 244–5; *WH*, pp. 400–1.
39. *The treatise of Walter de Milemete De nobilitatibus, sapientiis, et prudentiis regum . . .* ed. M. R. James (Oxford, 1913) p. l.
40. PRO E101/358/17; also Tout, *Edward II*, pp. 279–80.
41. *Fleta* ed. H. G. Richardson and G. O. Sayles (Selden Society, 72, 89, 99; 1955, 1972, 1983) i, pp. 114–15.
42. Given-Wilson, *Royal household*, p. 60.
43. *EC*, pp. 15, n. 50; 41; 97.
44. *RW*, p. 28.
45. MCO Fastolf paper 8, m. 2r; Fastolf paper 43, f. 16r.
46. *HBJH*, pp. xxix–xlii; *MHE*, pp. 394, 496; *HBJDN*, pp. 174, 199, 210, 230, 335, 364, 376, 558–9.
47. P. J. P. Goldberg, 'Female labour, service and marriage in the late medieval urban north' *Northern History* 22 (1986) pp. 24–8.
48. For prosopographies of servants, J. C. Ward, *English noblewomen in the later Middle Ages* (1992) pp. 52–7; Aston, *Arundel*, pp. 217–61; L. H. Butler, 'Robert Braybrooke, Bishop of London (1381–1404) and his kinsmen' (University of Oxford D. Phil. thesis, 1951) pp. 251–418; R. G. K. A. Mertes, *The English noble household 1250–1600: good governance and politic rule* (Oxford, 1988) pp. 52–74.
49. *MHE*, pp. 14, 53, 71; PRO E101/505/25–6.
50. Phillips, *Aymer*, pp. 256, 296, 307; H. Ridgeway, 'William de Valence and his *familiares*' *Historical Research* 65 (1992) pp. 244, 246–7, 250; *HAME* i, pp. 170–3, an account for Aymer de Valence (Matilda, the wife of Henry de Middleton, the joint accountant, subsequently married John Gascelin: *VCH Surrey*, iii, p. 423); N. Saul, 'A "rising" lord and a "declining" esquire: Sir Thomas de Berkeley III and Geoffrey Gascelyn of Sheldon' *Historical Research* 61 (1988) pp. 345–65.
51. A. R. Myers 'The household of Queen Elizabeth Woodville, 1466–7' in A. R.

Myers, *Crown, household and Parliament in fifteenth century England* (1985) p. 259.

52. Given-Wilson, *Royal household*, pp. 57–8; McFarlane, *England*, p. xiv.

53. H. G. Richardson, 'A French treatise on letter writing by Thomas Sampson' in *Formularies which bear on the history of Oxford c. 1204–1420* ed. H. E. Salter, W. A. Pantin and H. G. Richardson (Oxford Historical Society, new series, 4 and 5; 1942) ii, pp. 371–2.

54. C. Carpenter, *Locality and polity: a study of Warwickshire landed society, 1401–1499* (Cambridge, 1992) pp. 68–70.

55. Fleming, 'Household servants', pp. 27–8.

56. *SL*, p. 270.

57. H. S. Bennett, *The Pastons and their England* (2nd edition, Cambridge, 1932) pp. 82–3.

58. *HAME* ii, p. 537.

59. *HBJH*, p. xlii; *MHE*, pp. 309, 493–9, 585.

60. *HBJH*, pp. xxxix, xli–xlii; *MHE, passim*; *HBJDN*, p. 470.

61. Aston, *Arundel*, pp. 236–7.

62. *HAME* i, pp. 48–9.

63. *The English works of Wyclif* ed. F. D. Matthew (EETS, OS, 74; 1880) p. 168; for men in orders as administrators: PRO C47/3/3; Phillips, *Aymer*, p. 257.

64. Tout, *Chapters* iii, pp. 199, 233, 254; iv, pp. 149–57; vi, p. 27; also cited by Ward, *English noblewomen*, p. 57.

65. *Chaucer life-records* ed. M. M. Crow and C. C. Olson (Oxford, 1966) pp. 13–22, 94–143.

66. *NHB*, pp. 53–4.

67. B. F. Harvey, 'Work and *festa ferianda* in medieval England' *Journal of Ecclesiastical History* 23 (1972) pp. 289–308.

68. PRO E101/505/26, mm. 10r–11r, 15r.

69. *WW*, p. 243; below, pp. 86–90.

70. *NHB*, pp. 297–318.

71. *RW*, pp. 219–20, 330, 364–5.

72. *HAME* ii, p. 589.

73. Compare also Tout, *Edward II*, p. 276; R. B. Dobson, *Durham Priory, 1400–1450* (Cambridge, 1973) p. 121.

74. Dobson, *Durham Priory*, p. 121; Harvey, *Living*, p. 153.

75. *WH*, pp. 400–3; Tout, *Edward II*, p. 275.

76. *WW*, p. 243.

77. PRO E101/505/26, m. 11r; one page also in an account for Aymer de Valence: *HAME* i, p. 171.

78. *WW*, pp. 245–6.

79. Tout, *Edward II*, p. 276; *BB, passim*.

80. PRO E101/92/23, m. 3r; Ward, *English noblewomen*, p. 54; *RW*, p. 29.

81. Aston, *Arundel*, p. 414; CUL EDR D5/6, m. 3d.

82. WCM 1; *HAME* i, pp. 376, 428–9.

83. *MM*, p. 191.

84. *SL*, pp. 330–1.

85. J. M. Beattie, *The English court in the reign of George I* (Cambridge, 1967).

86. Fleming, 'Household servants', p. 25.

87. *SL*, p. 278.

88. *OED*; *MM*, p. 320.

89. *HAME* ii, pp. 595, 600, 603.

90. PRO E101/546/18, f. 29r.

91. *OED*; Nicolas, 'Observations', pp. 85, 92; Tout, *Edward II*, p. 269; Given-Wilson, *Royal household*, p. 32.

92. *Expeditions*, pp. 164, 166, 171, 176, 225, 284.

93. *RW*, p. 220.

94. *HAME* ii, pp. 655, 657.

95. *SR* ii, p. 402.

96. PRO E101/546/18, f. 37r.

97. Somerset RO DD/L P37/7, part 1, mm. 9r, 12r.

98. *BB*, pp. 126–7.

99. *WW*, p. 247.

100. Thurley, *Royal palaces*, pp. 176–7.

101. S. M. Newton, *Fashion in the age of the Black Prince: a study of the years 1340–1365* (Woodbridge, 1980) pp. 2–3.

102. E. Crowfoot, F. Pritchard and K. Staniland, *Medieval finds from excavations in London: 4. Textiles and clothing c. 1150–c. 1450* (1992) pp. 150–98.

103. *WH*, pp. 408–9; for the spirit of the late fifteenth-century English royal court, Griffiths, 'King's court', pp. 50–2.

104. *Fleta* i, pp. 109–14, 117, 120; W. R. Jones, 'The court of the verge: the jurisdiction of the steward and marshal of the household in later medieval England' *Journal of British Studies* 10 (1970–1) pp. 1–29.

105. *FCCB*, pp. 15–16.

106. *Leges Henrici Primi* ed. L. J. Downer (Oxford, 1972) pp. 35–6. 102–3, 148–9, 184–5.

107. *Leges Henrici Primi*, pp. 252–3.

108. *WW*, p. 242.

109. PRO E101/357/16.

110. PRO E101/355/14/1.
111. *BB*, pp. 104–5.
112. *HO*, pp. 89, 91.
113. *HO*, pp. *32–3.
114. Cited in A. Claxton, 'The sign of the dog: an examination of the Devonshire hunting tapestries' *JMH* 14 (1988) p. 162.

CHAPTER 4
Space and Residences

1. B. P. Hindle, 'Seasonal variations in travel in medieval England' *Journal of Transport History* 2nd series, 4 (1978) pp. 170–8.
2. *HKW* i, pp. 85, 112, 242–8; Steane, *Archaeology*, pp. 81–3.
3. PRO DL28/1/14; Maddicott, *Thomas of Lancaster*, pp. 25–6, 345–6.
4. PRO E101/510/17, E101/372/4, E101/505/17.
5. *Swinfield* i; analysis in Harvey, 'Consumer', p. 25.
6. N. D. McGlashan and R. E. Sandell, 'The Bishop of Salisbury's house at his manor of Potterne' *Wiltshire Archaeological and Natural History Magazine* 69 (1974) pp. 86–9; *HAME* i, pp. 264–430.
7. L. H. Butler, 'Robert Braybrooke, Bishop of London (1381–1404) and his kinsmen' (University of Oxford D. Phil thesis, 1951) pp. 219–50.
8. E. Roberts, 'William of Wykeham's house at East Meon, Hants' *ArchJ* 150 (1993) pp. 456–81; also the Bishops of Worcester: C. Dyer, *Lords and peasants in a changing society: the estates of the bishopric of Worcester, 680–1540* (Cambridge, 1980) p. 202.
9. I am grateful to Barbara Harvey for this point. R. B. Dobson, *Durham Priory 1400–1450* (Cambridge, 1973) pp. 94–7.
10. Northants RO Westmorland (Apethorpe) 4. xx. 4.; Rawcliffe, *Staffords*, pp. 66–8; N. W. Alcock, P. A. Faulkner and S. R. Jones, with G. M. D. Booth, 'Maxstoke Castle, Warwickshire' *ArchJ* 135 (1978) pp. 195–233.
11. J. Blair, 'Hall and chamber: English domestic planning 1000–1250' in *Manorial domestic buildings in England and Northern France* ed. G. Meirion-Jones and M. Jones (Society of Antiquaries of London, occa-

sional paper 15; 1993) pp. 1–21.
12. Salzman, *Building*, pp. 413–556.
13. *HKW* i, p. 121; ii, pp. 864–88, 910–18; *Clarendon Palace: the history and archaeology of a medieval palace and hunting lodge near Salisbury, Wiltshire* ed. T. B. James and A. M. Robinson (Reports of the research committee of the Society of Antiquaries of London, 45; 1988) pp. 1–31.
14. *HKW* ii, pp. 735–7; Challenger, 'Marlborough', pp. 1–49.
15. *HKW* i, p. 246; ii, pp. 934–5, 991.
16. *MM*, pp. 175–80.
17. Giuseppi, 'Bogo', p. 29.
18. PRO E101/505/27, m. 5r.
19. For some elements of this discussion, P. A. Faulkner, 'Castle planning in the fourteenth century' *ArchJ* 120 (1963) pp. 215–35; B. M. Morley, 'Aspects of fourteenth-century castle design' in *Collectanea historica: essays in memory of Stuart Rigold* ed. A. Detsicas (Maidstone, 1981) pp. 104–13; D. J. Turner, 'Bodiam, Sussex: true castle or old soldier's dream house?' in *England in the fourteenth century. Proceedings of the 1985 Harlaxton symposium* ed. W. M. Ormrod (Woodbridge, 1986) pp. 267–77.
20. *HKW* ii, p. 678.
21. *CClR 1323–7*, pp. 272–7.
22. C. Platt, *The architecture of medieval Britain: a social history* (1990) pp. 105–7; on Goodrich, Faulkner, 'Castle planning', pp. 221–5; D. Renn, *Goodrich Castle* (1993).
23. *CClR 1279–88*, pp. 26, 171; *CClR 1288–96*, p. 286.
24. *HKW* i, pp. 299–301.
25. F. R. Lewis, 'William de Valence (*c.* 1230–1296)' *Aberystwyth Studies* 13 (1934) pp. 11–35; 14 (1936) pp. 69–92.
26. *HKW* i, p. 231, citing PRO E101/476/5; ii, pp. 720–1.
27. PRO E101/505/26, mm. 9r, 14r.
28. PRO E101/505/27, m. 4r.
29. PRO E101/505/26, mm. 6r, 10r, 16r–21r.
30. PRO E101/505/25, m. 14r.
31. PRO E101/505/26, m. 5r.
32. PRO E101/505/27, mm. 1r–5r.
33. PRO E101/505/26, mm. 7r–22r.
34. Jones and Walker, 'Indentures', pp. 37–9; Phillips, *Aymer*, p. 261; modified by two

further indentures, PRO E101/68/1/2 and 3: *Calendar of documents relating to Scotland, 1272–1357* ed. J. Bain (2 vols, Edinburgh, 1884–7) ii, nos 981, 1004.

35. J. R. Knight, *Chepstow Castle and Port Wall* (revised edition, Cardiff, 1991).

36. Hare, 'Bishop's Waltham', pp. 236–7.

37. *HKW* ii, pp. 872–82.

38. H. D. Barnes and W. D. Simpson, 'The building accounts of Caister Castle A. D. 1432–1435' *Norfolk Archaeology* 30 (1947–52) pp. 178–86; H. D. Barnes and W. D. Simpson, 'Caister Castle' *AntJ* 32 (1952) pp. 35–51; K. B. McFarlane, 'The investment of Sir John Fastolf's profits of war' in McFarlane, *England*, pp. 186, n. 55; 191; *HAME* ii, pp. 615–16.

39. MCO Fastolf paper 43 and the second inventory printed by Amyot, 'Transcript', pp. 254–79, are substantially the same and of the same date, but differ to some extent in order and detail; Fastolf paper 43 has additional information of a later date. McFarlane, 'Fastolf's profits of war', p. 189.

40. *PL* i, pp. 111–13.

41. Barnes and Simpson, 'Building accounts of Caister', pp. 182–3.

42. MCO Fastolf paper 8, m. 2r, for her status in the household in 1430–1.

43. MCO Fastolf paper 43, f. 9v; Amyot's text is confused at this point.

44. *PL* i, p. 253.

45. There is a later coincidence of bed-chamber, bath, study and library in the bayne tower at Hampton Court as the privy lodgings of the king: Thurley, *Royal palaces*, pp. 135–6, 141; *NHB*, pp. 365–6.

46. M. W. Thompson, 'The construction of the manor at South Wingfield, Derbyshire' in *Problems in economic and social archaeology* ed. G. de G. Sieveking, I. H. Longworth and K. E. Wilson (1976) pp. 418, 426.

47. PRO E101/511/15, mm. 4r-5r.

48. PRO E101/512/5, m. 2d.

49. *HKW* i, p. 246.

50. PRO E36/150, pp. 68–9, cited in P. A. Rahtz, *Excavations at King John's Hunting Lodge, Writtle, Essex, 1955–57* (Society for Medieval Archaeology, monograph series, 3; 1969) pp. 11–12; Rawcliffe, *Staffords*, p. 67.

51. *HKW* i, p. 246; ii, p. 703.

52. *MM*, p. 316.

53. C. A. R. Radford, 'Acton Burnell Castle' in *Studies in building history: essays in recognition of the work of B. H. St. J. O'Neil* ed. E. M. Jope (1961) pp. 94–103; M. W. Thompson, *The decline of the castle* (Cambridge, 1987) pp. 32–42; A. Goodman, *The Wars of the Roses: military activity and English society, 1452–97* (1981) pp. 181–95.

54. *Gawain*, p. 68.

55. C. C. Taylor, 'Somersham Palace, Cambridgeshire: a medieval landscape for pleasure' in *From Cornwall to Caithness: some aspects of British field archaeology. Papers presented to Norman V. Quinnell* ed. M. Bowden, D. Mackay and P. Topping (British Archaeological Reports, British series, 209; 1989) p. 219; A. Uyttebrouck, 'Les résidences des ducs de Brabant, 1355–1430' and W. Paravicini, 'Die Residenzen der Herzöge von Burgund, 1363–1477' in *Fürstliche Residenzen im spätmittelalterlichen Europa* ed. H. Patze and W. Paravicini (Sigmaringen, 1991) pp. 189–263.

56. J. Gage, 'Extracts from the household book of Edward Stafford, Duke of Buckingham' *Archaeologia* 25 (1834) pp. 312–13.

57. Boorde, *Dyetary*, pp. 237–9.

58. *Ladie Kateryne*, p. 73.

59. Salzman, *Building*, pp. 140–6; T. P. Smith, 'Rye House, Hertfordshire, and aspects of early brickwork in England' *ArchJ* 132 (1975) pp. 111–50.

60. HRO 11M59/Bp/BW/63, m. 4r; 11M59/Bp/BW/64, m. 4r; 11M59/Bp/BW/65, mm. 3r–4r; 11M59/Bp/BW/66/1, m. 4r.

61. E. S. Eames, 'Decorated tile pavements in English medieval houses' in *Rotterdam papers II: a contribution to medieval archaeology* ed. J. G. N. Renaud (Rotterdam, 1975) pp. 13–14.

62. BL Add. MS 34,213, f. 64r; Thurley, *Royal palaces*, p. 230.

63. *MM*, pp. 177, 179, 181.

64. CUL EDR D5/3, m. 2d; *HAME* i, p. 421; Steane, *Archaeology*, pp. 144–5; *MM*, p. 183; PRO E101/546/18, f. 115Er.

65. *HKW* i, p. 87; Steane, *Archaeology*, p. 99.

66. *HAME* ii, p. 534.

67. PRO SC6/991/1.
68. *Baldricus Burgulianus: carmina* ed. K. Hilbert (Editiones Heidelbergenses, 19; 1979) pp. 149–74.
69. PRO DL28/1/13, m. 4d.
70. S. McKendrick, 'Tapestries from the Low Countries in England during the fifteenth century' in *England and the Low Countries in the late Middle Ages* ed. C. Barron and N. Saul (Stroud, 1995) pp. 43–60; *RW*, p. 72.
71. S. McKendrick, 'Edward IV: an English royal collector of Netherlandish tapestry' *Burlington Magazine* 129 (1987) pp. 521–4; Appendix I to HMC, *Eighth report* (3 vols, 1881) i, pp. 628–9.
72. *Ladie Kateryne*, pp. 72, 160–1.
73. PRO E101/546/18, f. 68r.
74. T. Borenius, 'The cycle of images in the palaces and castles of Henry III' *JWCI* 6 (1943) pp. 40–50; *Building accounts of King Henry III* ed. H. M. Colvin (Oxford, 1971) pp. 190, 238, 327.
75. *HKW* i, p. 528; iv, p. 227; *Ladie Kateryne*, pp. 72, 160.
76. R. Hayes, 'The "private life" of a late medieval bishop: William Alnwick, Bishop of Norwich and Lincoln' in *EFC, 1992*, p. 5.
77. PRO E101/546/18, ff. 56v, 66v.
78. Thurley, *Royal palaces*, pp. 158–9, 254.
79. *Building accounts of King Henry III*, p. 196.
80. *HKW* i, p. 246; ii, p. 974.
81. MCO Fastolf paper 43, f. 10r.
82. Northants RO Westmorland (Apethorpe) 4. xx. 4., ff. 17r, 32r.
83. *NHB*, pp. 364–71.
84. *HKW* i, pp. 497–8.
85. Eames, *Furniture*, pp. 73–107.
86. PRO E101/505/25, mm. 9r, 16r; E101/505/26, mm. 3r, 5r, 7r, 18r, 22r, 24r, 27r.
87. Giuseppi, 'Bogo', p. 28.
88. Nicolas, 'Observations', pp. 53, 77–8.
89. Salzman, *Building*, p. 261 for furze (*gorst*).
90. Tout, *Edward II*, p. 257.
91. *MM*, p. 313.
92. PRO E101/546/18, ff. 35r, 38v.
93. M. F. Braswell, 'Sin, the lady and the law. The English noblewoman in the late Middle Ages' *Medievalia et Humanistica* new series, 14 (1986) p. 89.
94. *HO*, pp. 121–2.
95. PRO DL28/1/13, m. 5d.
96. *HO*, p. 148.
97. Tout, *Edward II*, p. 254.
98. *MM*, p. 182.
99. A similar change was made at Westminster Abbey: Harvey, *Living*, pp. 89, 166–7; Salzman, *Building*, p. 261.
100. *SL*, p. 131.
101. HRO 11M59/Bp/BW/63, m. 3r.
102. *HAME* i, p. 178; K.-U. Jäschke, *Nichtkönigliche Residenzen im spätmittelalterlichen England* (Sigmaringen, 1990) pp. 275–82.
103. C. M. Barron, 'Centres of conspicuous consumption: the aristocratic town house in London 1200–1550' *London Journal* 20 (1995) pp. 1–16.
104. PRO E101/505/26, mm. 2r, 23r–24r.
105. *HAME* i, p. 173.
106. BL Add. MS 34,213, ff. 63v, 123r; J. Schofield, *Medieval London houses* (1994) pp. 210–12.
107. PRO E101/546/18, ff. 2r, 8r, 16v, 78–9, 92r.
108. Nottingham UL MS Manvers C57.
109. Nottingham UL MS Manvers C56.
110. M. Carlin, *Medieval Southwark* (1996) p. 52.
111. Barron, 'Centres', p. 7.

CHAPTER 5

The Rhythms of the Household

1. *NHB, passim.*
2. *RW*, p. 129.
3. LPL ED 1973.
4. D. S. Landes, *Revolution in time: clocks and the making of the modern world* (Cambridge, Mass., 1983) pp. 6–9, 67–97, 191–200; G. Dohrn-van Rossum, *History of the hour: clocks and modern temporal orders* trans. T. Dunlap (1996) pp. 32–40, 134–5, 169; Harvey, *Living*, pp. 154–6; J. Geddes, 'Iron' in *EMI*, pp. 178–9; R. P. Howgrave-Graham, 'Some clocks and jacks, with notes on the history of horology' *Archaeologia* 77 (1927) pp. 257–312.
5. *HKW* ii, pp. 802, 975, 996, n. 8; R. A. Brown, 'King Edward's clocks' *AntJ* 39 (1959) pp. 283–6; J. B. Post and A. J. Turner, 'An account for repairs to the Westminster Palace clock' *ArchJ* 130 (1973) pp. 217–20.

6. *HKW* ii, p. 802, n. 7.

7. A. R. Myers, 'The captivity of a royal witch: the household accounts of Queen Joan of Navarre 1419–21' in A. R. Myers, *Crown, household and Parliament in fifteenth century England* (1985) p. 125.

8. *BI*, pp. 90, 367.

9. *HAME* ii, pp. 589, 593, 595; Northants RO Westmorland (Apethorpe) 4. xx. 4., ff. 6v, 11r.

10. *FCCB*, p. 12.

11. *HO*, pp. *37–9; C. A. J. Armstrong, 'The piety of Cicely, Duchess of York: a study in late medieval culture' in C. A. J. Armstrong, *England, France and Burgundy in the fifteenth century* (1983) pp. 140–3.

12. *HO*, p. 89.

13. R. G. K. A. Mertes, 'The household as a religious community' in *People, politics and community in the later Middle Ages* ed. J. Rosenthal and C. Richmond (Gloucester, 1987) pp. 123–39.

14. *NHB*, pp. 311–13, 354–63.

15. *HAME* i, p. 31.

16. Harvey, *Living*, p. 157.

17. PRO E101/505/25, m. 17r.

18. PRO E101/366/28, Roger atte Becche, *cocus de gentaculo regis*.

19. *RWH, 1286–9*, p. 213.

20. Cornwall RO AR37/55, f. 1v.

21. It was, however, eaten by manual workers: BL Add. MS 34,213, f. 41r; Salzman, *Building*, pp. 61–6.

22. *Bryene, passim*.

23. J. Gage, 'Extracts from the household book of Edward Stafford, Duke of Buckingham' *Archaeologia* 25 (1834) pp. 320–3, from Staffs. RO D1721/1/5, p. 58; above, p. 24.

24. PRO E101/546/18, f. 45v.

25. *HO*, p. *39.

26. PRO E101/546/18, ff. 22v, 57v.

27. *NHB*, pp. 73–8.

28. *HO*, p. *29; BL MS Harley 6815, f. 29r.

29. T. More, *The apologye of Syr Thomas More knyght* ed. J. B. Trapp (*The Yale edition of the complete works of St Thomas More* (Yale, 1963–) ix) p. 106; Harvey, *Living*, pp. 156–9.

30. *PL* ii, p. 548.

31. *MM*, p. 181.

32. *HAME* i, p. 397.

33. PRO E101/546/18, f. 6r; Staffs. RO D1721/1/5, p. 31.

34. BL MS Harley 6815, ff. 36v-37r.

35. 'Ralph of Shrewsbury', pp. 85–133.

36. Staffs. RO D1721/1/5, p. 53.

37. *NHB*, pp. 22, 42, 242.

38. *BB*, pp. 90, 184, 200, 204, 237; *HO*, pp. *28, 90, 109.

39. *MM*, pp. 182, 314–15, 327, mention a mortar of wax, also *BB*, p. 90; but tallow was more usual, PRO E101/512/17, m. 1d; E101/513/2, m. 4d; BL Add. MS 34,213, f. 89r.

40. PRO E101/505/25, m. 1r; *MHE*, p. 12; *WH*, pp. 282–3; *RWH, 1285–6*, p. 210.

41. *HO*, pp. 90–1.

42. *MM*, p. 196.

43. *BB*, pp. 132, 200.

44. Harvey, *Living*, pp. 158–9.

45. Salzman, *Building*, pp. 61–6, and *Building accounts of King Henry III* ed. H. M. Colvin (Oxford, 1971) pp. 9–10, shorten lunch time to one hour. While there is force to the arguments about the equation of the service of Nones with lunch time, its simultaneous equation with 12 o'clock, noon, is misplaced.

46. *SL*, pp. 298–9.

47. *SL*, pp. 262–4.

48. *HAME* i, p. 134.

49. PRO E101/505/26–7.

50. *BB*, pp. 108–10.

51. Woolgar, 'Diet', p. 19.

52. *HAME* i, p. 420; ii, p. 578; *MHE*, pp. 339, 509; *HBJDN*, pp. 179–80.

53. PRO E101/505/25–7.

54. PRO E101/505/25, mm. 10r–11r; E101/505/26, m. 5r.

55. PRO E101/505/26, mm. 8r–12r.

56. WCM 1.

57. *Bryene, passim*.

58. Duffy, *Altars*, pp. 41–2.

59. For example, BL Add. MS 34,213, ff. 47r, 104r.

60. PRO E101/546/18.

61. Staffs. RO D1721/1/5.

62. LPL ED 1973.

63. PRO E101/505/26, mm. 9r, 15r.

64. *EC*, p. 80, n. 99.

65. *HAME* i, pp. 407–8.

66. *MHE*, p. 331; *NHB*, p. 321.

67. PRO E101/513/2, mm. 2d, 5d.

68. *HBQI*, pp. 120–1.

69. *NHB*, pp. 322–3; for Holy Week cere-

monies, Duffy, *Altars*, pp. 22–37.

70. Duffy, *Altars*, pp. 11–52.
71. G. C. Homans, *English villagers of the thirteenth century* (New York, 1960) pp. 353–81.
72. *Bryene*, pp. 85–92.
73. PRO E101/400/28, dorse; for the custom of the boy bishop, N. Orme, 'The culture of children in medieval England' *PP* 148 (1995) pp. 70–1.
74. Nottingham UL, Middleton MS Mi A1.
75. Nicolas, 'Observations', pp. 37–8, 43; discussed in Staniland, 'Clothing', pp. 228–9.
76. S. Westfall, *Patrons and performance: early Tudor household revels* (Oxford, 1990) pp. 34–42; S. Anglo, 'The court festivals of Henry VII: a study based upon the account books of John Heron, Treasurer of the Chamber' *BJRL* 43 (1960–1) pp. 12–45, especially pp. 21–2.
77. Somerset RO DD/L P37/7, part 1, m. 10r.
78. *HAME* i, pp. 414, 418–21, 426.
79. Westfall, *Patrons*, pp. 13–62.
80. *NHB*, p. 22; I. Lancashire, 'Orders for Twelfth Day and Night circa 1515 in the second Northumberland Household Book' *English Literary Renaissance* 10 (1980) pp. 7–45.
81. *HBJDN*, p. 517.
82. Westfall, *Patrons*, pp. 66–74.
83. Staffs. RO D1721/1/5, p. 45.
84. Anglo, 'Court festivals', p. 40.
85. *NHB*, pp. 331–2.
86. *RWH, 1285–6*, p. 196.
87. *EC*, p. 80.
88. *HAME* i, pp. 420, 422–3.
89. *HAME* ii, pp. 597–8.
90. *HO*, p. 120.
91. 'Isabel of Lancaster', p. 494.
92. *MHE*, p. 258. For the feast in the mid-fourteenth century, Nicolas, 'Observations', pp. 1–163; Staniland, 'Clothing', pp. 223–34.
93. *NHB*, p. 324.
94. PRO E101/512/5, m. 2r.
95. Anglo, 'Court festivals', pp. 31, 33, 36, 39, 41–3.
96. *MHE*, p. 275.
97. Harvey, *Living*, p. 106; Salzman, *Building*, p. 61, on the monastic year.
98. *HO*, pp. 91, 103–4, 162; *BB*, p. 148.
99. *HO*, p. *39; *MM*, p. 311.
100. PRO E101/505/25, m. 2r.
101. *HAME* i, pp. 283–4.
102. H. Johnstone, 'Poor-relief in the royal households of thirteenth-century England' *Speculum* 4 (1929) p. 159, n. 1.
103. *HBJDN*, pp. 509–10.
104. P. J. P. Goldberg, 'Female labour, service and marriage in the late medieval urban north' *Northern History* 22 (1986) pp. 25–6; K. Dockray, 'Why did fifteenth-century English gentry marry?: the Pastons, Plumptons and Stonors reconsidered' in *Gentry and lesser nobility in late medieval Europe* ed. M. Jones (Gloucester, 1986) pp. 61–80, at p. 65; S. Payling, 'The politics of family: late medieval marriage contracts' in *The McFarlane legacy: studies in late medieval politics and society* ed. R. H. Britnell and A. J. Pollard (Stroud, 1995) pp. 21–47.
105. Phillips, *Aymer*, p. 6.
106. *SL*, pp. 262–4.
107. R. E. Archer, 'Rich old ladies: the problem of late medieval dowagers' in *Property and politics: essays in later medieval English history* ed. A. Pollard (Gloucester, 1984) pp. 15–35; McFarlane, *Nobility*, pp. 143–53.
108. *EC*, pp. 109–10, 126–7.
109. Somerset RO DD/L P37/11, m. 3d.
110. *SL*, pp. 201–2.
111. Staniland, 'Clothing', p. 228.
112. *EC*, pp. 6–7; N. Orme, *From childhood to chivalry: the education of the English kings and aristocracy 1066–1530* (1984) pp. 1–80.
113. W. O. Massingberd, 'Notes on the pedigree of Multon of Frampton, co. Lincoln' *The Ancestor* 2 (1902) pp. 205–7; *HAME* i, pp. 227–45.
114. PRO E101/511/15, m. 4r; N. W. Alcock, 'The Catesbys in Coventry: a medieval estate and its archives' *Midland History* 15 (1990) p. 3.
115. *SL*, pp. 32–3, 55.
116. P. P. A. Biller, 'Birth-control in the West in the thirteenth and early fourteenth centuries' *PP* 94 (1982) pp. 3–26; J. M. Riddle, 'Oral contraceptives and early-term abortifacients during Classical Antiquity and the Middle Ages' *PP* 122 (1991) pp. 3–32.
117. *HAME* i, p. 113.
118. *HBQI*, pp. xxv–xxvi.
119. *WPR 1301–2*, p. 144.
120. PRO E101/365/20, mm. 3r, 8r; C. Peers and L. E. Tanner, 'On some recent discov-

eries in Westminster Abbey' *Archaeologia*
93 (1949) pp. 151–5.

121. *HO*, pp. 125–8; *MHE*, p. 18; PRO
E101/372/4, m. 2r; *NHB*, p. 43.

122. Nicolas, 'Observations', pp. 50–1.

123. PRO E101/505/27, m. 5r; for other
examples, *EC*, pp. 98, 113–14.

124. PRO E101/365/20, m. 8r.

125. Nicolas, 'Observations', pp. 50–1;
Staniland, 'Clothing', p. 228.

126. PRO E101/365/20, m. 8r; E101/365/17,
m. 2r; B. F. Harvey *Westminster Abbey
and its estates in the Middle Ages*
(Oxford, 1977) p. 376, n. 3; Peers and
Tanner, 'Recent discoveries', pp. 151–5.

127. Nicolas, 'Observations', p. 50.

128. *RWH, 1286–9*, pp. 186–7.

129. P. P. A. Biller, 'Childbirth in the Middle
Ages' *History Today* 36 no. 8 (1986)
pp. 42–9.

130. The statements about his age are contra-
dictory: *CIPM* iii, pp. 116, 122–3, 444;
PRO E101/505/25, mm. 4r–7r; E101/
505/26, mm. 10r, 14r, 18r–19r, 21r.

131. Orme, 'Culture of children', pp. 51–8; G.
Egan, *Playthings from the past: toys from
the A. G. Pilson collection c. 1300–1800*
(1996).

132. *HKW* i, p. 202, n. 2; *RWH, 1286–9*,
pp. 411–12.

133. C. Bullock-Davies, *Register of royal and
baronial domestic minstrels 1272–1327*
(Woodbridge, 1986) pp. 111–12.

134. A. Gransden, 'Childhood and youth in
medieval England' *NMS* 16 (1972) p. 3;
Orme, 'Culture of children', pp. 48–88.

135. *HAME* ii, pp. 599–600; Orme, 'Culture
of children', pp. 67–8; McFarlane,
Nobility, p. 130.

136. Anglo, 'Court festivals', p. 14.

137. Orme, *Childhood to chivalry*, pp. 181–
210.

138. P. W. Fleming, 'Household servants of
the Yorkist and early Tudor gentry' in
Early Tudor England ed. D. Williams
(Woodbridge, 1989) pp. 25–6.

139. Aston, *Arundel*, pp. 411–14.

140. *BB*, pp. 136–7.

141. *HBJDN*, p. 145. For other chapels, *HO*,
pp. *29, 92.

142. *BB*, pp. 137–8.

143. *BB*, pp. 126–7.

144. Orme, 'Culture of children', p. 85.

145. G. Platts, *Land and people in medieval
Lincolnshire* (Lincoln, 1985) pp. 265–6;
HAME i, pp. 236–7.

146. PRO E101/511/15, mm. 4r–5r; E101/
512/5, mm. 2r–3r.

147. *SL*, p. 138.

148. P. R. Coss, *The knight in medieval England
1000–1400* (Far Thrupp, 1996) pp. 61,
67, 69.

149. PRO E101/505/27, mm. 1r, 5r; Phillips,
Aymer, p. 22.

150. Orme, *Childhood to chivalry*, pp. 190–1.

151. Jones and Walker, 'Indentures', pp. 43–4.

152. *HAME* i, pp. 232, 245.

153. C. M. Woolgar and B. O'Donoghue,
'Two Middle English poems at Magdalen
College, Oxford' *Medium Aevum* 52
(1983) p. 221.

154. F. M. Powicke, *King Henry III and the
Lord Edward* (2 vols, Oxford, 1947) ii,
pp. 562, 603–4.

155. *Expeditions*, pp. lxxvi–lxxvii.

156. *HAME* i, p. 157; J. R. Maddicott,
'Follower, leader, pilgrim, saint: Robert
de Vere, Earl of Oxford, at the shrine of
Simon de Montfort, 1273' *EHR* 109
(1994) pp. 641–53.

157. PRO E101/505/25, mm. 3r, 4r and
schedule, 7r–8r; Phillips, *Aymer*, pp. 8–9.

158. PRO E101/505/25, mm. 4r–5r.

159. C. Rawcliffe, *Medicine & society in later
medieval England* (Far Thrupp, 1995)
pp. 105–6, 133–7; *HAME* i, pp. 301–430.

160. Crawford, 'Private life', p. 12.

161. A. C. Reeves, 'Some of Humphrey
Stafford's military indentures' *NMS* 16
(1972) p. 91.

162. *MHE*, pp. 31, 33; PRO E101/400/28,
dorse; CUL EDR D5/6, m. 2d.

163. G. E. Trease, 'The spicers and apothecaries of the royal household in the reigns
of Henry III, Edward I and Edward II'
NMS 3 (1959) pp. 46–7.

164. *NHB*, p. 371.

165. *PL* ii, pp. 538, 566–7.

166. *RW*, p. 98.

167. *HO*, pp. 129–33; P. W. Hammond, 'The
funeral of Richard Neville, Earl of
Salisbury' *The Ricardian* 6 (1984)
pp. 410–16.

168. P. Binski, *Westminster Abbey and the
Plantagenets: kingship and the representa-
tion of power 1200–1400* (1995) pp. 108,

113.

169. PRO E101/505/26, m. 24r.
170. PRO E101/505/25, mm. 9r–13r, 17r, 21r; *EC*, pp. 88, 132–3.
171. PRO E101/505/25, m. 13r; E101/505/26, m. 28r.
172. PRO E101/505/26, m. 23r; P. J. Lankester, 'A military effigy in Dorchester Abbey, Oxon.' *Oxoniensia* 52 (1987) pp. 145–72.
173. H. Jenkinson, 'Mary de Sancto Paulo, Foundress of Pembroke College, Cambridge' *Archaeologia* 66 (1914–15) pp. 401–46.
174. Harvey, *Living*, pp. 23–33.
175. Turner, 'Humphrey de Bohun', p. 341.
176. *RW*, p. 44; J. Catto, 'Religion and the English nobility in the later fourteenth century' in *History and the imagination: essays in honour of H. R. Trevor-Roper* ed. H. Lloyd-Jones, V. Pearl and B. Worden (1981) pp. 50–1.
177. *RW*, p. 217.
178. *HAME* i, pp. 402–3, 405, 424, 430.
179. *HAME* ii, pp. 658, 661, 664–5, 679–82.
180. M. Campbell, 'English goldsmiths in the fifteenth century' in *EFC, 1986*, p. 51.
181. Hammond, 'Funeral of Richard Neville', p. 411.
182. C. Carpenter, 'The religion of the gentry of fifteenth-century England' in *EFC, 1986*, p. 61.
183. *Ladie Kateryne*, pp. 92–3.

Chapter 6
Food and Drink

1. Dyer, *Standards*, p. 70.
2. PRO E101/505/25–7.
3. *WH*, pp. 396–9.
4. Crawford, 'Private life', p. 9.
5. Harvey, 'Consumer', pp. 29, 32–6.
6. Norfolk RO, NH 3–5, 7–8, 10–12.
7. BL Add. MS 34,213, ff. 5v, 6v, 7v, 9v, 11r, etc.
8. *WH*, pp. 398–9, 411.
9. PRO E101/505/27, m. 5r.
10. C. Dyer, 'The consumer and the market in the later Middle Ages' in Dyer, *Everyday life*, pp. 257–81.
11. PRO E101/505/26, mm. 6r–7r and dorse.
12. Nottingham UL, Middleton MS Mi A1, m. 3r.

13. 'Ralph of Shrewsbury', p. 137; BL Add. MS 34,213, ff. 72v, 84v.
14. Note 5, above; Woolgar, 'Diet', p. 21.
15. Somerset RO DD/L P37/7, part 1, mm. 4r–5r, 7r.
16. Northants RO Westmorland (Apethorpe) 4. xx. 4., ff. 3v, 4v, 32r.
17. PRO E101/505/26, mm. 25r–27r.
18. WCM 1, under 30 June.
19. PRO E101/372/4, m. 1r.
20. BL Add. MS 34,213, ff. 14r, 99r.
21. PRO E101/546/18, ff. 42r, 67r.
22. Northants RO Westmorland (Apethorpe) 4. xx. 4., f. 12v.
23. The department known as the poultry looked after young animals of all sorts. PRO E101/505/17, m. 2r.
24. *HAME* i, p. 167; PRO DL28/1/13, m. 4d.
25. Woolgar, 'Diet', p. 22; J. McCann, 'An historical enquiry into the design and use of dovecotes' *Transactions of the Ancient Monuments Society* 35 (1991) pp. 89–160.
26. Cornwall RO AR37/55, f. 7v.
27. Northants RO Westmorland (Apethorpe) 4. xx. 4., f. 19r.
28. *HAME* i, pp. 403, 429.
29. PRO E101/546/18, f. 27v.
30. Harris, 'Buckingham', p. 35.
31. 'Ralph of Shrewsbury', pp. 97, 135.
32. *RWH, 1286–9*, p. 389; *HAME* i, pp. 182, 206; ii, p. 553.
33. Woolgar, 'Diet', pp. 22–3.
34. D. Serjeantson, 'A dainty dish: consumption of small birds in late medieval England' in *Man and animals in the past: Festschrift for Anneke Clason* ed. H. Buitenhuis (forthcoming).
35. *RWH, 1285–6*, pp. 225, 229, 237; *RWH, 1286–9*, p. 321; F. J. Tanquerey, 'Lettres du roi Edward I à Robert de Bavent, King's yeoman, sur des questions de vénerie' *BJRL* 23 (1939) pp. 487–503.
36. PRO E101/505/25, m. 9r; E101/505/26, m. 20r.
37. PRO E101/505/25, m. 20r; E101/505/27, m. 1r.
38. PRO E101/505/25–7; for salting venison, *RWH, 1286–9*, p. 330.
39. Woolgar, 'Diet', p. 22; J. Birrell, 'Deer and deer farming in medieval England' *AgHR* 40 (1992) pp. 112–26.
40. On two occasions only: half on Easter Sunday 1297; and the gift of a boar to Joan

around Christmas 1296, PRO E101/505/26, m. 20r, and dorse.

41. PRO *Keeper's Annual Report 1995–6*, p. 20, citing E32/43; Steane, *Archaeology*, pp. 138, 148; O. Rackham, *Ancient woodland* (1980) p. 181.
42. *HAME* ii, p. 500.
43. PRO E101/505/26, dorse.
44. 'Ralph of Shrewsbury', pp. 92–101.
45. BL Add. MS 34,213, ff. 62v, 67r.
46. *HAME* i, pp. 187, 224.
47. Norfolk RO, NH6–7.
48. PRO E101/510/17, E101/372/4; E101/505/17, m. 1r.
49. *HAME* ii, p. 515.
50. Harvey, 'Consumer', p. 28.
51. Somerset RO DD/L P37/7, part 1, m. 10r.
52. G. G. Astill, 'An early inventory of a Leicestershire knight' *Midland History* 2 (1974) p. 280.
53. *SL*, p. 131.
54. Northants RO Westmorland (Apethorpe) 4. xx. 4., f. 16v.
55. PRO E101/505/26, dorse.
56. *HAME* i, p. 295.
57. *HAME* ii, p. 520.
58. *HAME* ii, pp. 527–42.
59. PRO E101/512/17, m. 2d.
60. *HAME* i, pp. 229, 256.
61. CUL EDR D5/3, m. 1d; *HAME* i, p. 231; *The overseas trade of London: Exchequer customs accounts 1480–1* ed. H. S. Cobb (London Record Society, 27; 1990) p. 187; L. Wright, *Sources of London English: medieval Thames vocabulary* (Oxford, 1996) pp. 102–5.
62. *Overseas trade of London*, pp. 1, 4, 14, 17, 20.
63. S. Godbold and R. C. Turner, 'Medieval fishtraps in the Severn estuary' *MA* 38 (1994) pp. 19–54.
64. 'Ralph of Shrewsbury', pp. 94–133.
65. Somerset RO DD/L P37/7, part 1, mm. 6r–7r.
66. H. S. A. Fox, 'Fishing in Cockington documents' in *Devon documents in honour of Mrs Margery Rowe* ed. T. Gray (Exeter, 1996) pp. 76–82.
67. Woolgar, 'Diet', pp. 24–5.
68. Woolgar, 'Diet', p. 25; A. J. F. Dulley, 'The early history of the Rye fishing industry' *Sussex Archaeological Collections* 107 (1969) pp. 36–64; R. W. Unger, 'The Netherlands

herring fishery in the late Middle Ages: the false legend of Willem Beukels of Biervliet' *Viator* 9 (1978) pp. 333–56.
69. *Building accounts of King Henry III* ed. H. M. Colvin (Oxford, 1971) p. 56, n. 1.
70. PRO E101/505/26, mm. 14r–15r.
71. PRO E101/505/26, m. 8r.
72. 'Ralph of Shrewsbury', pp. 126, 134, 146.
73. Norfolk RO, NH3, m. 4r.
74. *The brokage book of Southampton from 1439–40* ed. B. D. M. Bunyard (Southampton Record Society, 20; 1941) pp. 95, 110–11, 115; *The brokage book of Southampton 1443–1444* ed. O. Coleman (Southampton Record Series, 4, 6; 1960–1) ii, p. 170.
75. PRO E101/505/25, mm. 13r–15r; E101/505/26, mm. 2r, 10r.
76. BL Add. MS 34,213, ff. 5v, 6v, 7v, 9v, 11r, etc.; 21r, 101v; Dyer, 'Consumer', pp. 264–5.
77. Aston, *Arundel*, p. 230; *HAME* ii, p. 528.
78. J. M. Steane, 'The royal fishponds of medieval England' in *Medieval fish, fisheries and fishponds in England* ed. M. Aston (British Archaeological Reports, British series, 182 (i) and (ii); 1988) i, pp. 39–68.
79. *RWH, 1286–9*, pp. 15, 33.
80. Challenger, 'Marlborough', p. 47.
81. E. Roberts, 'The Bishop of Winchester's fishponds in Hampshire, 1150–1400: their development, function and management' *Proceedings of the Hampshire Field Club and Archaeological Society* 42 (1986) pp. 125–38.
82. PRO E101/505/26, m. 14r.
83. PRO E101/505/25, mm. 10r, 20r–21r; E101/505/26, mm. 1r–2r.
84. PRO E101/505/26, m. 19r.
85. *MHE*, pp. 15, 39.
86. Northants RO Westmorland (Apethorpe) 4. xx. 4., ff. 21v, 26v, 31v, 45v.
87. HRO 11M59/Bp/BW/61.
88. R. C. Hoffman, 'Fishing for sport in medieval Europe: new evidence' *Speculum* 60 (1985) pp. 877–902.
89. *MHE*, pp. 560–4; C. F. Hickling, 'Prior More's fishponds' *MA* 15 (1971) pp. 118–23.
90. 'Ralph of Shrewsbury', pp. 157–9.
91. PRO E101/505/25, mm. 1r, 12r, 15r. On freshwater fish generally, C. Dyer, 'The

consumption of freshwater fish in medieval England' in Dyer, *Everyday life*, pp. 101–11; Woolgar, 'Diet', pp. 17–31.

92. *HAME* i, pp. 265, 267–9, 367, 370, 382, 400, 404, 415, 418, 421.

93. *WPR 1301–2*, pp. 312, 322.

94. BL Add. MS 34,213, ff. 63v, 65r, 108r; *MHE*, p. 381.

95. BL Add. MS 34,213, f. 119v.

96. BL Add. MS 34,213, f. 21r.

97. Northants RO Westmorland (Apethorpe) 4. xx. 4, f. 13v; BL Add. MS 34,231, f. 60r; PRO E101/546/18, f. 83v.

98. *HAME* ii, p. 528.

99. Roberts, 'Bishop of Winchester's fishponds', p. 127; Steane, *Archaeology*, p. 138; *RWH, 1285–6*, p. 18; PRO E101/546/18, f. 46v.

100. Roberts, 'Bishop of Winchester's fishponds', p. 130; Le Strange, 'Household accounts', p. 116.

101. PRO E101/354/30, recto.

102. PRO E101/353/28, E101/364/16; Tout, *Edward II*, pp. 257–8.

103. *HAME* ii, p. 514.

104. Bodl. MS Fairfax 24, f. 62v.

105. PRO E101/372/4, m. 2r.

106. Norfolk RO, NH8.

107. *HAME* i, pp. 188–9.

108. *HAME* ii, p. 500.

109. Bodl. MS Fairfax 24, f. 62r.

110. *Medieval Framlingham: select documents 1270–1524* ed. J. Ridgard (Suffolk Records Society, 27; 1985) p. 106.

111. *WH*, pp. 404–5.

112. 'Ralph of Shrewsbury', p. 126.

113. PRO E101/400/28, m. 3r; E101/510/27, m. 2r; CUL EDR D5/2, m. 1r; D5/3, m. 1r; D5/5, m. 4r.

114. Based on 276 lb. of fine flour per quarter of wheat, with a reduction of about 20% in baking: M. Prestwich, 'Victualling estimates for English garrisons in Scotland during the early fourteenth century' *EHR* 82 (1967) pp. 536–43. Dyer, *Standards*, pp. 55–7, suggests a loaf of about 2 lb. per person; Harvey, *Living*, p. 59, a conventual loaf of about the same weight after baking; B. M. S. Campbell, J. A. Galloway, D. Keene and M. Murphy, *A medieval capital and its grain supply: agrarian production and distribution in the London region c. 1300* (Institute of British Geo-

graphers, Historical Geography Research Series, 30; 1993) pp. 191–2.

115. *HAME* i, pp. 245–58, 264–404.

116. *HAME* i, pp. 264–87.

117. CUL EDR D5/5.

118. *MM*, p. 120.

119. Nottingham UL, MS Middleton Mi A1, m. 1r; Harvey, *Living*, p. 59, for wastel bread.

120. 'Ralph of Shrewsbury', pp. 134–6.

121. *HO*, pp. 91–2.

122. *BB*, p. 166.

123. PRO E101/505/26, mm. 5r–6r.

124. PRO E101/505/25–7.

125. Tout, *Edward II*, pp. 257–8.

126. Archives Départementales, Loire-Atlantique, E 206/1, mm. 1r–2r.

127. PRO E101/546/18, ff. 35v, 83v.

128. PRO E101/505/25, mm. 3r, 16r–17r, 18 (schedule), 21r; E101/505/26, mm. 12r, 26r.

129. PRO E101/505/26, mm. 6r–12r.

130. *HAME* i, pp. 333–49, 409.

131. Archives Départementales, Loire-Atlantique, E 206/1, m. 1r; PRO E101/546/18, f. 6r.

132. *MM*, pp. 125–8.

133. BL Add. MS 34,213, f. 123v.

134. Woolgar, 'Diet', p. 20; PRO E101/511/15, m. 5d; E101/512/5, mm. 2r–3r.

135. PRO E101/505/26, mm. 18r–20r; E101/505/27, m. 5r.

136. *HAME* i, pp. 180–95.

137. *HAME* i, pp. 264–404.

138. *MM*, pp. 128–9.

139. Campbell *et al.*, *Medieval capital*, p. 206, suggests ½ gallon. Bishops Mitford and Wykeham provided *c.* 1 gallon per *ferculum*: *HAME* i, pp. 264–404; WCM 1.

140. *HO*, p. 90; *BB*, p. 214.

141. *HAME* ii, p. 672; *The customs accounts of Hull 1453–1490* ed. W. R. Childs (Yorkshire Archaeological Society, Record Series, 144; 1986) pp. 5–6, 60–1.

142. *HAME* ii, pp. 514, 521.

143. BL Add. MS 34,213, ff. 22v, 59r, 96v; PRO E101/546/18, ff. 85r, 90v, 95v.

144. *HBJDN*, p. 56; he had also bought beer in 1468, *MHE*, pp. 512–15, 517.

145. PRO E101/505/26–7.

146. PRO E101/505/17, m. 3r.

147. Longleat House MS 4050, m. 1r.

148. Dyer, *Standards*, p. 93.

149. *RWH, 1286–9*, p. 20; *HBQI*, p. 112.

150. PRO E101/505/26, m. 19r; E101/505/27, mm. 3r–4r.
151. PRO E101/505/26, m. 13r.
152. *HAME* i, pp. 126–50; PRO E101/505/26–7.
153. *EC*, p. 82.
154. *HBQI*, p. 132.
155. *MM*, p. 123.
156. Harvey, *Living*, pp. 61–2; *HAME* i, pp. 268, 272, 281, 291, 381–2.
157. *HAME* ii, p. 465.
158. Above, pp. 90–2.
159. *Swinfield* i, pp. 64, 115–16.
160. Dyer, *Standards*, p. 63; Woolgar, 'Diet', pp. 29–30.
161. *Seyntz medicines*, pp. 19–20.
162. Below, p. 167.
163. *Gawain*, pp. 78–9.
164. Aston, *Arundel*, p. 379; Kingsford, 'Forfeitures', p. 97; *BI*, p. 57.
165. *RWH, 1286–9*, p. 357.
166. *RWH, 1285–6*, p. 55.
167. *CI*, pp. 12–14; B. Laurioux, 'Modes culinaires et mutations du goût à la fin du Moyen Âge' in *Artes mechanicae en Europe médiévale* ed. R. Jansen-Sieben (Brussels, 1989) pp. 199–222.
168. PRO E101/505/26, mm. 10r, 24r, dorse.
169. *HAME* i, pp. 229–30, 232–3, 245.
170. *HAME* i, pp. 408–9.
171. Harris, 'Buckingham', p. 44.
172. BL Add. MS 34,213, ff. 95v–96v.
173. Giuseppi, 'Bogo', pp. 25–6.
174. *BB*, pp. 188, 190.
175. *MM*, pp. 122–3.
176. M. Hyman, 'Les "menues choses qui ne sont de neccessité": les confitures et la table' in *DMT*, pp. 279–80.
177. G. E. Trease, 'The spicers and apothecaries of the royal household in the reigns of Henry III, Edward I and Edward II' *NMS* 3 (1959) pp. 45–6; *RWH, 1285–6*, pp. 11, 66.
178. Northants RO Westmorland (Apethorpe) 4. xx. 4., ff. 15r, 15r, 16v, 19v, 22v, 27v.
179. PRO E101/546/18, ff. 32v, 61r.
180. *HAME* ii, pp. 507, 578.
181. PRO E101/546/18, f. 46v.
182. *HAME* i, p. 418; ii, pp. 498, 520.
183. C. Dyer, 'Gardens and orchards in medieval England' in Dyer, *Everyday life*, p. 115.
184. *SL*, p. 223.
185. 'Isabel of Lancaster', p. 498; *HAME* i,

pp. 234, 240.
186. Woolgar, 'Diet', p. 29.
187. BL Add. MS 34,213, ff. 116r, 120r; *NHB*, p. 108.
188. *MM*, p. 124.
189. Southampton City RO, SC5/4/2, f. 5v; BL Add. MS 34,213, f. 93r; Archives Départementales, Loire-Atlantique, E 206/1; 206/3.
190. BL Add. MS 34,213, ff. 21v, 36r, 46r.
191. Northants RO Westmorland (Apethorpe) 4. xx. 4., f. 46r.
192. *Swinfield* i, pp. 25, 59; ii, pp. cxxxi–cxxxii.
193. *HAME* ii, pp. 522, 526, 540.
194. *HKW* ii, pp. 967–8, 972, 992, 1042.
195. T. Scully, *The art of cookery in the Middle Ages* (Woodbridge, 1995) pp. 40–65; *CI*, p. 20; M. Weiss-Amer, 'The role of medieval physicians in the diffusion of culinary recipes and cooking practices' in *DMT*, pp. 69–80.
196. *BB*, p. 123.
197. Dyer, *Standards*, p. 56, illustrates a similar pattern.
198. Woolgar, 'Diet', pp. 24–5.
199. Duffy, *Altars*, pp. 405–6; W. E. Tate, *The parish chest: a study of the records of parochial administration in England* (3rd edition, Cambridge, 1969) p. 156.
200. Steane, *Archaeology*, pp. 138–40; for the practice of feeding harvest workers debilitated livestock, C. Dyer, 'Changes in diet in the late Middle Ages: the case of harvest workers' in Dyer, *Everyday life*, pp. 89–90.
201. Boorde, *Dyetary*, pp. 272–4.
202. Dyer, 'Changes in diet', pp. 97–8.
203. PRO E101/546/18, f. 65.
204. Staffs. RO D641/1/3/8.
205. *NHB*, pp. 5–6, 102–7.
206. *JLBC* vi, pp. 2–4, 16–32.
207. B. Laurioux, 'Table et hiérarchie sociale à la fin du Moyen Âge' in *DMT*, p. 94; Dyer, *Standards*, pp. 105–6, quoting a Venetian observer of *c.* 1500.

CHAPTER 7

Cooking and the Meal

1. PRO E101/505/25–7.
2. PRO C47/3/33.
3. Above, p. 34.
4. Tout, *Edward II*, p. 262.

5. MCO Fastolf paper 8, m. 5r.

6. *HAME* ii, p. 513.

7. Above, pp. 30, 33; for substantial bequests to cooks, Aston, *Arundel*, p. 247.

8. *Plaisirs et manières de table aux xive et xve siècles* ed. D. Milhau and M. Rey-Delqué (Toulouse, 1992) pp. 54–6.

9. P. Aebischer, 'Un manuscrit valaisan du "Viandier" attribué à Taillevent' *Vallesia* 8 (1953) pp. 73–100.

10. Dyer, *Standards*, p. 63; J. L. Flandrin, 'Le goût et la nécessité: sur l'usage des graisses dans les cuisines d'Europe occidentale (xive–xviiie siècle)' *Annales ESC* 38 (1983) pp. 369–401; J. L. Flandrin, 'Internationalisme, nationalisme et régionalisme dans la cuisine des xive et xve siècles: le témoignage des livres de cuisine' in *Manger et boire au Moyen Âge* ed. D. Menjot (Publications de la faculté des lettres et sciences humaines de Nice, 1st series, 27–8; 1984) ii, pp. 75–91.

11. *Libre de Sent Soví* ed. R. Grewe (Barcelona, 1979) pp. 53–4, 61.

12. *MM*, p. 149.

13. C. B. Hieatt, C. Lambert, B. Laurioux and A. Prentki, 'Répertoire des manuscrits médiévaux contenant des recettes culinaires' in *DMT*, pp. 315–88.

14. Somerset RO DD/L P37/7, part 1, m. 5r; BL Add. MS 34,213, f. 9r.

15. Tout, *Edward II*, pp. 241–81.

16. J. R. Kenyon, *Medieval fortifications* (Leicester, 1990) p. 138.

17. PRO DL28/1/13, m. 3d.

18. Harvey, *Living*, pp. 51–6, 216–30.

19. PRO E101/372/4, m. 2r.

20. *CI*, p. 62, number 5.

21. *MM*, pp. 144, 147, 150, 152.

22. T. Scully, *The art of cookery in the Middle Ages* (Woodbridge, 1995) pp. 88, 92; Harris, 'Buckingham', p. 42.

23. *HO*, p. 148.

24. Thurley, *Royal palaces*, p. 153.

25. Giuseppi, 'Bogo', p. 26.

26. Kenyon, *Medieval fortifications*, pp. 141, 144–5.

27. P. A. Rahtz, *Excavations at King John's Hunting Lodge, Writtle, Essex, 1955–57* (Society for Medieval Archaeology, monograph series, 3; 1969) pp. 20; 22, n. 57; 42–51.

28. Salzman, *Building*, p. 455; *GMH* i,

pp. 303–12.

29. J. R. Kenyon, *Raglan Castle* (revised edition, Cardiff, 1994) pp. 34–41.

30. Hare, 'Bishop's Waltham', pp. 228–30; HRO 11M59/B1/140, m. 30r; 11M59/B1/141, m. 21v; 11M59/Bp/BW/65, m. 3r.

31. PRO E101/505/26, m. 23r.

32. BL Add. MS 34,213, ff. 77–8r, 88, 103v.

33. Eames, *Furniture*, pp. 55–72; Hare, 'Bishop's Waltham', pp. 228–9.

34. PRO E101/505/25, mm. 2r, 6r; E101/505/26, mm. 20r, 22r.

35. PRO E101/513/2, m. 9d.

36. *MM*, p. 322.

37. WCM 1.

38. *HBQI*, p. 36; Northants RO Westmorland (Apethorpe) 4. xx. 4., f. 14r.

39. *BB*, p. 184.

40. MCO Fastolf paper 43, f. 11r.

41. Hare, 'Bishop's Waltham', pp. 227, 236.

42. Northants RO Westmorland (Apethorpe) 4. xx. 4., ff. 20r, 38v, 46r.

43. *BB*, p. 72.

44. *HO*, p. 95; Thurley, *Royal palaces*, pp. 144–61.

45. *HKW* i, pp. 549–50.

46. Kenyon, *Medieval fortifications*, p. 161.

47. *RWH, 1286–9*, p. 212.

48. PRO E101/510/21, m. 1r.

49. *Ladie Kateryne*, pp. 71–2.

50. PRO E101/546/18, ff. 35v, 42v, 47r, 51r, 57r.

51. Hare, 'Bishop's Waltham', p. 229; J. N. Hare, *Bishop's Waltham Palace, Hampshire* (2nd edition, 1990) pp. 8–11.

52. *WH*, pp. 406–7.

53. William Langland, *The vision of Piers Plowman: a critical edition of the B-text based on Trinity College Cambridge MS B. 15. 17* ed. A. V. C. Schmidt (1987) p. 103.

54. M. Wood, *The English medieval house* (1965) pp. 91–4.

55. *WH*, pp. 402–7.

56. *WW*, p. 243.

57. Jones and Walker, 'Indentures', p. 55.

58. *The register of the common seal of the Priory of St Swithun, Winchester, 1345–1497* ed. J. Greatrex (Hampshire Record Series, 2; 1978) pp. 8–9.

59. *FCCB*, pp. 11–17.

60. HRO 11M59/Bp/BW/63, m. 3r.

61. *The Domesday of St Paul's in the year MCCXXII* ed. W. H. Hale (Camden

Society, 1st series, 69; 1858) p. 137, cited in Eames, *Furniture*, p. 56, n. 137; on tables, pp. 215–27.

62. *FCCB*, p. 13.

63. Eames, *Furniture*, p. 225.

64. Eames, *Furniture*, pp. 181–214.

65. PRO DL28/1/13, m. 4d.

66. HRO 11M59/Bp/BW/65, m. 4r.

67. *MM*, p. 302.

68. Tout, *Edward II*, p. 255; *BB*, p. 112.

69. Eames, *Furniture*, pp. 56–72.

70. *BI*, pp. 45, 56–60, 215–20, 341–8, 374; for the later history of the Royal Gold Cup, M. Campbell, 'Gold, silver and precious stones' in *EMI*, pp. 107–66, at p. 129.

71. *Ladie Kateryne*, pp. xlviii, 55, 58, 76, 148–9.

72. PRO DL28/1/13, m. 5r.

73. D. M. Mitchell, '"By your leave my masters": British taste in table linen in the fifteenth and sixteenth centuries' *Textile History* 29 (1989) pp. 49–77.

74. *HO*, pp. 103–4.

75. MCO Fastolf paper 43, f. 11v, attached paper.

76. *MM*, pp. 130–1, where the identification of 'towaile of Raynes' with Rennes, in Brittany, is mistaken.

77. PRO E101/546/18, ff. 47r, 67v.

78. *FCCB*, pp. 13–14; *MM*, pp. 129–32.

79. *MM*, pp. 131–2.

80. *MM*, p. 324.

81. HMC, *Report on the manuscripts of Lord Middleton . . .* (1911) pp. 84–6.

82. Nottingham UL Middleton MS Mi A1, dorse.

83. *MHE*, pp. 3–5, 13, 38, etc.

84. PRO E101/372/4, m. 3r.

85. *The registers of John de Sandale and Rigaud de Asserio, Bishops of Winchester (A. D. 1316–1323)* ed. F. J. Baigent (Hampshire Record Society, 8; 1897) p. xlix.

86. R. F. Homer, 'Tin, lead and pewter' in *EMI*, p. 67.

87. Somerset RO DD/L P37/7, part 1, mm. 5r–7r.

88. BL Add. MS 34,213, f. 49r.

89. PRO E101/546/18, f. 114v.

90. *NHB*, p. 58.

91. D. Gaimster and B. Nenk, 'English households in transition *c.* 1450–1550: the ceramic evidence' in *The age of trans-*

ition: the archaeology of English culture 1400–1600 ed. D. Gaimster and P. Stamper (Oxford, 1997) pp. 171–95.

92. A. R. Malden, 'The will of Nicholas Longespee, Bishop of Salisbury' *EHR* 15 (1900) p. 526; W. H. St. John Hope, 'On the English medieval drinking bowls called mazers' *Archaeologia* 50 (1887) pp. 129–93.

93. *HAME* i, p. 406.

94. *MM*, p. 323.

95. *HAME* ii, p. 532.

96. PRO E101/511/15, m. 4r; J. Munby, 'Wood' in *EMI*, p. 400.

97. *HAME* ii, pp. 511–12.

98. J. Cherry, 'Leather' in *EMI*, pp. 312–14.

99. *NHB*, p. 57.

100. G. Beresford, 'The medieval manor of Penhallam, Jacobstow, Cornwall' *MA* 18 (1974) pp. 138–9; R. J. Charleston, 'Vessel glass' in *EMI*, pp. 244, 256–62.

101. D. B. Harden, 'Table-glass in the Middle Ages' in *Rotterdam papers II: a contribution to medieval archaeology* ed. J. G. N. Renaud (Rotterdam, 1975) pp. 36–8.

102. Kingsford, 'Forfeitures', p. 89.

103. *The local port book of Southampton for 1439–40* ed. H. S. Cobb (Southampton Records Series, 5; 1961) p. 11; *The overseas trade of London: Exchequer customs accounts 1480–1* ed. H. S. Cobb (London Record Society, 27; 1990) pp. 7, 53.

104. Harvey, *Living*, p. 73, for the gift of Abbot Litlington of 48 trenchers and 24 salt-cellars in 1378.

105. M. Camille, 'Labouring for the lord: the ploughman and the social order in the Luttrell Psalter' *Art History* 10 (1987) pp. 423–54.

106. *RW*, pp. 50–1, 112, 114.

107. Above, p. 129.

108. *WH*, pp. 404–5.

109. BL MS Harley 6815, ff. 32v–35v.

110. Aston, *Arundel*, p. 380.

111. Amyot, 'Transcript', p. 244.

112. *The antient kalendars and inventories of the treasury of His Majesty's Exchequer . . .* ed. F. Palgrave (3 vols, 1836) iii, p. 136.

113. *HBQI*, p. 222. There was some continental usage of the *nef* for alms: *MOM* iv, pp. 3, 22.

114. C. Oman, *Medieval silver nefs* (Victoria and Albert Museum, monograph 15;

1963) pp. 2–7; Nicolas, 'Observations', p. 79; Turner, 'Humphrey de Bohun', p. 348; PRO E101/91/30, m. 1r; *RW*, p. 30.

115. *RW*, pp. 112–14.

116. MCO Fastolf paper 43, f. 11v, schedule; Amyot, 'Transcript', pp. 240, 243.

117. BL MS Harley 6815, f. 30r.

118. J. Cowgill, M. de Neergaard and N. Griffiths, *Medieval finds from excavations in London: 1. Knives and scabbards* (1987) pp. 51–6.

119. *RWH, 1286–9*, p. 385.

120. *MHE*, p. 9; Cowgill *et al.*, *Knives and scabbards*, pp. 42–50.

121. *MHE*, p. 8.

122. Malden, 'Will of Nicholas Longespee', p. 526.

123. G. G. Astill, 'An early inventory of a Leicestershire knight' *Midland History* 2 (1974) p. 279.

124. *WPR 1301–2*, p. 235.

125. T. H. Turner, 'Usages of domestic life in the Middle Ages. 1. The dining table' *ArchJ* 2 (1846) p. 179; Kingsford, 'Forfeitures', p. 88.

126. Bodl. MS Fairfax 24, f. 62.

127. *FCCB*, p. 15; *HO*, p. 93.

128. M. A. Michael, 'A manuscript wedding gift from Philippa of Hainault to Edward III' *Burlington Magazine* 127 (1985) pp. 582–99; M. A. Michael, 'The iconography of kingship in the Walter of Milemete treatise' *JWCI* 57 (1994) pp. 35–47.

129. *Le secré de secrez by Pierre d'Abernun of Fetcham* ed. O. A. Beckerlegge (ANTS, 5; 1944) pp. xviii–xxvi.

130. *The treatise of Walter de Milemete De nobilitatibus, sapientiis, et prudentiis regum . . .* ed. M. R. James (Oxford, 1913) pp. xli–lxiii, 159–86.

131. *Gawain*, p. 75.

132. *MM*, pp. 321–6.

133. *WH*, pp. 402–7.

134. *JLBC* vi, pp. 36–7; *SR* i, pp. 278–9.

135. K. Brush, 'The *Recepta jocalium* in the wardrobe book of William de Norwell, 12 July 1338 to 27 May 1340' *JMH* 10 (1984) pp. 249–70.

136. G. L. Harriss, *King, Parliament and public finance in medieval England to 1369* (Oxford, 1975) pp. 231–52.

137. *Two fifteenth-century cookery-books* ed. T. Austin (EETS, OS, 91; 1888) pp. 58–9.

138. *MM*, pp. 164–71.

139. *SR* i, pp. 380, 382.

140. Harvey, *Living*, pp. 48–9, 216–30.

141. J. L. Flandrin, 'Structure des menus français et anglais aux xive et xve siècles' in *DMT*, pp. 173–92; *CI*, pp. 4–5.

142. *FCCB*, p. 17.

143. Silver dishes *pro interferculis regis*, *RWH, 1286–9*, p. 20.

144. A. Lafortune-Martel, 'De l'entremets culinaire aux pièces montées d'un menu de propagande' in *DMT*, pp. 121–9; *Ladie Kateryne*, pp. 55–8.

145. *Two fifteenth-century cookery-books*, p. x; BL Add. MS 34,213, f. 95r.

146. *MM*, pp. 140–8, 153–61; B. Laurioux, 'Table et hiérarchie sociale à la fin du Moyen Âge' in *DMT*, pp. 87–108.

147. BL MS Harley 6815, ff. 29r–36r.

148. *BB*, pp. 65–6.

149. *BB*, p. 214.

150. *HO*, p. 90.

151. *MM*, p. 120.

152. *HO*, p. 95.

153. *MM*, pp. 130–1.

154. *MM*, p. 133.

155. BL MS Harley 6815, ff. 31v–34r; *BB*, p. 183.

156. Flandrin, 'Structure des menus français et anglais', pp. 191–2.

157. *The travels of Leo of Rozmital through Germany, Flanders, England, France, Spain, Portugal and Italy 1465–1467* ed. M. Letts (Hakluyt Society, 2nd series, 108; 1957) pp. 46–7; above, p. 88.

158. *HO*, p. 112. Rozmital's description of the English court came soon after a visit to the Duke of Burgundy, where the practices of courtesy seem less extreme, but nonetheless magnificent: *Travels of Leo of Rozmital*, pp. 26–8, 33–5.

159. BL Add. MS 34,213, f. 42r.

160. E. Roberts, 'Edward III's lodge at Odiham, Hampshire' *MA* 39 (1995) pp. 91–106.

161. Thurley, *Royal palaces*, p. 243.

CHAPTER 8
The Senses, Religion and Intellectual Life

1. *MM*, pp. 130–2.

2. *MM*, pp. 134–6.

3. *MM*, p. 120.

4. *MM*, p. 158.
5. *Seyntz medicines*, pp. 13–14, 47.
6. M. Stoddart, *The scented ape: the biology and culture of human odour* (Cambridge, 1990), *passim*.
7. *MM*, p. 181.
8. *RW*, p. 129.
9. *CClR 1254–1256*, p. 326; D. J. A. Ross, 'A lost painting in Henry III's palace at Westminster' *JWCI* 16 (1953) p. 160.
10. *RW*, p. 50.
11. PRO E101/546/18, f. 67r.
12. Turner, 'Humphrey de Bohun', pp. 344–5.
13. M. F. Braswell, 'Sin, the lady and the law. The English noblewoman in the late Middle Ages' *Medievalia et Humanistica* new series, 14 (1986) p. 89; *HO*, p. 215.
14. *MM*, pp. 182–5.
15. *MHE*, pp. 8, 33.
16. PRO E101/505/25, m. 2r.
17. *MM*, pp. 182–3.
18. *HKW* i, p. 550.
19. Salzman, *Building*, pp. 276–7.
20. *Seyntz medicines*, pp. 194, 202–3.
21. Thurley, *Royal palaces*, pp. 167–73.
22. *HAME* i, p. 240.
23. *RWH, 1286–9*, p. 393.
24. *EC*, p. 85.
25. *MM*, p. 180.
26. *BB*, p. 126; *HAME* ii, p. 451.
27. PRO E101/505/25–6.
28. PRO E101/505/26, m. 3r.
29. BL Add. MS 34,213, ff. 7v, 28r, 57v, 90r, 123v.
30. *HBQI*, p. 98.
31. *BB*, pp. 192, 196.
32. S. M. Newton, *Fashion in the age of the Black Prince: a study of the years 1340–1365* (Woodbridge, 1980) p. 17.
33. *MM*, p. 176.
34. PRO E101/546/18, ff. 51v, 67v, 68v.
35. *RWH, 1285–6*, p. 42; *RWH, 1286–9*, p. 213.
36. *MM*, p. 180.
37. *Executors*, p. 6.
38. *Liber quotidianus contrarotulatoris garderobae anno regni regis Edwardi primi vicesimo octavo . . .* ed. J. Nichols (1787) p. 58.
39. P. A. Kennedy, 'A gentleman's house in the reign of Henry VII' *Northamptonshire Past and Present* 2 (1954–9) pp. 17–28.
40. *BB*, pp. 118, 120.
41. PRO E101/546/18, f. 87v.
42. PRO E101/505/27, m. 4r.
43. *WPR 1301–2*, pp. 206–7.
44. Aston, *Arundel*, pp. 181, 183.
45. MCO Fastolf paper 43, f. 16v.
46. BL Add. MS 34,213, f. 78v.
47. *Seyntz medicines*, pp. 99–101.
48. For example, Northants RO Westmorland (Apethorpe) 4. xx. 4., f. 41r.
49. Northants RO Westmorland (Apethorpe) 4. xx. 4., ff. 13v, 32r.
50. Harvey, *Living*, pp. 130–2.
51. HRO 11M59/Bp/BW/65, m. 4r; *HBJDN*, p. 514.
52. HRO 11M59/Bp/BW/65, m. 4r; for other latrines, Thurley, *Royal palaces*, pp. 171–7.
53. Salzman, *Building*, p. 261.
54. *Seyntz medicines*, pp. 226–7.
55. Steane, *Archaeology*, p. 116.
56. *MM*, pp. 179–80.
57. Dyer, *Standards*, p. 70.
58. Newton, *Fashion*, pp. 3–4; Staniland, 'Clothing', pp. 223–34; F. Lachaud, 'Textiles, furs and liveries: a study of the material culture of the court of Edward I (1272–1307)' (University of Oxford D. Phil. thesis, 1992) pp. 135–47.
59. *MM*, pp. 177–8, 181.
60. *HO*, p. 151; Lachaud, 'Textiles, furs and liveries', p. 162.
61. D. D. Egbert, *The Tickhill Psalter and related manuscripts: a school of manuscript illumination in England during the early fourteenth century* (New York, 1940) p. 142. Monks, however, remained clothed in bed, either in their undergarments or in their habits as well: Harvey, *Living*, pp. 130–2.
62. *MHE*, p. 25.
63. PRO E101/505/25, mm. 2r, 5r, 15r; E101/505/26, m. 3r.
64. PRO E101/505/26, m. 4r.
65. PRO E101/505/26, mm. 10r, 20r, 21r, 26r, 27r; dorse; Giuseppi, 'Bogo', pp. 50–5.
66. F. Lachaud, 'Liveries of robes in England, c. 1200–c. 1330' *EHR* 111 (1996) pp. 279–98; *WH*, pp. 402–3.
67. *MHE*, pp. 299, 365. The livery distributed by Clarence was given out in the form of cloth, not garments: *HO*, p. 105.
68. PRO E101/511/15, mm. 3r–5r: these figures may underestimate both the expense and the receipts.

69. F. Lachaud, 'An aristocratic wardrobe of the late thirteenth century: the confiscation of the goods of Osbert de Spaldington in 1298' *Historical Research* 67 (1994) pp. 91–100.
70. Kennedy, 'A gentleman's house', p. 25.
71. Lachaud, 'Textiles, furs and liveries', p. 152.
72. Dillon and Hope, 'Inventory', pp. 303–5.
73. MCO Fastolf paper 43, ff. 1v-2r.
74. W. P. Baildon, 'A wardrobe account of 16–17 Richard II, 1393–4' *Archaeologia* 62 (1911) pp. 497–514.
75. BL Add. Ch. 13,972, m. 2r.
76. G. R. Owst, *Literature and pulpit in medieval England* (Oxford, 1961) p. 283, quoting BL Add. MS 41,321.
77. T. F. Ruiz, 'Festivités, couleurs et symboles du pouvoir en Castille au xvᵉ siècle. Les célébrations du mai 1428' *Annales ESC* 46 (1991) pp. 521–46; A. Page, *Vêtir le Prince: tissus et couleurs à la Cour de Savoie (1427–1447)* (Cahiers lausannois d'histoire médiévale, 8; Lausanne, 1993).
78. *SR* i, pp. 280–1.
79. *SR* i, pp. 380–2.
80. *SR* ii, pp. 399–402.
81. *SR* ii, pp. 468–70.
82. *SR* iii, pp. 8–9.
83. *HAME* ii, pp. 576–7.
84. F. Lachaud, 'Embroidery for the court of Edward I (1272–1307)' *NMS* 37 (1993) pp. 33–52.
85. K. B. McFarlane, 'The investment of Sir John Fastolf's profits of war' in McFarlane, *England*, pp. 187, 190 and n. 81; A. Smith, '"The greatest man of that age": the acquisition of Sir John Fastolf's East Anglian estates' in *Rulers*, p. 137.
86. *BB*, pp. 205, 217.
87. Above, pp. 39–40.
88. *MM*, pp. 3–4, 134–7, 300.
89. *BB*, p. 161.
90. *The travels of Leo of Rozmital through Germany, Flanders, England, France, Spain, Portugal and Italy 1465–1467* ed. M. Letts (Hakluyt Society, 2nd series, 108; 1957) p. 47.
91. *HO*, p. *37.
92. BL MS Harley 6815, ff. 29r–36r; *FCCB*, p. 15.
93. *WH*, pp. 402–5.
94. *HO*, pp. 98, 121.
95. Harris, 'Buckingham', p. 42.
96. Above, pp. 76–7.
97. PRO E101/505/25–7; above, p. 91.
98. J. Catto, 'Religion and the English nobility in the later fourteenth century' in *History and imagination: essays in honour of H. R. Trevor-Roper* ed. H. Lloyd-Jones, V. Pearl and B. Worden (1981) pp. 43–55; C. Carpenter, 'The religion of the gentry of fifteenth-century England' in *EFC, 1986*, p. 63.
99. *Liber regie capelle: a manuscript in the Biblioteca Publica, Evora* ed. W. Ullmann (Henry Bradshaw Society, 92; 1961) pp. 8, 56–9.
100. *HAME* ii, pp. 645, 651; M. K. Jones, 'Collyweston – an early Tudor palace' in *EFC, 1986*, p. 134, n. 25.
101. *The register of the common seal of the priory of St Swithun, Winchester 1345–1497* ed. J. Greatrex (Hampshire Record Series, 2; 1978) p. 74. I am grateful to Dr J. Hare for this reference.
102. *NHB*, p. 242.
103. *GMH* i, pp. 144–50.
104. Hare, 'Bishop's Waltham', pp. 229, 232–4; HRO 11M59/Bp/BW/63, m. 2r; 11M59/Bp/BW/65, m. 4r.
105. MCO Fastolf paper 43, f. 10v.
106. *RWH, 1286–9*, pp. 31–2.
107. *EC*, pp. 9, 11; *HBQI*, pp. 138–9; 'Isabel of Lancaster', pp. 487–98.
108. H. Jenkinson, 'Mary de Sancto Paulo, Foundress of Pembroke College, Cambridge' *Archaeologia* 66 (1914–15) pp. 401–46.
109. Catto, 'Religion and the English nobility', pp. 49–50.
110. *SL*, p. 252.
111. *HAME* ii, p. 645.
112. P. J. P. Goldberg, 'Lay book ownership in late medieval York: the evidence of wills' *The Library* 6th series, 16 (1994) pp. 181–9; Duffy, *Altars*, pp. 210–65.
113. *MHE*, pp. 9, 24.
114. PRO E101/505/25, m. 17r.
115. PRO E101/512/5, m. 3r.
116. Goldberg, 'Lay book ownership', p. 186.
117. *RWH, 1286–9*, pp. 379, 386; *EC*, pp. 63–4, 84, 87, 131.
118. J. Stratford, 'The royal library in England before the reign of Edward IV' in *EFC, 1992*, pp. 189–90.

119. Dillon and Hope, 'Inventory', pp. 298–303.
120. A. I. Doyle, 'English books in and out of court from Edward III to Henry VII' in *English court culture in the later Middle Ages* ed. V. J. Scattergood and J. W. Sherborne (1983) p. 165; C. Revard, 'Richard Hurd and MS Harley 2253' *Notes and Queries* 224 (1979) pp. 199–202; T. Turville Petre, *England the nation: language, literature, and national identity, 1290–1340* (Oxford, 1996) pp. 192–8; *HAME* i, pp. 173–7.
121. *The Harley lyrics: the Middle English lyrics of MS. Harley 2253* ed. G. L. Brook (4th edition, Manchester, 1968) p. 38.
122. C. M. Woolgar and B. O'Donoghue, 'Two Middle English poems at Magdalen College, Oxford' *Medium Aevum* 52 (1983) pp. 217–22.
123. *Executors*, pp. 50–1.
124. MCO Fastolf paper 43, f. 10r.
125. *The epistle of Othea translated from the French text of Christine de Pisan by Stephen Scrope* ed. C. F. Bühler (EETS, OS, 264; 1970) pp. xi–xxix.
126. *The dicts and sayings of the philosophers: the translations made by Stephen Scrope, William Worcester and an anonymous translator* ed. C. F. Bühler (EETS, OS, 211; 1941) pp. xii, xxiv; K. B. McFarlane, 'William Worcester: a preliminary survey' in McFarlane, *England*, pp. 199–224.
127. J. T. Rosenthal, 'Aristocratic cultural patronage and book bequests' *BJRL* 64 (1981–2) pp. 522–48; McFarlane, *Nobility*, p. 244; K. B. McFarlane, *Lancastrian kings and Lollard knights* (Oxford, 1972) pp. 233–8.
128. *Seyntz medicines*; *Scalacronica: the reigns of Edward I, Edward II and Edward III as recorded by Sir Thomas Gray* ed. H. Maxwell (Glasgow, 1907) pp. vii–x; McFarlane, *Nobility*, p. 242.
129. In general, A. S. G. Edwards and C. M. Meale, 'The marketing of printed books in late medieval England' *The Library* 6th series, 15 (1993) pp. 95–112.
130. McFarlane, *Nobility*, pp. 238–41; *HAME* i, pp. 49, 58–61; Dyer, *Standards*, p. 94.
131. *PL* i, pp. xxxvi–xxxix.

CHAPTER 9
Travel, Horses and Other Animals

1. *HO*, p. 97.
2. Nicolas, 'Observations', pp. 71–83.
3. *RWH, 1286–9*, p. 70.
4. PRO DL28/1/13, m. 4d.
5. J. Langdon, *Horses, oxen and technological innovation: the use of draught animals in English farming from 1066 to 1500* (Cambridge, 1986) pp. 142–55.
6. Langdon, *Horses*, pp. 77–9.
7. *HAME* i, p. 246.
8. *HAME* ii, pp. 664–5.
9. *HAME* i, pp. 282, 406–7, 427, 429. The other references in this account to seven horses pulling the wagon remove any doubt that the *carectis* mentioned on p. 427 were just one vehicle, describing what is earlier called *charietta*.
10. *HAME* ii, pp. 449, 529.
11. *HBQI*, p. 234.
12. *RW*, p. 35.
13. *HAME* ii, p. 667.
14. Langdon, *Horses*, pp. 225–6; J. F. Willard, 'Inland transportation in England during the fourteenth century' *Speculum* 1 (1926) p. 368; J. Masschaele, 'Transport costs in medieval England' *EconHR* 2nd series, 46 (1993) pp. 266–79, at pp. 269–70.
15. *HAME* i, pp. 304, 307–8, 340, 354, 371, 415, 417, 427.
16. *Bryene*, pp. 2–100.
17. BL Add. MS 34,213, ff. 63v, 77r; PRO E101/546/18, f. 27v.
18. PRO E101/505/25, mm. 11r, 13r; E101/505/26, mm. 3r, 13r–14r, 23r.
19. PRO E101/505/26, mm. 3r, 18r.
20. PRO E101/505/26, mm. 13r, 25r, 27r.
21. PRO E101/505/25, mm. 10r, 14r.
22. As, for example, *HAME* ii, p. 679, *le thil-horsse*.
23. PRO E101/505/25.
24. PRO E101/505/26, mmm. 3r, 7r, 10r–11r, 14r–15r, dorse.
25. PRO E101/505/25, m. 14r.
26. PRO E101/505/25, m. 19r.
27. PRO E101/505/26, m. 5r.
28. PRO E101/505/26, m. 31r; E101/505/27, m. 4r.
29. PRO E101/505/25, m. 15r.
30. *WH*, pp. 396–7; Harvey, 'Consumer', p. 35.
31. *NHB*, pp. 372–7.

32. PRO E101/546/18, ff. 51r, 115Er.
33. *MHE*, pp. 4, 18, 31, 39, 57.
34. *EC*, pp. 73, 75.
35. C. Dyer, 'The consumer and the market in the later Middle Ages' in Dyer, *Everyday life*, p. 262; Masschaele, 'Transport costs', pp. 271–7; J. F. Edwards and B. P. Hindle, 'The transportation system of medieval England and Wales' *JHG* 17 (1991) pp. 123–34.
36. Northants RO Westmorland (Apethorpe) 4. xx. 4, f. 7r.
37. CUL EDR D5/7, m. 2r; D5/7a, m. 2d; PRO E101/400/28, m. 2d; Aston, *Arundel*, pp. 218–19.
38. *HAME* ii, pp. 532, 537.
39. PRO E101/546/18.
40. Kingsford, 'Forfeitures', pp. 73, 89.
41. *RWH, 1286–9*, p. 40.
42. *HAME* ii, pp. 663, 666.
43. Distances as the crow flies: the actual distances may be a little longer, but the distortion is proportionately at its greatest for short distances, say, under 5 miles. Masschaele, 'Transport costs', pp. 270–1; *MHE*, pp. 1–86.
44. PRO E101/505/25–7.
45. E. J. S. Parsons *The map of Great Britain circa A. D. 1360 known as the Gough Map: an introduction to the facsimile* (Oxford, 1958) pp. 2–15; J. B. Mitchell, 'Early maps of Great Britain: the Matthew Paris maps' *Geographical Journal* 81 (1933) pp. 27–34; F. M. Stenton, 'The road system of medieval England' *EconHR* 1st series, 7 (1936–7) pp. 1–21; B. P. Hindle, 'The road network of medieval England and Wales' *JHG* 2 (1976) pp. 207–21.
46. B. P. Hindle, 'Seasonal variations in travel in medieval England' *Journal of Transport History* 2nd series, 4 (1978) pp. 170–8; M. Sommé, 'Vie itinérante et résidences d'Isabelle de Portugal, duchesse de Bourgogne (1430–1471)' *Revue du Nord* 79 (1997) pp. 25–7.
47. PRO E101/505/26, m. 4r.
48. Northants RO Westmorland (Apethorpe) 4. xx. 4., f. 6r.
49. *HAME* ii, p. 596; N. Saul, *Richard II* (1997) pp. 428–9.
50. *RWH, 1286–9*, p. 41.
51. For timings of meals, especially on Fridays, above, pp. 85, 87–8.
52. Northants RO Westmorland (Apethorpe) 4. xx. 4., ff. 5–7.
53. PRO E101/505/26, m. 24r.
54. *MHE*, p. 42.
55. PRO E101/505/26, mm. 8r, 11r; for other examples, *RWH, 1285–6*, p. 14; PRO E101/505/17, m. 8r; *MHE*, p. 160.
56. W. H. St John Hope, 'The loss of King John's baggage train in the Wellstream in October 1216' *Archaeologia* 60 (1906) pp. 94–110; *EC*, p. 66; PRO E101/505/25, m. 19r.
57. 'Ralph of Shrewsbury', pp. 151–4.
58. PRO E101/505/25, m. 20r.
59. F. Heal, *Hospitality in early modern England* (Oxford, 1990) pp. 83–5.
60. *PL* i, p. 306.
61. Tout, *Edward II*, pp. 277–9.
62. *Seyntz medicines*, p. 101.
63. Cornwall RO AR37/55; W. A. Pantin, 'Medieval inns' in *Studies in building history: essays in recognition of the work of B. H. St. John O'Neil* ed. E. M. Jope (1961) pp. 166–91.
64. *RWH, 1286–9*, pp. 190, 205–6; *HAME* ii, p. 678.
65. *RWH, 1285–6*, pp. 6, 15.
66. Above, p. 114, for maintenance of supplies of poultry, etc. within the household.
67. PRO E101/505/17, m. 3, schedule.
68. *RWH, 1286–9*, p. 87.
69. J. Clark, *Medieval finds from excavations in London: 5. The medieval horse and its equipment c. 1150–c. 1450* (1995) pp. 10–11, 22–32.
70. Langdon, *Horses*, pp. 272–3, for the analogy.
71. A. Ayton, *Knights and warhorses: military service and the English aristocracy under Edward III* (Woodbridge, 1994) p. 46, n. 117.
72. For some values of horses, c. 1308, HMC, *Report on the manuscripts of Lord Middleton . . .* (1911) p. 85.
73. PRO E101/505/25, m. 1r and dorse.
74. PRO E101/372/4, m. 3, schedule.
75. Staffs. RO D1721/1/5, p. 57.
76. 'Ralph of Shrewsbury', pp. 92–119.
77. *HAME* i, pp. 289–397.
78. BL Add. MS 34,213, ff. 8v, 28r.
79. J. R. Kenyon, *Medieval fortifications* (Leicester, 1990) p. 156.

80. HRO 11M59/B1/140, m. 30d.
81. HRO 11M59/Bp/BW/66/1, m. 3r.
82. PRO E101/505/25, mm. 10r–14r; E101/505/26, mm. 26r–29r; E101/ 505/17, m. 8a, dorse; *MHE*, pp. 43–62.
83. PRO E101/372/4, m. 8r.
84. 'Ralph of Shrewsbury', p. 110.
85. *EC*, p. 68.
86. PRO E101/505/25–7.
87. 'Ralph of Shrewsbury', p. 95.
88. *HAME* i, pp. 264–404.
89. *MM*, p. 319.
90. *Swinfield* i, pp. 113, 193.
91. *HAME* ii, pp. 655–6, 658, 662.
92. *RWH, 1286–9*, p. 404; Nicolas, 'Observations', p. 82.
93. 'Ralph of Shrewsbury', p. 108.
94. PRO E101/505/26, m. 3r.
95. PRO E101/505/25, m. 1r; E101/505/26, m. 26r.
96. PRO E101/505/26, m. 5r.
97. PRO E101/372/4, m. 8r; E101/505/17, m. 7r; *RWH, 1285–6*, p. 13; PRO DL28/1/13, m. 4d.
98. *RWH, 1285–6*, pp. 8, 38; *CI*, p. 212.
99. B. Johnston, 'The dogs of yesteryear' *History Today* 29 (1979) p. 118; *The Master of Game by Edward, second Duke of York: the oldest English book on hunting* ed. W. A. and F. Baillie-Grohman (1909) pp. 75–127.
100. *BB*, p. 169; *HO*, pp. 90, 150.
101. *MM*, pp. 182, 302; *BB*, pp. 120–1.
102. PRO E101/505/25, mm. 1r, 9r, 18r.
103. *MHE*, pp. 27, 36.
104. *BB*, p. 66.
105. 'Ralph of Shrewsbury', pp. 115–16.
106. *HAME* i, pp. 264–404, 416–17.
107. Above, p. 125, for bread for dogs; *BB*, p. 165; *HAME* ii, pp. 490, 493–4, 500, 532, 538; Nottingham UL Middleton MS Mi A1, m. 2r and dorse.
108. *Gawain*, pp. 112–13.
109. *Master of Game*, pp. 105–22; above, pp. 115–16.
110. *Executors*, pp. 2, 7.
111. *HAME* i, p. 240.
112. *HAME* ii, p. 589.
113. 'Isabel of Lancaster', p. 498.
114. *MHE*, p. 558; for one of his expeditions, pp. 277–9.
115. *Seyntz medicines*, pp. 104–5; *Master of Game*, pp. 64–7; J. Cummins, *The hound*

116. *and the hawk: the art of medieval hunting* (1988) pp. 1–152; *RWH, 1285–6*, p. 211; *RWH, 1286–9*, p. 326.
116. *RWH, 1286–9*, pp. 319–20.
117. *RWH, 1286–9*, p. 327.
118. Johnston, 'Dogs of yesteryear', pp. 113–18.
119. *Master of Game*, pp. 125–6.
120. *HBJDN*, p. 508.
121. Northants RO Westmorland (Apethorpe) 4. xx. 4., f. 46r.
122. PRO E101/505/25–7.
123. *HAME* i, pp. 415–16.
124. BL Egerton Charter 7352.
125. *RWH, 1286–9*, pp. 336–7, 405.
126. *HKW* ii, p. 991.
127. W. P. Baildon, 'A wardrobe account of 16–17 Richard II, 1393–4' *Archaeologia* 62 (1911) pp. 506–8; Given-Wilson, *Royal household*, pp. 165, 282–7: John Littlebury was a King's knight by this date, but not a knight of the chamber until the reign of Henry IV.
128. B. Morley, 'Aspects of fourteenth-century castle design' in *Collectanea historica: essays in memory of Stuart Rigold* ed. A. Detsicas (Maidstone, 1981) pp. 104–13.
129. *MHE*, p. 8.
130. *HAME* i, pp. 183, 186–7.
131. *RWH, 1285–6*, p. 16; *BB*, pp. 65, 161.
132. *EC*, p. 112 and n. 172; C. Bullock-Davies, *Register of royal and baronial domestic minstrels 1272–1327* (Woodbridge, 1986) p. 74; *Expeditions*, p. 286; A. R. Myers, 'The captivity of a royal witch: the household accounts of Queen Joan of Navarre 1419–21' in A. R. Myers, *Crown, household and Parliament in fifteenth century England* (1985) p. 125.
133. Longleat MS Misc. IX; Staffs. RO D1721/1/5.
134. *RWH, 1286–9*, pp. 338–9; for the later menagerie, *BB*, p. 116 and n. 148.
135. *RWH, 1286–9*, p. 108.

CHAPTER 10
Conclusion

1. *MM*, pp. 185–94; Bodl. MS Fairfax 24, f. 62.
2. At the same time, in Richard's case, personal approaches to the King became more relaxed outside the formal setting:

N. Saul, *Richard II* (1997) pp. 344–65; S. Walker, 'Richard II's views on kingship' in *Rulers*, p. 57.

3. McFarlane, *Nobility*, pp. 83–101; Dyer, *Standards*, pp. 86–108.

4. *Manorial records of Cuxham, Oxfordshire, circa 1200–1359* ed. P. D. A. Harvey (HMC, Joint Publications Series 23; 1976) pp. 15–16, 56–7; *HAME* i, pp. 43–6.

5. *WH*, pp. 388–99.

6. *Executors*, pp. 1–3; P. A. Kennedy, 'A gentleman's house in the reign of Henry VII' *Northamptonshire Past and Present* 2 (1954–9) pp. 17–28.

7. G. D. Duncan, 'An introduction to the accounts of Corpus Christi College' in *The history of the University of Oxford* iii: *The collegiate university* ed. J. K. McConica (Oxford, 1986) p. 575.

8. Boorde, *Dyetary*, pp. 241–2.

9. Aston, *Arundel*, p. 17; McFarlane, *Nobility*, p. 91.

10. Given-Wilson, *Royal household*, pp. 268–9.

11. *RW*, p. 145.

12. Amyot, 'Transcript', pp. 232–51.

13. Harris, 'Buckingham', pp. 20–31, 46–55.

14. PRO E101/505/26, m. 25r.

15. PRO E101/505/25, m. 15r; E101/505/26, mm. 5r, 7r.

16. PRO E101/505/26, m. 10r.

17. PRO E101/505/26, dorse.

18. PRO E101/505/25, m. 12r.

19. Dyer, *Standards*, pp. 79–83; *HAME* i, pp. 234–41.

20. For building costs, A. Emery, *Dartington Hall* (Oxford, 1970) p. 116.

21. *HKW* ii, pp. 859, 879.

22. *HKW* ii, p. 1029.

23. Maddicott, *Thomas of Lancaster*, pp. 26–7.

24. Hare, 'Bishop's Waltham', pp. 230, 235.

25. K. B. McFarlane, 'The investment of Sir John Fastolf's profits of war' in McFarlane, *England*, p. 187; H. D. Barnes and W. D. Simpson, 'The building accounts of Caister Castle A. D. 1432–1435' *Norfolk Archaeo-*

logy 30 (1947–52) pp. 181–6; M. Carlin, *Medieval Southwark* (1996) p. 52.

26. A. Smith, ' "The greatest man of that age": the acquisition of Sir John Fastolf's East Anglian estates' in *Rulers*, p. 138.

27. W. D. Simpson, 'Herstmonceux Castle' *ArchJ* 99 (1942) p. 110.

28. *The building accounts of Tattershall Castle 1434–1472* ed. W. D. Simpson (Lincoln Record Society, 55; 1960); M. W. Thompson, 'The construction of the manor at South Wingfield, Derbyshire' in *Problems in economic and social archaeology* ed. G. de G. Sieveking, I. H. Longworth and K. E. Wilson (1976) pp. 417–38; M. K. Jones, 'Collyweston – an early Tudor palace' in *EFC, 1986*, p. 132; A. Emery, 'Ralph, Lord Cromwell's manor at Wingfield (1439–c. 1450): its construction, design and influence' *ArchJ* 142 (1985) pp. 276–339.

29. A. H. Thompson, 'The building accounts of Kirby Muxloe Castle, 1480–1484' *Transactions of the Leicestershire Architectural and Archaeological Society* 11 (1913–20) p. 212.

30. *SL*, p. 354.

31. *Household accounts and disbursement books of Robert Dudley, Earl of Leicester, 1558–1561, 1584–1586* ed. S. Adams (Camden, 5th series, 6; 1995) p. 25.

32. *The household book of Lady Grisell Baillie 1692–1733* ed. R. Scott-Moncrieff (Scottish History Society, 2nd series, 1; 1911); *The housekeeping book of Susanna Whatman 1776–1800* introduced by C. Hardyment (1987).

33. Cf. the remarks of R. H. Hilton, 'Rent and capital formation in feudal society' in R. H. Hilton, *The English peasantry in the later Middle Ages* (Oxford, 1975) pp. 177–81.

34. C. Wainwright, 'Patronage and the applied arts in early nineteenth-century London' in *London – world city: 1800–1840* ed. C. Fox (1992) pp. 111–28.

Glossary

All Saints	1 November
almoner	a domestic officer, often a cleric, responsible for handing out alms
assay	the formal tasting of food or drink or testing of bedding or other service before the lord or lady partook of it
avenar	a domestic officer, usually in the stables, in charge of oats
banker	a cushion for a bench or seat
board-end	the end of the lord's table or other table used by those of high rank in the household
bouche of court	the right to food and drink in the household
bushel	a measure of dry capacity, usually 8 to the quarter; note also differences in size between the heaped and the struck bushel
butler	the domestic officer in charge of the buttery, ale, beer and wine, and the cellar
calendar	a list of members of the household
Candlemas (also Purification)	2 February
celure	a canopy over a bed
chamber	a room or suite of rooms; a set of hangings for a room or bed; a department of the household looking after finance
chamberlain	the officer in charge of all things to do with the chamber
chandlery	the domestic office responsible for wax and candles
confectionary	the domestic office, often a sub-department of the kitchen, responsible for making desserts, sweetmeats and subtleties
controller	one who keeps a duplicate account
corrody	a right to food, drink, accommodation and related allowances in a religious house
demesne	landed property owned by the lord
dorser/dosser	a covering for the back of a seat; a measure of the amount fresh marine fish carried on the back of a pack-horse
ewery	the domestic office responsible for water and vessels for drinking or washing the person (not laundry)
ferculum	a course or portion
garderobe	a privy: *see also* wardrobe
groom	a grade of household servant, ranking above a page and below a yeoman or valet
hanap	a cup
larderer	the official responsible for the larder, that is, for preserved meat or fish

mark	currency: 13s. 4d.
marshal	the official responsible for supervision of the stables (marshalsea) and for household discipline
marshalsea	the stables
Martinmas	11 November
mess	the unit in which food was usually prepared
Michaelmas	29 September
napery	table linen
offices	the household departments
out of court	away from the household
page	the lowest rank of household servant
pantler	the official responsible for the pantry, typically for bread, cheese and napery
peck	dry measure, usually 4 pecks to the bushel
pentice	a lean-to covering a walk way
porter	one who keeps the gate; *see also* usher
poultry	the household department responsible for fowl and young animals of all sorts
quarter	dry measure, usually containing 8 bushels
reward	a position of honour at the upper end of the lord's table; additional rations
saucery	the household department, often a sub-department of the kitchen, responsible for making sauces
scullery	the household department, often a sub-department of the kitchen, responsible for cleaning utensils
serjeant *de mester*	grade of officer in charge of a household department
serjeanty	tenure of land by performance of personal service
sester	measure of liquid capacity, commonly between 14 and 20 gallons
steward	an official responsible for the overall conduct of the household's domestic business, sometimes jointly with, or subordinate to, the marshal
tester	the cloth hangings for a bed, for the head end
trencher	a slice of bread (or dish on which to place the bread) onto which food was commonly served
tresance	a corridor, covered way
usher	a household servant, keeping the door (as opposed to the porter, who kept the main gate), admitting and escorting people to rooms
valet	a grade of household servant, of a medium rank
verge	the area in which the jurisdiction of the marshal of the royal household prevailed, called after his wand (*virga*) of office
wardrobe	the department of the household responsible for cloth and clothing, wax and spices (called the Great Wardrobe in the English royal household); a financial office. Also a privy, called here a garderobe, although the sources employ the same word without distinction
yeoman	a grade of household servant, above a groom

Index

Places in the United Kingdom have been identified by their pre-1974 counties. Peers have been numbered following *CP*, with the addition of dates in a small number of cases.